# *His*
# INSTRUMENTS

## If God Could Use
## Them...He Can Use Us

# Sebastian Myladiyil, S.V.D.

### Foreword by Most Reverend Roger Paul Morin, D.D.

E*v*ergreen
PRESS

Mobile, AL

*His Instruments: If God Could Use Them...He Can Use Us*
Copyright © 2012 by Sebastian Myladiyil

Scripture is taken from: New American Bible, St. Joseph Edition, Catholic Book Publishing Corp., New York, 1991.

ISBN 978-1-58169-413-0
For Worldwide Distribution
Printed in the U.S.A.

Evergreen Press
P.O. Box 191540 • Mobile, AL 36619
800-367-8203

# Contents

# Foreword

This book, *HIS INSTRUMENTS: If God Could Use Them...He Can Use Us,* by Reverend Sebastian Myladiyil, SVD, presents the reader with a very interesting series of meditations presenting major biblical personages from the Old Testament. From Adam and Eve in Genesis, to Jesus of Nazareth in the Gospels, the subjects of meditation are presented as those especially chosen humans, with the exception of Jesus Christ, whose lives are radically changed by responding to God's call for action in the world by boldly witnessing to divine love and mercy. Jesus, Son of God, the Incarnate Word, makes divine love present to all through His unique mission as Redeemer of the world.

Father Sebastian, through his thoughtful creative writing, is able to enliven individual biblical personalities as he casts them in roles of daily conversations with God as they ponder the mystery of the divine plan for them. By God's plan, each person is challenged to be faithful and loving in order to be redeemed. The mechanism and the content of the dialogical construct beckon the reader to reflect on the ways in which he or she may have talked to God about personal triumphs and tragedies, successes and failures, experienced in daily living. The inevitable discovery is that a deep personal faith forms the basis for acceptance of God's will for us. The cornerstone of unwavering faith in God's freely given infinite love is the foundation for a blessed life that is constantly enriched by patient, consistent faithfulness.

This book of meditations is spiritual reading that will bring blessings to those who read it. I recommend Father Sebastian's meditations to those who strive for a closer relationship to God as they aspire to higher levels of perfection in the Christian life.

Most Reverend † Roger Paul Morin, D.D.
Bishop of Biloxi
January 1, 2012

# Acknowledgments

Ministry in a foreign land is always challenging. God's grace and support from people are vital elements for keeping the passion for ministry alive and vibrant. God's grace is ever present. I have experienced tremendous support and encouragement from many people. Tragedies and moments of crisis often bring people together. That has been my experience since Katrina hit the Gulf Coast. In coming together, I have witnessed tremendous faith, resilience, and courage in many people, which in turn has deepened my own faith and strengthened my convictions.

I am so very grateful to the wonderful people of three different parishes where I have had the privilege of ministering: St. Edwards/St. Jude in New Iberia, Louisiana; St. Rose de Lima in Bay St. Louis, Mississippi; and Immaculate Conception in Liberty, Texas. Words are not adequate enough to express my appreciation and love for all of you for all your support in my ministry.

The members of the Society of the Divine Word have always offered support and encouragement. Thanks to Very Rev. James Pawlicki, SVD, for his motivating words.

A special thank you to Most Rev. Roger Paul Morin, the Bishop of Biloxi, for his enthusiastic support in this endeavor. I was elated when he agreed to write the Foreword for this book. I am grateful for his careful reading of the text and valuable suggestions.

A number of other individuals have played important roles in this effort. My classmate and friend Fr. Jaison Magalath, SVD, gave me valuable insights about some of the characters in the Bible. Ms. Di Fillhart's simple words of wisdom redirected some of my thoughts about certain characters. Mr. Bruce Northridge has been very meticulous about proofreading and making the required corrections. Thanks to all who have encouraged me to undertake this endeavor.

# Introduction

Occasionally one may hear the questions: "Can we not leave Adam, Eve, Abraham, Jacob, Moses and all others in the Old Testament alone, and just focus on Jesus? Why bother bringing them into our lives? After all, they lived in another era. Their lives were totally different from ours; their situations have nothing in common with us." My response is simple. We still need to consider them today, both for introspection and reassurance. They can help us face ourselves honestly and help us to be cognizant of our own mistakes, weaknesses, and vulnerabilities, and gain insights so we can advance in our spiritual journey. They can also give us the reassurance that just as God was present in their lives and guided them, the living God continues to be present with us and guides us.

Even though they lived in another era and their experiences were different, they still have a story to tell us, based on their relationship with God. We can come to know their strengths and weaknesses, their dreams and aspirations, their struggles and triumphs, their victories with God or failures without God. We can marvel at the faith and resilience of some, or we can wonder about the wrong choices of others. But after reflecting upon their lives and experiences, one thing is certain: they have a lesson to teach us today that can transform us for the better. So this venture is nothing less than journeying with them, so they can give us insights as to how we can walk without faltering.

It is said, "If you see a good person, imitate him or her. If you see a bad person, examine your conscience." The forty persons described in this book will present before us qualities to emulate, and/or weaknesses that will lead us to an examination of our conscience. At the end of the journey when we meet the Lord, we want to be able to face Him just as we are, without any fear or shame.

We can all attest to this:

I was afraid to look at the Lord,
For I feared condemnation and judgment.
After all, I deserved it
For three times I denied the Lord.

I looked within, only to find hopelessness
All that I hoped for turned to nothingness.
Denial was seen as momentary escape
Only to find it had removed my peace.

So in the restlessness of my being, I decided
To look into the eyes of my Lord.
Fearing judgment and condemnation, I looked
Only to hear Him say gently, "I love you more."
*(Author's reflection on Peter's act of denial)*

Maybe we fear to look up and face the Lord today. Maybe we fear to face ourselves honestly. Perhaps beyond our gentle face there exists an ugly face; beyond our familiar world there exists a hidden world; beyond our loving nature there exists a hateful nature; beyond our composed demeanor there exist tempestuous personalities. Journeying with these persons in the Bible will tell us that only when we honestly face our vulnerabilities, weaknesses, and limitations, can we stand before the fountains of grace, strength, holiness, and perfection and hear Him say, "I love you more."

Holiness and perfection are essential attributes of God. He is holy and in Him there are no imperfections. Standing before God, who is absolutely holy and perfect, we are certainly humbled by our lack of holiness and our imperfections. Yet God invites and challenges us to move toward holiness and perfection. Leviticus 11:44 says, "For I, the Lord, am your God; and you shall make and keep yourself holy, because I am holy."

Jesus says in Matthew 5:48, "So be perfect, just as your heavenly Father is perfect." None of us can possibly make that claim at this time of being absolutely holy and perfect. But we can all take steps daily to come closer to this vision of God for ourselves.

Many of us are timid to take that first step because of our understanding of God or ourselves. Some say, "I am not worthy; I am not good enough; I am too weak and sinful; I have a horrible past; I am not capable." When Peter encountered Jesus and witnessed the miraculous catch of the fish, his response was, "Depart from me, Lord, for I am a sinful man" (Luke 5:8). Jesus was not discouraged by the words of Peter, but rather He told him, "Do not be afraid; from now on you will be catching men" (Luke 5:10). God is not put off by our unworthiness, failures, sinful past, limitations, and imperfections. He has shown repeatedly in history that whenever men and women have responded with trust and faith, they have succeeded in accomplishing His purpose.

This book can be used in many ways for our spiritual renewal. It could be an awesome resource for daily reflection during Lent; it could serve as a resource for group sharing, Bible study, or for spiritual, inspirational, and motivational reading. I have realized that the key figures in the Bible, both good and bad, have valuable lessons to teach us daily. We can proclaim loud and clear that "If God could work with them, He can work with us." The persons in the following chapters will tell us a lot about ourselves, maybe about our strengths and resoluteness, or maybe about our sinfulness and weaknesses. Reflecting on their lives will help us both with resolving our convictions of Him and with correcting our ways, so that we can renew our strength in Him and continue our life's journey in pursuit of eternal life.

# ADAM:

## Called for Greater Responsibility

*"The Lord God formed man out of the clay of the ground and blew into his nostrils the breath of life, and so man became a living being"* (Genesis 2:7).

There are two creation accounts in Genesis, the first book of the Bible. The focus of our reflection is the second story of creation in the second chapter of Genesis. The first narrative in chapter 1 is a very brief, simultaneous creation of man and woman: "God created man in His image, in the divine image He created him; male and female He created them" (Genesis 1:27). The second creation story is more descriptive in the creation of human beings. It is as if God were taking His time in fashioning the crown of creation. Even the theory of evolution supports the notion of the passage of time before the appearance of man.

God is seen here like a Master Potter, using the clay and water to create His masterpiece. The complex anatomy of the human body required careful comprehension of its details along with delicate engineering skills and deliberate exercise of all powers to fashion this being into perfection. Just look at each part of the human anatomy and see how they are carefully shaped and formed for the marvelous functions they perform. God must have taken tremendous care to fashion Adam's heart and brain, as these organs have both physical and spiritual functions. The faculties of these organs would enable man to reach new levels of awareness about himself, his origin, his purpose, and his destiny. This awareness entailed his unique status as the crown of creation, God as the source of his life, fullness of life as his purpose, and life with God as his destiny. For God, the creation of man must have been a supreme act of love as the Master Craftsman was engaged fully in the creation of this masterpiece.

God is not only the designer, He is also the source of life. That is the difference between God and all the other master craftsmen the world has produced. Let us consider Michelangelo sculpting the statue of David, chiseling away everything that was unnecessary in order to create a perfect statue. The perfect statue still remains intact for the whole world to see with that same majesty and grandeur but without life! God, on the other hand, bends down to the newly created master-piece and imparts the greatest gift—a part of His being—LIFE, so man can become a living being! The breath of life that was blown into the nostrils of Adam would forever separate him from the rest of creatures. The breath of life will enable Adam to possess not only his physical body but also his immortal soul.

What an act of love from God! How much joy it must have given Him when He saw Adam coming to life! Finally, God had created someone in His image and likeness! Adam is not left hanging in his newly formed existence, but he is soon given a task that would lead him to a new level of consciousness and awareness of his being. Having created the Garden of Eden and all living creatures, God brings the creatures to Adam, who has the task of naming them.

God entrusts Adam with this responsibility, and He eventually would entrust the whole of creation into his care. Adam completes the task of naming the creatures beautifully and in the process realizes a few things about himself: his superiority, his differences, and his lone-liness. He realizes that he can name the creatures and that they will be known from then on by those names. Having power to name entails a sense of superiority over that which is named. Yet Adam knew that he did not have the right to abuse any aspect of creation for his own grati-fication. He had realized from the beginning that he was vested with the responsibility of being a good steward of creation. He also must have felt that he possessed certain special qualities that separated him from the rest of the creatures. He looked at all the creatures of the world and saw himself as different from them. He may have seen the creatures in pairs and compatible with one another. However, he saw nothing suitable for him. This might have created in him a sense of longing for friendship and companionship.

It is as if God recognizes this loneliness in man. God, who is a communion of persons (Father, Son, and Holy Spirit), is able to see this aspiration of man for communion, and goes to work immediately with a desire to satisfy this longing. This is a challenging task, but fruitful, nonetheless, at the end. The creation of woman fulfills the deep longing of Adam for communion, as he exclaims with joy upon seeing her, "This one, at last, is bone of my bones and flesh of my flesh" (Genesis 2:23). Though they were different, they were perfectly compatible and made for each other. By bringing Eve to Adam, God unites man and woman to form a permanent, loving, and self-giving relationship.

Things should have been pretty good for the first man and woman, and indeed they were. They were able to give themselves to each other completely and totally. They were able to give and receive love from each other. They were able to enjoy each other's company and friendship tremendously. They were able to communicate with each other with utmost respect and love. However, Genesis 3 speaks about the fall of the first parents. The conversation between the serpent and the woman leads to an act of disobedience. Adam seems to be a silent witness to this but a greater culprit in the act nonetheless, as it was specifically to him that God said what he could eat and what he should refrain from: "You are free to eat from any of the trees of the garden except the tree of knowledge of good and bad. From that tree you shall not eat; the moment you eat from it you are surely doomed to die" (Genesis 2:16–17).

God had given both man and woman a supreme gift of free will to decide for themselves the right choices in life. He had not made them like robots, with no power to decide what should be done in life. God did not intend the crown of His creation to act purely on instincts and impulse, rather in freedom. The God of life demonstrated from the beginning His unfathomable love when He gave human beings the gift of freedom, even if it meant they could rebel against Him. There should have been moments when the man and the woman talked about it and felt fully satisfied with God's stipulation. Why then did Adam just listen to the tempting words of the serpent without asserting himself? Did the word of the serpent have such convincing power that man thought God did not tell him everything?

Adam forgot his responsibility to protect and care for the whole creation that was entrusted to him. God had made man the steward, and therefore a protector and defender of creation when "He took the man and settled him in the Garden of Eden to cultivate and care for it" (Genesis 2:15). It was his duty to protect the creation from the invasion of evil. He should have defended the creation, even if it cost him his life. God would never have let Adam vanish into extinction but would have raised him up like He did with Christ, the new Adam who surrendered Himself totally to the will of His Father. But Adam did not show that level of trust and confidence, and he let the evil one intimidate him.

The failure of Adam consists of abandoning God's command by being a silent spectator initially, and then by disobeying Him eventually. By his silence he let the influence of evil grow and eventually consume them. He should have resisted the enticement of the evil one and protected his spouse from being lured into sin. Rather, he let Eve engage in an ominous conversation with the evil one. He did not prevent her when she approached the tree and plucked the forbidden fruit. He watched her as she delightfully caressed the fruit and ate it. He willingly accepted it from her when she offered him one and ate it himself. He knew well that he was disobeying God's specific instructions. His rebellious action brought punishment upon him at once as he lost that special bond that kept him united with God. His peace of mind was lost instantly and he sought to hide in shame and fear. He hid like a thief, and there was no visible remorse or repentance seen in his actions, only shame and guilt. The sin of Adam led to a breach in the harmony that existed between him and God, between him and Eve, and between him and nature. Adam lost his friendship with God and was banished from the Garden of Eden along with his wife. They also lost their access to the Tree of Life because God knew that having access to it would doom them to live forever in a fallen state, and that was not the destiny God intended for man, the crown of creation.

The Tree of Life would once again become accessible to man through the cross upon which God's beloved Son would offer the ultimate sacrifice: "And when I am lifted up from the earth, I will draw everyone to myself" (John 12:32). Adam's sinful act had brought in death: "Through one person sin entered the world, and through sin death to all" (Romans 5:12). In contrast, Jesus remained totally obedient to the will of His Father; He would triumph over the power of evil by His death and resurrection and restore eternal life for all. Jesus, by His death and resurrection, would defeat the power of evil and death. As the new Adam, Jesus would totally abandon Himself to the will of the Father and in that act of surrender would bring about redemption and restoration of friendship between God and humans.

We might be quick to point out Adam's sin and blame his failure for the reality of original sin and our own fallen state. Certainly, Adam had the right knowledge and clear instructions from God as to how he should live his life and conduct his affairs. Nevertheless, he failed miserably and was quick to blame Eve for his sin. Human beings seem to have acquired a tendency from Adam to point an accusatory finger at the shortcomings of others to justify one's own failures. It might serve us better to realize that we have an abundance of resources that can give us directives for right believing and right living. In our lives, we not only have the right knowledge, clear instructions, and teachings of Jesus, but we also have the example of millions who have said either yes or no to God, and the results of their choices.

*Sin begins with tolerating evil, grows with compromise, and matures in embracing it.*

## For Further Reflection and Discussion

1.   Love is a dynamic principle. It is generative. Can creation be seen as the result of the everlasting love of God?
2.   The "blame game" is very common in our society. Adam blamed Eve, and Eve blamed the serpent. Failure to own responsibility for one's actions further escalates the gravity of a situation. Blame leads to further division, whereas acceptance of one's failure leads to reconciliation. Discuss.
3.   Freedom is true freedom only when you choose what is right. Discuss.
4.   Human beings were created to be good stewards of God's creation. Often God's blessings—"Be fertile and multiply; fill the earth and subdue it. Have dominion over the fish of the sea, the birds of the air, and all the living things that move on the earth" (Genesis 1:28)—are misinterpreted to justify the abuse of natural resources. Discuss.
5.   Compared to Adam and Eve, we possess a multitude of resources that can guide our lives: right knowledge, the life and example of Jesus, the teachings of the church, and the witness of millions of people of faith. How are these sources guiding our lives today?

# EVE:

## Promise of a New Beginning

*"The Lord God said, 'It is not good for the man to be alone. I will make a suitable partner for him'"* (Genesis 2:18).

With bringing Eve to life, God completed creation. It may be that God saved the best for last. Seeing no suitable partner for man, God got down to the challenging task. He put man into a deep sleep, almost to a state of unconsciousness, and performed the first surgery. He took one rib out of man. The rib cage protects the heart and many other vital organs that preserve life. God knew the result of His creation should be dear and close to the heart of man. Couldn't God have chosen any other bone? He certainly could have. He did not choose a bone from Adam's foot, lest she be trampled under. He did not take a piece of bone from Adam's head, that she could rule over him. No, God took one of Adam's ribs that protects his heart. The symbolism is great. She has to be at the side of her man—a true fitting helper, a companion in every sense of the word. In God's mind, the role of the helper, companion, and spouse is to lead the other to holiness. It is the role of the spouse to protect the other from all forms of harm and to lead each other to eternal life.

Eve—woman, as she was destined to bear children—demanded diligent and careful attention from God during the process of creation. Oh, with what tenderness and love He fashioned her! Tenderness and love then, would also become inevitable qualities of her being. God must have taken such great care in creating her because the approval also had to come from Adam. When God brought Eve to Adam, he looked at her and fell in love with her instantly. He exclaimed, "This one at last is bone of my bones and flesh of my flesh; this one shall be called 'woman,' for out of her 'man,' this one has been taken" (Genesis 2:23). They are of the same flesh and same bone, meant to complete each other's existence. Eve must have at once experienced compatibility in seeing Adam. Yes, they were true soul mates!

They were given a perfect world. There existed perfect harmony in that original setting—between the Creator and the creation, perfect harmony within creation, and perfect harmony between man and woman, the crown of creation. Genesis 2:25 says, "The man and his wife were both naked, yet they felt no shame." Scripture is not talking about physical shame that comes from being naked but points to the perfect harmony that permeated the original setting. There existed perfect love and acceptance between man and woman, and in that state of grace there was no room for shame. Their love for each other was pure and innocent, as there existed no sin that distorts purity and innocence.

The perfect unity between man and woman should have led to perfect communication between them. One of the first things Adam might have told Eve as they walked through the Garden of Eden would have been about the two trees: the Tree of Life and the Tree of Knowledge of Good and Evil (Genesis 2:9). Eve wholeheartedly may have agreed with Adam as to how they would obey this command of God. Eve may have said that they shouldn't even set their eyes on those trees. They lacked nothing, so why go in search for anything more? They were in a state of happiness and bliss.

So how did the serpent get Eve's attention? Was she praised by the serpent in an unusual way? Did the cunningness of the serpent break down her defenses? Whatever the case, we find Eve and the serpent in serious conversation that could be detrimental to every form of harmony. Questions are subtly posed by the serpent, and when Eve answers them, the serpent gives them a twist and makes them all sound appealing without any trace of danger. The Serpent, the Father of Lies, assures her that eating the fruit will not cause them death but would be greatly beneficial to them as they would become like gods who know the difference between good and evil. The serpent subtly suggested to her that God did not tell them the whole truth. The idea of being like gods must have appealed to her, for who wants to be a creature if you have the option to be a creator? Who wants to be obedient if you can be above the law?

The Serpent, the Father of Lies, seems to take advantage of the beautiful feminine qualities of tenderness, affection, and trust in Eve. By telling her, "You will not die, you will be like gods," he succeeds in planting seeds of doubt in her heart. She trusted God and His word, but now she began to feel that God had betrayed her trust. Since she had no experience with deceit, she trusted the Serpent. At that moment, seeking the knowledge of good and evil appealed to her more than being obedient to God's commands. The cunning Serpent had enticed her to look at the beautiful fruit, assured her that it tasted delicious, and most importantly convinced her that she would gain greater knowledge. When she looked at the forbidden fruit, she found it extremely appealing, and she could not resist the temptation to touch it, hold it, and eat it. The Serpent had succeeded in planting in her the desire that could lead to sin and to death. Eve's experience is beautifully captured by St. James, "Then desire conceives and brings forth sin, and when sin reaches maturity it gives birth to death" (James 1:15).

One might wonder, "Where was Adam?" The horrible reality was that he was right there, like a silent spectator. Was that not the first sign of the fall? Being the "man of the house," he was exposing the love of his life to danger. This probably was the first indication of failure in his responsibility. He did not stop her from setting her eyes on the tree, touching the appealing fruit, and worse still, he silently witnessed her eat the forbidden fruit, and, alas, ate it himself! In the whole story, Adam was not deceived by the Serpent. He knew what he was doing and deliberately chose his action in freedom. It was a conscious act of rebellion on the part of Adam.

Shame, guilt, anger, frustration, and accusatory tones and gestures all result from their failure. The perfect harmony was broken. Their experience of innocence and purity suddenly vanished. They experienced the strange feelings of shame and guilt and they hid in fear. Love disappeared instantly, and the blame game began: "it's not my fault; it's *your* fault." Adam wanted to put the blame on Eve, and in a subtle way blamed God for giving Eve to him. Eve, on the other hand, wanted to blame the serpent, whose words she believed!

Was Eve unjustly punished with the pain of childbearing and childbirth? Certainly for a woman, these can be painful and sacrificial moments in her life. She has to sacrifice her comfort in many ways to nurture the child growing in her womb. But these could also be the most fulfilling moments of her life, when the child growing within her is the result of true love and commitment. Childbearing and childbirth can become painful moments of curse when there is lack of true com-

8

mitment and total self-giving of oneself to another. When there is no total self-giving and love, what was intended as life-giving could turn out to be sinful and evil.

In pregnancy and childbirth, a woman becomes extremely vulnerable and undergoes pain and suffering. However, none of that takes away her desire to be in union with her husband. What once was presumed as part of the fullness of Adam and Eve—pure love—now has to be realized in the midst of pain and sacrifice. The pain and sacrifice are eased when there exist unconditional self-giving and love. Here "the desire for her husband" would not lead to greater pain and suffering but can become an expression of responsibility and pure love for one another. What appears to be a curse was, in fact, a call to greater responsibility and the promise of a new beginning.

The reality of sin had entered human existence. There would exist an ongoing struggle between evil and the human race until evil would be destroyed by the promised Savior. This becomes clear from God's word to the serpent: "He will strike at your head, while you strike at his heel" (Genesis 3:15). The new Eve, Mary, who would constantly say yes to God and no to evil, would bring forth the Savior who would crush the head of the serpent. God knew that, left to themselves, human beings would not survive the struggle against evil in a fallen state. The sin was so great that no repentance or reparation on the part of human beings could restore the original state of innocence and remove guilt and shame from human experience.

The prophet Isaiah would proclaim that the Suffering Servant—the promised Messiah—would be the One who would take away the shame and guilt: "Yet it was our infirmities that He bore, our sufferings that He endured, while we thought of Him as stricken, as one smitten by God and afflicted. But He was pierced for our offenses, crushed for our sins, upon him was the chastisement that makes us whole, by His stripes we were healed" (Isaiah 53:4–6). Love propels God to bear upon Himself the wounds of human sin. Jesus said, "No one has greater love than this, to lay down one's life for one's friends" (John 15:13). God, who created human beings to be His friends, restores the original friendship through the sacrificial death of His Son, Jesus.

In our own lives the attraction of evil can be so powerful that it can often make us forget God and His love. Feelings such as pleasure, thrill, and fleeting excitement that are often connected with human misdeeds make sin very attractive to our senses and minds. When these feelings take over human minds, willpower loses its strength, discipline is set aside, and morality is forgotten. How often have we fallen prey to the short-term benefits and immediate gratification as a result of yielding to the tempting moments of sin? Many times short-term benefits and immediate gratification have led to greater pain and suffering in life. On the other hand, conquering the temptation of sin and attractions of evil has led to the realization of one's true character and ultimate dependency on God's grace.

*What is right and what is wrong is already decided. It is not arbitrary. By choice we either accept or reject it.*

## For Further Reflection and Discussion

1.  Strong communication strengthens relationships. Did our first parents maintain a strong line of communication between them?
2.  What are the situations in which beautiful feminine qualities such as tenderness, affection, and trust work against a woman?
3.  Short-term benefits and immediate gratification can lead to greater pain and suffering in the long run. Discuss.
4.  Adam blamed Eve and she has been blamed ever since. Does she deserve to be blamed?
5.  Can a failure lead to a new beginning?

# CAIN:

## Consumed by Jealousy and Anger

*"Why are you so resentful and crestfallen? If you do well, you can hold up your head; but if not, sin is a demon lurking at the door…yet you can be his master"* (Genesis 4:6–7).

Life had become tougher for Adam and Eve. They had lost their privileged place in the Garden of Eden. Due to their disobedience and their attempt to become like gods, they had lost their friendship with God. It was not that God had moved out of their lives, but rather, by their deliberate choice, they had moved away from God. As a result they experienced disharmony among themselves. While they were trying to make sense of their new form of existence, God was at work, planning for the redemption of human beings. Genesis 3:21 states, "For the man and his wife the Lord God made leather garments, with which He had clothed them." Some innocent animals were killed and their blood was shed to cover the shame and guilt of Adam and Eve. Adam and Eve had vainly attempted to cover their nakedness when "they. sewed fig leaves together and made loincloths for themselves" (Genesis 3:7). The sin of Adam and Eve should have led to their death. But instead, the innocent lambs were killed in their place, and God clothed them with the skin taken from these animals. God's plan for human redemption would totally be realized when the innocent Lamb of God, Jesus Christ, would shed His blood for the sins of mankind.

God had not taken away the procreative power from them. One of God's most beautiful blessings to Adam and Eve was, "Be fertile and multiply; fill the land and subdue it" (Genesis 1:28). God wanted them to participate in His creative power through love and total uncondi- tional self-giving to one another. The fall had brought pain into child- bearing. There loomed the danger of lust replacing love at any moment, momentary satisfaction replacing commitment, and self-gratification replacing unconditional self-giving for the joy of one another. The first- born in their relationship was Cain. In fact, he was the first human being born naturally in this world. God had created Adam from the clay of the earth. He had brought Eve to life from the rib taken from Adam. Both of them were generated from God's pure love. Could Cain have been the result of his parents' unconditional love, lust, or an "accident"? He seemed to have come into this world with a lot of baggage. The birth of his brother may have made him bitter when he lost the attention of his mother.

Cain learned the art of tilling the soil from his father. We can imagine that he was good at what he did. The young Cain must have been a great help to his father, who battled the thorns and thistles to grow food for the family. Cain rose to the challenge and possessed natural abilities to become the first farmer. Did his success make him generous? No, as he preferred to keep the best for himself. His parents might have told him about bringing the best to God as an act of thanksgiving. But then, what might have been Cain's feelings toward God? Did he blame God for their condition? Adam might have been silent about the whole situation, and Cain might not have listened to Eve when she tried to tell him about God. To make matters worse, lately she seemed to be preoccupied with the younger son. Abel, the younger son, opted to care for the animals in the family. Cain and Abel became the forerunners of two important careers: farming and sheepherding. Millions and millions of people, even up to this day, continue to choose these careers.

Abel seemed to have a special relationship with God and was enthusiastic about bringing an offering from his flock. Cain did not believe in it, but still out of duty, to fulfill an obligation, he brought an offering to the Lord from the fruit of the soil. He looked at his brother, Abel, and saw him bringing the best firstlings of his flocks. He must have laughed in his heart and called his brother a fool for "wasting" such a precious creature. He could have done better, but he chose to keep the best for himself and bring something to God out of sheer obligation. He might have considered himself smarter for keeping the best for himself. *Why burn up some good food for God, who lacks nothing?* he must have thought. Cain was not aware that the omniscient God was able to know the deepest thoughts of his heart.

He was horrified at what the Lord did. God looked favorably upon the offering of Abel but ignored Cain's. It was not an act of preference of meat over grains and vegetables. Rather it was God's acceptance of the one who approached Him with love and gratitude than out of sheer duty and obligation. Abel had demonstrated his love and gratitude to God by bringing the best to Him, while Cain's gesture of keeping the best for himself and reluctantly bringing the leftovers clearly indicated his attitude of negligence toward God. Their attitudes clearly separated them in their relationship with God. God, who could clearly understand the thoughts of these two brothers, joyfully accepted the offering of Abel, and painfully rejected what Cain brought.

However, Cain was not ready for God's response. He thought God was overly partial to his brother. He felt totally rejected, and rage began to seep through his being. He became angry at God, at his parents, at the world, and at his brother. In his mind, everybody else was at fault and he was innocent. Then he began to see a possibility to put an end to this unhappy situation. He probably did not know that the power of sin was taking a strong hold on him as he began to forget about relationships and what the consequences of his horrible act might be. The hatred in him was so great that he did not pay any attention to the reality—that the possible act of murder would deprive his parents of their children—Abel to death, and he himself to evil.

Then he heard the gentle voice of God and His warning, "Why are you so resentful and crestfallen? If you do well, you can hold up your head; but if not, sin is a demon lurking at the door: his urge is toward you, yet you can be his master" (Genesis 4:6–7). He did not fully understand that the gentle voice of God he was hearing in his heart was, in fact, his conscience propelling him to think and act right. For a moment, he attempted to shake off his anger and hostility. He tried to remember the many warnings he had heard about sin and its consequences. But nothing gave him peace, and he allowed the demon of sin to take control over him.

We see God making an attempt to reach out to Cain when He said, "If you do well, you can hold up your head." God was showing His mercy and compassion to Cain, whose attitudes and actions demonstrated indifference and lack of appreciation toward God. God was gently reminding Cain that if he did what was right, he would be acceptable to Him. God also warned Cain when He said, "Sin is a demon lurking at the door." Cain had the opportunity to realize that his weak human nature could easily be susceptible to the enticement of sin, especially when he had allowed hatred to take over his heart. God also gently urged Cain to take control over the situation when He said, "His (sin's) urge is towards you, yet you can be his master." Cain had all the opportunity to discipline his thoughts, change his attitude, and correct his ways. But he let hatred grow rapidly in his heart, and rage consume his being, and he took pleasure in wanting to murder his only brother. Cain had successfully silenced the gentle voice of his conscience when he totally and fully embraced hate and rage in his life.

Cain had never invited Abel to his field. In fact, Cain had warned his brother to keep away from entering his garden. He was always on the lookout for any of his brother's sheep that entered his orchard. He surprised Abel when he invited him to join him. As he walked with his brother, Abel, to the field, he appeared calm on the outside, but fury was raging within him. He knew that he was preparing himself for the horrible act of murdering his only brother in a cold-blooded fashion. It was not an act of self-defense, nor was he trying to protect anything important to him. The violence that was raging within him resulted from allowing himself to be taken over by his passions, jealousy, and hatred. The fact that his brother was innocent meant nothing to him. Cain had allowed sin and demonic power to take control over his faculties.

Cain had failed to realize that sin, to which he now had given power, not only affected him but inflicted unwanted pain and suffering on others. The destructive force of sin was about to take away the life of an innocent person and cause agony and pain to their parents. Cain attacked his brother with such violent force that he killed him in an instant. With a triumphant heart and victorious smile he walked away when he heard the gentle voice of God again, "Where is your brother, Abel?" Taken aback he thought, *No one knows about it. I did it in secret.* Whatever Cain did, luring his brother into the field secretly, away from their parents, was clearly seen by God. There is nothing that is hidden from God's sight, not even one's innermost thoughts.

Frustration and fury are evident in his words: "I do not know. Am I my brother's keeper?" (Genesis 4:9). Cain made a futile attempt to escape his responsibility. He clearly knew where his brother was. He had cold-bloodedly murdered his brother. But when he was confronted by God for the horrible act he committed, Cain realized that the consequences of his act—the murder of his innocent brother—would hound him for the rest of his life. The feeling of victory was short-lived, and it

14

was replaced with fear and emptiness. Cain realized that he could never be at peace, having killed an innocent person and depriving him of his future.

God's mercy was greater than the great sin of Cain, and He promised Cain protection even though he did not deserve it. How much suffering has been brought into human life because of uncontrolled emotions? In Cain's case it was anger, caused by his jealousy, that led to his brother's murder. "You have heard that it was said to your ancestors, 'you shall not kill; and whoever kills will be liable to judgment.' But I say to you, whoever is angry with his brother will be liable to judgment" (Matthew 5:21–22). Jesus was warning His listeners about the danger of this natural emotion—anger. When anger takes over a person, it leads to the death of a relationship. One can cut the other person off from one's life due to the emotion of the anger. Cain had already killed the relationship due to his anger even before he actually murdered Abel.

Human passions, left uncontrolled, can bring enormous pain and unforeseen misery in life. Human beings are not called to be slaves to those passions. Every human passion can at the same time be channeled into a positive energy for the right actions in life: anger can be turned into an enthusiastic passion for justice, and jealousy can be turned into positive ambition to advance in life.

*Anger begins with folly and ends in repentance.*

## For Further Reflection and Discussion

1.  Why didn't God accept Cain's offering but accepted Abel's offering? Can Genesis 3:21 shed light on God's acceptance and rejection?
2.  Psychologists say that anger is a secondary emotion. Anger is generated from frustration, hurt, fear, or disappointment. Discuss.
3.  "Sin is a demon lurking at the door; his urge is toward you, yet you can be his master" (Genesis 4:7). Cain lost the spiritual battle and became the slave of sin. Discuss.
4.  "Am I my brother's keeper?" (Genesis 4:9) What are the implications of this question today?
5.  Genesis 4:17 speaks about Cain's wife. Who was Cain's wife? Can Genesis 5:5 give us a possible answer?

# ABEL:

## Pure and Innocent

*"Abel, for his part, brought one of the best firstlings of his flock"*
(Genesis 4:4).

Abel, the younger son of Adam and Eve, was a happy child. He loved his parents dearly but soon became attached to his mother. Abel loved to listen to the many stories his mother told him about the Garden of Eden. The power and splendor of God constantly amazed him. He heard with sadness the story of the fall and decided never to do anything to offend God. He never blamed his parents for their failure. Neither did he feel that God was uncharacteristically cruel to his parents. He clearly knew what to despise—sin, and the cause of sin, a defiled heart.

Abel saw remorse, shame, and guilt in his mother whenever she narrated the story of the fall. Never did Eve complain that God was cruel, but she always emphasized how ungrateful and naïve she had been. Neither did she blame her husband nor the serpent. However, she constantly warned her sons about the power of evil and the need to keep away from his lies and empty promises. Cain, on the other hand, was not interested in listening to her stories and frequently walked away whenever she tried to relate her experience and warn them of evil and sin.

Abel adored his big brother, Cain. His strong, masculine figure and hard work always amazed him. He loved to go to Cain's field to taste the delicious fruits from his garden, but he was seldom allowed there. He thought Cain was very protective of his orchards and fields. Though he was hurt by the attitude of his brother, he did not let any ill feeling defile his heart. He knew that any form of ill-feeling—be it anger, jealousy, or greed—could take away the joy of one's heart. He did not complain, even when Cain gave him the leftovers or spoiled fruits. He was grateful to get any attention from his brother.

As time went on, he decided to take care of the flocks of the family. It was a great help to his father, Adam. He loved those lambs and took great pride in tending them. They always responded to his voice. He was sad to leave his mother and the coziness of their home and go with the flocks to the pastures. There were many dangerous wild animals searching for food and even they seemed harmless around him. As time went on, the moments in the open fields gave him time to think of God and enjoy the beauty of creation. He was no longer afraid of anything, not even the wild animals, as he felt a sense of God's protection all around him. Abel often reminisced about the breathtaking scenes of the Garden of Eden described by his mother. Yet he marveled at the beauty of nature and wondered if creation were to be so beautiful, how splendid the Creator would be. He would be lost in his thoughts of God, his heart erupting with joy at the thought of being with God forever.

When it was time to offer God the gift, he remembered vividly what his parents had told them. One day, out of curiosity, he had inquired about the leather garments they wore. In his mind, he did not see any value in killing animals to obtain their skins. With tears in their eyes, his parents explained to both brothers about how their sin should have resulted in their death. God had clearly warned them about the consequence of eating the forbidden fruit: "From that tree you shall not eat; the moment you eat from it you are surely doomed to die" (Genesis 2:16). "Our sin should have resulted in death," Eve recounted. "But sin had killed our relationship with God and suddenly we were consumed with guilt, shame, and fear."

"We tried to cover our shame with leaves of the fig tree," Adam added. "The innocent lambs had to die in our place, and God took their skin and clothed us, as if to say the death of the lambs have spared ours." He reminded his sons that each year they had to offer an animal as a sacrifice to God for any sins they might have committed. None of them knew then that the Lamb of God, Jesus Christ, would shed His blood for the remission of human sins and end all forms of animal sacrifice by His death on the cross.

Abel knew that he had to do everything right before God. Though he was not aware of any sins he committed, he knew there were elements of sinful tendencies in him. At times he felt unworthy to stand before the presence of God, who is absolutely holy. As time drew near to offer the sacrifice to God, he wanted to choose the best from his flock. But the best was also his favorite. There were tears in his eyes, yet joy and gratitude in his heart, as he offered his favorite lamb to the Lord. He prayed ardently for forgiveness from his gracious and merciful God. He could see the gracious and loving look on God's face, and he felt his sadness lifted away and his heart experienced inexplicable joy.

He looked at his brother with a joyful smile, only to find him frowning and breathing heavily. Then he noticed spoiled fruits and wasted grains as part of his brother's offering. He had asked his brother to choose any lamb from his flock to offer to God. Cain had chastised his brother by stating that he was man enough to bring the fruit of his own labor to God. Now Abel felt sad for Cain and asked God to accept his offering on his brother's behalf as well. But God gently reminded Abel that Cain should fulfill his own responsibilities in life. Abel told his brother how sorry he was, but Cain walked away, apparently cursing under his breath.

When he narrated the whole experience to his parents, they assured him that he had done what was right before God. His parents reminded him that human beings can never outdo God in generosity. When we offer the best from our part, we receive from God tenfold in return. They also warned him to have the correct disposition and attitude toward God, before whom nothing can be concealed. They explained to him that, although his gracious act of pleading for his brother was indeed noble, Cain was not exempt from his duties and responsibilities before God. Eve encouraged Abel to have a pure heart and to keep on doing what was good and appropriate before God. Adam assured them that he would make Cain understand the importance of sacrifice to God.

Cain had seldom invited Abel to his garden. So it was thrilling for him to hear the words from Cain, "Let us go out in the field." *Oh yes, I will get to see his beautiful garden. Maybe he wants me to pick the fruits and grains and help him make the offering to God,* Abel thought. He wanted nothing more than God's gracious smile and favor on his brother. Then he also panicked, *Could one of my lambs have escaped my attention and destroyed any part of Cain's field?* There were times when he could be lost in his thoughts as the beauty of creation reminded him of God's splendor and magnificence. There were a few sheep in his flock that could cause troubles. *Well, no,* he reassured himself. *Cain would have told me if anything like that had happened.*

He was greatly pleased to see the beautiful garden and its produce. The fruits were so lovely and large, and they looked delicious. He turned to his brother with such great admiration and pride and told him how magnificent his garden was, how the fruits looked lovely and wonderful. He pointed to a few huge ripened fruits and suggested that those could be the best offerings for God along with a lamb from his flock. As he turned to face Cain, he saw the dangerous look in his eyes. It was like the cunning look of the wild animals that often came after his flocks.

He heard a thunderous roar and saw the flashing of a huge club that came crashing down on his skull, and he fell instantly at this heavy blow. Abel did not even have a chance to defend himself before his mighty brother. Even in pain, he thought, *No, this is only a dream; my brother would never do such a thing.* He smiled at his brother, his eyes offering him forgiveness and his heart pleading to God to be merciful to his brother. He prayed that the blood that was gushing out from his head onto the ground would not seek vengeance but rather would cry out to God to help his brother become a better person. There was another growl and a heavy blow on his head and then absolute darkness. Then he saw a ray of light, which became brighter and brighter, enveloping him totally and fully as if in a loving embrace. The blood of the innocent Abel that cried out to the Lord was not seeking vengeance but forgiveness for his brother, because blood that seeks vengeance only multiplies violence. On the other hand, forgiveness offered in place of thirst for blood can prevent further bloodshed and lead to reconciliation.

Abel stands as first in the long line of innocent victims whose lives are taken away by the cruelty of human hearts. The moment of violence that demonstrates a murderer's highest form of hate has also become the moment when the best quality of human spirit is demonstrated through love and forgiveness.

The innocent Lamb of God, Jesus, would go through the mockery of a trial and be condemned unjustly to be crucified. From the cross, Jesus would pray for His executioners, "Father, forgive them, they know not what they do" (Luke 23:34). When the centurion who stood facing Him saw how He breathed His last, he said, "Truly this man was the Son of God" (Mark 15:39).

"As they were stoning Stephen, he called out, 'Lord Jesus, receive my spirit.' Then he fell to his knees and cried out in a loud voice, 'Lord do not hold this sin against them'; and when he said this, he fell asleep" (Acts 7:59–60). Living an innocent and righteous life does not always mean one will not be exposed to the cruelties of this world. Life is often not fair, and even the most amiable can be a victim of the viciousness of evil forces. But a righteous person has the conviction that even in such situations, evil can only destroy the mortal body, not the immortal soul and life with God.

> *"Forgiveness is the fragrance the violet sheds on the heel that has crushed it."* —Mark Twain

## For Further Reflection and Discussion

1.  Creation tells the glory of the Creator. Discuss.
2.  Attitudes and dispositions are everything when we approach the throne of God. Discuss this premise using episodes of the sacrifices of Abel and Cain.
3.  Jesus said, "Blessed are the clean of heart, for they will see God" (Matthew 5:8). Abel was able to see God in creation and in others. Discuss.
4.  Through His death, Jesus ended all forms of animal sacrifices offered to God for the remission of sin. Do you agree? Why or why not?
5.  "Forgiveness is not a sign of the weak, but a weapon of the strong." Discuss this as it relates to the episodes of Abel, Stephen, and Jesus.

# NOAH:

## Righteous Among the Wicked

*"Go into the ark, you and all your household, for you alone in this age have I found to be truly just"* (Genesis 7:1).

Noah is introduced in the book of Genesis as a righteous person. The world at that time was in turmoil and lawlessness, caused by the wickedness of human beings. Sin was reigning supreme in all affairs of human beings. As a result, God had no place in human hearts. Every conceived desire was of evil, and sin multiplied in the world as a result. The evil in the world was so rampant that it made the Creator regret His decision to bring forth creation, an extension of His love. God had created everything good, and His desire was to see goodness pervading in all realms of human life. However, gripped with the power of evil and sin, human beings strayed away from the path of God. They had freely chosen to be enticed by the devil and constantly perpetuated evil ways in their lives. God grieved in His heart and decided to undo the creation to initiate a new beginning.

Noah stood as an exception, and this was pleasing to the Lord. He was a just person and led a righteous life. "I love my Lord," he said often. Some laughed; some shook their heads; some looked aloof; some called him old-fashioned; and occasionally some said he was crazy. But deep in his heart Noah knew his words were simple but true expressions of his devotion to the Lord. He was a man of faith who sought to do God's will at all times. From early on, Noah had realized the destructive effect of sin and sought the power of God to refrain from the attraction of evil. It was not easy, especially when people around him were lawless and immoral. It was a great challenge to swim against the current. There was always the tendency to go with the flow and become involved in the sinful affairs of the world. But Noah stood firm in his faith in the Lord.

Things were not pretty during his days. Noah was not the one to judge by a long shot, but human action often indicated that they had either forgotten about God, felt He was too distant or too busy for them and unconcerned about human affairs, or that He was a myth. The more people distanced themselves from God, the less human and humane they became. There was much bloodshed, violence, shameless exploitation, immorality, corruption, and a litany of other evils. Noah felt sad for the people in his heart because he was convinced that if they knew the Lord, they would act differently. But there existed a bond between God and Noah that helped him to live a good and peaceful life.

Occasionally, Noah would ask the Lord, "Why is there so much corruption, so much violence, so much immorality, and so much lawlessness?" He could hear God say with a sigh, "They still haven't learned." Noah could hear pain in God's voice. It echoed the painful acceptance of reality when your best-laid plans were going to ruins. One day God and Noah walked for a long time in silence. Noah was so glad to be in God's company. Being with God always gave Noah a sense of peace that surpassed all understanding of the human heart, and brought inexplicable joy and contentment. When he looked into God's eyes, he could see disappointment, compassion, sympathy, and determination. He knew that God was about to give him a message of pivotal significance. Noah suspected the words that would come forth from God might not be too good. Sure enough, Noah heard, "They have taken My mercy and patience for granted for such a long time. It is time for a fresh start."

Noah knew when to speak up and when to be silent, and so he accepted the painful reality that God was going to destroy all mortals of the earth because of their wickedness and lawlessness. God startled Noah when He said, "You are going to build an ark, not just for you and your household, but for a pair of every living creature." He had never even imagined such a huge ark, let alone seen one. God made it clear that Noah was to save a pair of every living species, as His intention was not to eliminate creation altogether but to remake it in a new direction. Unfortunately the new direction involved destruction, the inevitable result of evil and sin.

In faith Noah began the monumental task of building the ark with the help of his sons. There was no possibility of hiring anyone for this gigantic endeavor. This unusual task attracted the attention of many people, who were inquisitive about what Noah was doing. Now everyone began to think he was truly crazy. *Why would any sensible person build a 440-foot boat on the land?* they wondered. There was a great deal of distance between the location where the ark was being built and the nearest river. The weather was gorgeous, and when he told them about the impending flood, they all laughed and ridiculed him.

Noah had tried sincerely for years to bring others to repentance, but what he received in return was scorn and mocking. Deep within, he believed that if people turned away from their wickedness and repented, the merciful God would withhold the impending punishment. But the people ignored the warnings of Noah completely. Some even tried to stop him from building the ark, but seeing how determined and obstinate he was, they left him alone. Quite a few times he wondered if this was such a great idea. But he knew his Lord would not ask him to do anything that would be meaningless and thus lead to shame. Noah believed that God's words and promises were always true and fulfilled in time. "The Lord is entering into a covenant with me," Noah reminded himself often.

His wife and daughters-in-law were to oversee the collection of all the food. Initially they were flabbergasted when Noah announced to them what God wanted him to do. However, these women knew Noah well enough to believe what he said. When the time came, Noah's wife and daughters-in-law carefully carried out his instruction to collect as much food as they could muster. Noah had no idea how they did it, but they got it all together for their household and for all the creatures.

Noah wondered about the task of gathering all the animals. He knew well that neither he nor his sons, who were all exhausted with the building of the ark, would be strong enough to gather the animals. More surprises were in store! As he and his sons were about to complete the ark, he saw animals, wild and tame, birds and creeping creatures, coming toward the ark, in pairs—male and female. It was as if the animals understood God's intentions, whereas human beings failed to read the signs of the times. Noah looked around, searching frantically to see if there was someone who might have had a change of heart and decided to join at the last moment. He was disappointed to realize that all his pleadings had fallen on deaf ears. Noah gathered his family together, asked God for protection, and went into the ark with them. Soon they were all in and the doors were closed. Noah knew that it was going to be the end of the world he had known, and he surrendered in faith to God's plans.

The flood was no ordinary one as the waters under the earth burst forth and the waters that were gathered behind the firmament of heaven collapsed onto the earth as if the floodgates of heaven were opened. For forty days and forty nights heavy rain fell, destroying every living creature and along with them all that was evil. God was purifying the earth for a new beginning. Noah wondered many times if the heavy rain that fell upon the ark were God's tears. His own heart ached with pain as he could hear the loud cries for help from all around the ark and imagined the devastating destruction that was happening in the world. He had tried for years to teach the people to be obedient, just, and righteous before God. However, his instruction and pleas were laughed at or totally ignored. He had to humbly admit that it was a moment of purification and that God was initiating a new creation.

The flood can be seen as a pre-figuration of baptism, a grace-filled moment through which one is purified of all evil and given a new beginning. After the rains ended, the dove returning with an olive branch indicated to Noah that the earth was habitable one again. At the moment of baptism, the Holy Spirit removes the destructive power of sin and makes the person a temple of God, habitable for grace to grow and mature.

When Noah came out of the ark, his first action was to build an altar and offer a sacrifice. Pleased with it, God blessed Noah and his sons and renewed the covenant He made with the first parents: "Be fertile and multiply and fill the earth" (Genesis 9:1). The sign of the covenant would be the rainbow, as a reminder that He would never again destroy the earth due to the sinfulness of human beings. Noah also believed that the rainbow would be a sign of God's presence in the world.

God made it clear to Noah that He saw sin as a serious matter—one that offended Him immensely to the point of nearly bringing creation to an end. But He is a God of second chances and offered another opportunity to humanity through Noah. The question still remains, "Did God know humans still would not learn?" God knew it well and understood that human hearts had become so perverse, no punishment would bring them to realize their failures. Yet God was so passionately in love with His creatures that He renewed the covenant and made the rainbow a sign of it. The rainbow in the horizon could remind people of God's love and care. Even this covenant would be neglected by the "I" of human independence apart from God—the result of sin—and God's love would once again be revealed on the cross. God was setting Himself up for greater pain that involved the self-emptying and sacrifice of His only begotten Son, Jesus.

In our human nature, we often fail to learn lessons from the past and neglect the warnings for the future. We live among many who seem to think that this world is their permanent home! Wisdom from above calls us to seek righteousness first and surrender to the will of God.

> *"But of that day and hour no one knows, neither the angels of heaven, nor the Son, but the Father alone. For as it was in the days of Noah, so it will be at the coming of the Son of Man. In those days before the flood, they were eating and drinking, marrying and giving in marriage, up to the day that Noah entered the ark. They did not know until the flood came and carried them all away. So will it be also at the coming of the Son of Man."* —Matthew 24:36–39

## For Further Reflection and Discussion

1. Genesis 6:9 states that Noah was a righteous and blameless man, who walked with God. Discuss the relationship between being righteous and walking with God.

2. Noah built an ark when there was no sign of rain or flood. What are the implications of Noah's faith for us today?

3. Is the experience of the flood compatible with our belief that God is merciful and kind?

4. The first act of Noah when he came out of the ark was to build an altar and offer a sacrifice to God. His actions demonstrated gratitude, trust, and belief in the power of God. Why is worship so important in our journey of life?

5. God made a covenant with Noah. The sign of the covenant was the rainbow. What are its implications for us today?

# ABRAHAM:

## Faith That Overcame All Barriers

*"Abram put his faith in the Lord, who credited it to him as an act of righteousness"* (Genesis 15:6).

Abraham did not hesitate to leave his father's house and land when the Lord asked him. Though he was seventy-five years old, he felt that this venture could be a new beginning. He had always experienced such a special friendship with God. Abraham was grateful that God had chosen him to be His special friend. He was able to talk to God like a close friend and felt safe and secure in His presence. No one could truly understand the depth of faith Abraham had in the Lord. There was a sense of peace that filled the heart of Abraham because of this love relationship.

God was always doing unexpected things in his life. He had no idea what God was up to at this time. The blessing of the Lord sounded wonderful and a little strange at the same time: wonderful, because it was the best he had heard in his life and this blessing could fulfill the greatest possible aspirations of a living being; strange, because it sounded a little unrealistic. He thought, *How could God make me a great nation when my wife and I are childless?* Never had he complained about this to the Lord, though God could see the sadness in His friend's heart. God knew what He was going to do. As Abraham listened to the blessing of the Lord, he felt strengthened by the promise and humbled at the words that echoed in his ears, "All the communities of the earth shall find blessing in you" (Genesis 12:3). This at the same time became the moment of realization for Abraham that there was only one true and living God, who was the Creator of the world, and that His love knew no boundaries.

Nothing stopped Abraham from setting forth on a journey to an unknown land. Sarah, his beloved wife, faithfully obeyed and followed Abraham to the new land. Abraham realized how painful it must have been for Sarah to leave behind her people whom she loved and her familiar surroundings to travel to an unknown land. However, he trusted and believed in the promises of the Lord. He never turned back. He assured Sarah that God's promises were always for their well-being. Twists and turns in life continued. He had to part with his nephew Lot and found himself in Egypt. Though Lot had taken the better portion of the land, Abraham moved on, trusting in God's providential care. As time went on, Abraham may have wondered about the promises of the Lord. He gathered up his strength and made his frustration known: "What good will your gifts be, if I keep on being childless?" (Genesis 15:2). To the delight of his ears, God answered him, "Your own issue shall be your heir" (Genesis 15:4). It is so beautiful to imagine God taking His friend Abraham and showing him the sky that was lit with the numberless stars and telling him, "Your descendants shall be as numerous as the stars" (Genesis 15:5).

What a promise! Optimism and freshness were returning to his life. He reassured Sarah, and trusting in God's promise, they moved on. However, Sarah was getting impatient with the passing time, and she probably thought God needed a little help on her part. *I am barren, but my husband must be capable, so why not give God a helping hand through my maidservant, Hagar?* she thought. The impatience of Sarah only led to greater trouble and pain for all. Though Abraham fathered Ishmael through Hagar, the whole family experienced strife, conflict, and division on account of the impatience of Sarah.

Though Abraham hoped and prayed for peace in the family, God lovingly reminded him that Sarah's impatience demonstrated her lack of faith and that what they were going through resulted from her impetuousness. Shamefully Abraham must have realized his own share in the problem as he had willfully endorsed the plan of Sarah. Abraham sought forgiveness from God and made a decision to trust in God in all situations. Centuries later, the writer of the letter to the Hebrews would sum up faith as "the realization of what is hoped for and evidence of things not seen" (Hebrews 11:1).

However, God was not going to let any human failure upset His plans. He performed the impossible, allowing Sarah to get pregnant in her old age and thereby making His promises come true. Jesus, reasserting the abilities of God, would state that, "All things are possible for God" (Matthew 19:26). Isaac, the love of their lives, was born. No words could fully express the feelings of joy that Sarah and Abraham experienced when they held their son. Looking at this tiny boy, Abraham may have thought proudly, *All the promises of the Lord will come through this little child.*

The greatest test of his life was yet to come. Abraham delighted in hearing the voice of the Lord. As usual he was ready to hear the loving words of God and obey them. As he listened to the words, he must have stood still for a moment thinking that it was a just a dream, and a bad one indeed! He vividly heard, "Take your son Isaac, your only one, whom you love, and go to the land of Moriah. There you shall offer him up as a holocaust on a height that I will point out to you" (Genesis 22:2). Reality soon set in on him that he was going to lose the love of his life, his only son, to the One he loved above all things. No further words were spoken. He did not speak a single word to his wife that night. Time must have stood still as he looked at the sleeping face of his little child. The thought that this was going to be the last night for the family to be together must have ripped through his aching heart.

He must have dreaded the moment when dawn set in. The three-day journey must have felt longer than all his previous journeys. But with every step they took, it was like closing in on the end of his hopes and dreams. He must have looked several times at his cheerful son, who was so happy to be with his father on this long journey, and more excited about offering sacrifice and worshiping God. Tears may have blinded Abraham often when he thought of the final moment. Repeatedly, he must have reassured himself that God knew what He was doing and that His plans were always for his well-being.

He must have been crestfallen when he saw the land of Moriah. Asking the servants to remain there, Abraham and Isaac continued their journey. He might have thought with sadness about his lone return trip. He had already lost Ishmael, his first son, born to Hagar, as he hesitantly obliged Sarah's obstinate demand to send him away. Now he was going to lose Isaac as well. What would he say to Sarah? He knew how deeply Sarah loved Isaac. Would she die of grief, or worse, curse God for this cruelty? Then he heard the sweet sound of his baby boy, "Father, here are the fire and the wood, but where is the sheep for the holocaust?" (Genesis 22:7). He must have choked when he said, "Son, God will provide." Helplessness must have filled his heart when he thought, *There will be no sheep, son, because God wants you to be the sacrifice.*

It must have been a painful experience to build the altar this time. He remembered the tremendous feelings of joy, awe, and unworthiness he felt whenever he had built an altar previously. There was no turning back. Resolved to obey God and trust in His promises, he completed the task. Isaac asked him numerous questions about building the altar, and excitedly told Abraham that he now knew how to build one. As Isaac was excitedly talking about offering sacrifice to God, Abraham was strenuously attempting to hold back his tears and focus on the final task ahead. With trembling hands, he held his son closer for one last time. Isaac must have been surprised at his father's unexpected show of emotions. Though he was totally surprised at his father's behavior, Isaac did not resist when his father tied his hands and placed him on the altar. With shaking hands, Abraham must have reached for the knife. His eyes must have caught the eyes of his son and locked in for what seemed like an eternity. What thoughts of God went through the mind of Isaac as he lay still, helplessly bound and waiting for the knife to pass through his body? Though Isaac had heard of human sacrifices demanded by other gods in surrounding cultures, never did he imagine it as part of the living God whom he loved and served. Still he tried to smile and reassure his father.

Abraham looked at the boy one last time and then turned his head in agony and raised the knife with trembling hands. There was tremendous pain and helplessness. Yet his determination to surrender himself totally to God's will steadied his hands and calmed his heart. He was about to lower the knife onto the tender body of Isaac when he heard the voice of the Lord's messenger, "Do not harm the boy. I know how devoted you are, since you did not withhold from me your own beloved son" (Genesis 22:12). The God of the unexpected and unimaginable things was doing it again. There again was the promise of blessings, and this time in abundance.

"Do not do this to me, my Friend," one might have said when faced with a similar situation. However, Abraham trusted and believed in God. On a human level, Abraham transcended all expressions of trust and faith by his constant acts of surrender. As a human being, he must have experienced tremendous heartache, anxiety, and helplessness. His faith was not just a sentimental feeling or a mere act of the mind but a reality that enabled him to act even in the most challenging situations.

No wonder he is called the Father of Faith and stands before us as the towering example of unconditional trust in the promises of the Lord.

The Father will hear the prayer of His beloved Son: "My Father, if it is possible, let this cup pass from me; it, not as I will, but you will" (Matthew 26:39). God must have turned to His friend Abraham and said with tears in His eyes, "There will be no sacrificial victim to replace him, because redemption of man requires the sacrifice of My beloved Son."

> *"If Columbus had turned back, no one would have blamed him. But we would not have remembered him either."*

## For Further Reflection and Discussion

1.   Abraham talked to God like a true companion. What are the implications of God being a friend of human beings?

2.   Did Abraham always demonstrate absolute faith in God?

3.   "Without a test, one will not have a testimony," goes the dictum. What were those tests that helped Abraham to give us lasting testimonies?

4.   God did not allow Abraham to sacrifice his son. However, Jesus totally surrendered to His Father's will when He died on the cross. Discuss.

5.   "We walk by faith, not by sight" (2 Corinthians 5:7). Discuss it in light of Abraham's life.

# SARAH:

## A Person of Paradoxes

*"God has given me cause to laugh, and all who hear of it will laugh with me"* (Genesis 21:6).

Sarai is introduced in the Bible as the loyal and obedient wife of Abram. In the patriarchal society, important decisions were made by the prominent male member of the family. When Abram's father, Terah, decided to leave the land of Ur, his son, Abram, followed suit, and so did the daughter-in-law, Sarai. It must have been painful for her to leave behind her loved ones and journey to an unknown land. She did not complain but rather followed in obedience. Soon life was to change dramatically for Sarai.

Sarai loved and obeyed her husband, Abram, unconditionally. She bore quietly a sense of shame and embarrassment for being a barren woman. During those days, society and family expected a woman to be productive by bringing forth new life into the world. A woman's worth was often measured by the number of sons to whom she was able to give birth. If she were unable to generate a son for whatever reason, it was deemed to be her fault and her fault alone. Yes, she was fortunate to have a husband who loved her for who she was, not for what she was able to bring into his life, their marriage, and into the world.

Abram had confided in Sarai about his special friendship with God. She was not able to fully understand the ways of God. Though people had a certain understanding of the prevailing presence of the supernatural, their ideas were greatly influenced by their culture and beliefs. However, Sarai noted a marked difference between Abram's faith in God and the general beliefs of other people. Sarai's own understanding of God began to change: from someone who demanded blind obedience and submission, and elicited fear and trembling, to someone who wanted to enter into a loving relationship with human beings.

Ever since the death of Terah, his father, Abram seemed to be too preoccupied and content in spending time alone. Initially Sarai thought that he was mourning over the death of his father. However, Abram did not demonstrate any sign of grieving. On the contrary he was increasingly becoming joyful and enthusiastic about life. Eventually Sarai understood that the cause of Abram's joy was his friendship with God. She was exceedingly happy as she believed that a person who truly loved his God would also care and love others, particularly his wife. Yet she was flabbergasted when Abram announced that they would be leaving the land of Haran for a new land God was going to give them. He was totally convinced that God was calling him out for a special purpose and wanted to cooperate with God completely to fulfill this plan. He shared God's plan with Sarai, the promise of new land and descendants, and the promise of Abram being the recipient and dispenser of blessings to all the nations. Sarai, who was a practical woman, began to be skeptical about the whole situation, greatly due to her barren status. However, Abram demonstrated his faith in God by venturing into his new adventure, and Sarai showed her obedience to Abram by faithfully following him.

Her obedience was not without a price. Their journey had reduced them to mere nomads, and they very often had to go through various forms of physical and emotional hardships. Famine brought them to the land of Egypt, where Sarai had to undergo a severe test. Abram commanded her to disguise her identity as his wife and presented her as his sister. Abram could justify his position as Sarai indeed was his half sister (Genesis 20:12). However, for Sarai, it was a bitter pill to swallow as it entailed the possibility of being taken as one of Pharaoh's concubines. In her mind she preferred famine to the humiliation of being a concubine. Her husband had placed her in such a precarious position, where she would have been forced to commit adultery. Abram's act of cowardliness made her wonder about the depth of his faith in God, who had promised to protect them from every form of danger. It was only logical for her to wonder why Abram, who believed in the power of God, was placing her in such a predicament. Yet she obeyed the command of her husband. For Abram, it was not a moment that was guided by his faith. Nevertheless, for Sarai, whose honor was at stake, it must have been a decisive moment that deepened her faith.

God is always on time; as it is said, "He is an on-time God!" God had set aside both Abram and Sarai for a specific purpose. He was not going to let the Egyptians defile His chosen ones. God inflicted a severe plague on the household of Pharaoh, who had no choice but to let Sarai go with Abram. The whole episode might have made Sarai a bit more convinced about the power of God. Probably that was the reason she agreed to go with Abram's suggestion a second time in the land of Gerar when he asked her to say "he is my brother" (Genesis 20:5). A woman places her trust in the one who protects her honor, and she was increasingly becoming convinced of God's mighty power.

Abram had shared God's amazing promise of blessing with Sarai. The promise entailed possession of the land and descendants as numerous as the stars of the sky and sand on the seashore. Though it all sounded exciting and wonderful, Sarai, a barren woman who had passed the childbearing years, could not fathom how such a promise would ever be materialized. Yet she was willing to wait and see if God would act favorably on her behalf. But with each passing month and year, she became convinced that her destiny was to die childless. She was tormented between the promise of God and her practical view of life. This is where Sarai began to think a little too hard and make decisions that would bring even greater pain for her. She must have reasoned that *probably God needs my help in this matter. After all, He saved me from precarious situations in Egypt and Gerar.* The memory of the events in Egypt brought her focus on to her Egyptian maid, Hagar.

Sarai reasoned that God's promise to Abram was to give him descendants as numerous as the sky. It could still be realized if she acted quickly and gave her maid over to Abram. Sometimes when the ultimate goal becomes the paramount priority, the means resorted to achieve the goal become less important. Though it was painful for her to imagine her husband in the embrace of another woman, she was willing to pay that price for obtaining the ultimate goal. She convinced Abram that this could fit well within the plan of God. Abram listened to Sarai and took Hagar as his concubine. Sarai's plan was being materialized as Hagar became pregnant. However, the knowledge of her pregnancy led Hagar to forget about her position as a slave in the family. Hagar's privileged status, which resulted from being impregnated by Abram, made her blind with disdain toward Sarai.

Sarai ruefully understood what impatience and lack of trust in God could result in. She had to learn her lesson the hard way. The result of

Sarai's mistake, which Abram willfully endorsed, became the source of trouble and conflict in the family. When Sarai voiced her complaints to Abram, he reminded her that she was still in charge and she could treat Hagar the way she chose to. Resentment, frustration, jealousy, and revenge were all visible in the way Sarai treated Hagar. Hagar, who endured severe punishment from Sarai, attempted to run away from her mistress. For Hagar, that painful moment became a source of blessing as God encountered her, persuaded her to return to Sarai, and unfolded His plans for her and her unborn child.

God's promise always comes to pass in its appropriate time. The realization of God's promise is not an act of chance, luck, or coincidence. Rather, it is made possible by the power of God at the most appropriate time. He was ready to act powerfully in the lives of Abram and Sarai. The first thing God did was to change the names of this chosen couple: Abram was changed to Abraham, which meant "father of nations," and Sarai ("princely") was changed to Sarah ("princess/queen"), and by extension "mother of the nations." God assured Abraham that His promise would pass through the child Sarah would bring forth. At that time Abraham was ninety-nine years old and Sarah was eighty-nine!

God was acting in history with a specific goal of forming His chosen people. He had called one man (and his wife), and from them He intended to create one nation, through whom the promised Messiah would be born. It is fascinating that for the first time God was revealing Himself as a community of persons (the three visitors to Abraham and Sarah are often seen as the pre-figuration of the Trinity: Father, Son, and Holy Spirit), for the creation of the chosen people, that inevitably entails a community and unity of people. The words of one of the three visitors resonated urgency and purpose: "I will surely return to you about this time next year, and Sarah then will have a son" (Genesis 18:10).

For a couple who longs for children, the knowledge of pregnancy is a matter of inexplicable joy. For a couple who is 100 and 90 respectively, the knowledge is ecstatic and fulfilling. What must have been the thoughts that ran through the mind of Sarah when she realized that she was pregnant? How eager must she have been to share the news with Abraham? For this elderly couple, the birth of a child not only meant protection for their old age but also entailed a powerful manifestation of God's power and fulfillment of His promises. They must have expressed their profound gratitude to God through their continuous praise and act of worship. They must have come to the realization that in Him and through Him all things are possible.

For Sarah each day must have brought a tremendous sense of joy as she experienced the growth of her baby in her womb. She must have been anticipating the day in which she would be able to hold him in her bosom. When finally the day arrived and the baby was born, she remembered God first when she said, "God has given me cause to laugh, and all who hear of it will laugh with me" (Genesis 21:6). Sarah was profoundly grateful in acknowledging the mighty deeds of God in her life.

There is a natural instinct in every mother to look after the best interest of her children. Sarah let her instinct dominate her thinking when she demanded Abraham to expel Ishmael, who was born to Hagar. She wanted all inheritance and blessings to go to Isaac, the legitimate son of Abraham. Though it was painful for Abraham, he conceded, and having received assurance from God of His plans for Ishmael, he sent Hagar and Ishmael away. Sarah was content and began to devote all of her attention to her son.

The hardest and longest days in her life probably were when Abraham took Isaac and went off to the land of Moriah to offer sacrifice to God. Though Abraham did not reveal the nature of God's command to his wife (to offer Isaac as a holocaust), she must have been anxious about the whole affair. She knew that journey to the mount of Moriah took at least three days. The thought of Isaac being away from her presence must have caused her great anguish, though her anguish was nothing in comparison to Abraham's agony. For Sarah those six days must have felt like six years in her life. What a relief it must have been for her to see her boy upon his return. She must have held her son in her tight embrace and shed tears of joy and gratitude. There must have been tears of joy and relief in the eyes of Abraham and Isaac for reasons different from hers. God must have been smiling on all three of them and preparing them for greater blessings.

*Impatience has great power to make
a situation go from bad to worse.*

### For Further Reflection and Discussion

1.  What were the positive qualities of Sarah?
2.  What were the negative qualities Sarah demonstrated?
3.  Sarah's practical thinking brought her great pain. How do you know your practical points of view on life are in conformity with God's will?
4.  What do you do when you do not see God's promises coming to pass?
5.  What were those moments when you had to pay a heavy price for your impatience?

> *"They that wait on the Lord will renew their strength, they will soar as with eagle's wings; they will run and not grow weary, walk and not grow faint."* —Isaiah 40:31

# HAGAR:

## Blessed Beyond Her Imagination

*"Go back to your mistress and submit to her abusive treatment. I will make your descendants so numerous"* (Genesis 16:9-10).

Hagar is often thought to be a naïve and powerless slave girl, who became a victim of cruelty in the household of Abraham and Sarah. In reality, she came from a sophisticated culture and civilization, as Egypt was recognized to be a land of progress. The fact that she was a slave in Pharaoh's court elevated her status and put her in the category of those who were beautiful, talented, and trustworthy. Becoming part of Abraham's household deprived her of the privileges that she had enjoyed at Pharaoh's palace and forced her to endure the status of a nomad. Though she had to undergo a tremendous amount of physical and emotional suffering, she became a recipient of God's special favors. Her life bore a powerful testimony of knowing God, growing in faith, and believing in the power of God. The story is also a reminder to us that no one is too insignificant for God, and that His love is extended to everyone.

The story of Hagar is inextricably linked with the story of Sarah. Scarcity of food had brought Abraham and Sarah to Egypt, a land of abundance. Abraham knew that his beautiful wife, Sarah, would attract the attention of the Egyptians. Hence he ordered her to disguise her identity as his wife and introduced her as his sister. Abraham's fears came true when Pharaoh took Sarah to his palace. Pharaoh handsomely rewarded Abraham with male and female slaves and various kinds of flocks and herds. Abraham probably received Hagar as one of the females slaves in exchange for Sarah. Abraham might never have imagined then that his wife, Sarah, who now was reduced to the status of Pharaoh's concubine, would one day give him one of the Egyptian slaves, Hagar, to be his concubine.

But the Lord let severe plagues affect all in Pharaoh's palace (Genesis 12:17). Pharaoh, inflicted with God's punishment, realized his mistake and allowed Abraham and Sarah to leave the land with all their possessions. Sarah was proud of her new possessions, particularly the female slaves. However, for Hagar, leaving Egypt meant leaving her culture and her people, being deprived of her privileges, and being made part of a household that seemed to wander through different lands. She grieved over her losses but decided to make the best of whatever came her way. Hagar was well aware of her physical beauty and charm. She was very skilled in all the tasks that were assigned to her. It was only a matter of time before Sarah took note of the efficient young slave girl and began entrusting her with important household tasks. She possessed several special qualities that helped her win over the trust of her new mistress, Sarah.

Though Hagar despised her current status as a slave in a Hebrew family, she did not explicitly demonstrate any such feelings. She kept all her thoughts to herself, like any other slave would in such circumstances. She was respectful toward Abraham and Sarah, and often found herself doing a multitude of chores for the couple. She was grateful that the couple had no children, as children would have increased her responsibilities. She had heard from her mistress some strange promise that they had received from some strange God. She must have laughed in her heart when she heard this elderly couple was hoping to have descendants as numerous as the stars in the sky. Though she secretly scoffed at their beliefs, she was impressed with their devotion and piety toward their God. Hagar was not particularly religious and could not care less about any practices of religion. She had no hesitation in blaming religious practices for perpetuating evils such as slavery.

However, she found a substantial difference between the way Egyptians and her new owners looked at the divine. Abraham and Sarah seemed to have an understanding of God based on their personal experiences. Abraham in particular talked about God as if He was a friend and constant companion. She knew that Abraham was different from anyone else, as he did not rule the slaves in his household with an iron fist. Female slaves in Abraham's house did not have to submit themselves to their master, which was a common practice at that time. It did not take her much time to realize that all of Abraham's actions were guided by his faith in God. She was intrigued at his unwavering trust in God's promises, that He would bless Abraham and make him a great nation. On the other hand, Sarah, who was a practical person, seemed skeptical about the whole affair. Hagar shared Sarah's skepticism about such a possibility, due to her mistress's age.

Hagar was flabbergasted when Sarah informed her that she had decided to give her as a concubine to Abraham. Sarah had engineered a plan and insisted that Abraham should accept Hagar as his concubine. She had explained clearly to Hagar that her role as Abraham's concubine would end upon the procreation of a child and her place as a slave would revert back to her. Hagar realized that she was powerless to resist the instruction of her mistress and submitted to her fate. She was not consulted about this arrangement but was commanded to comply. Though it was unrealistic for a slave to dream about the possibility of having a normal and independent life, Hagar had often hoped for the day when she would be free to have a loving husband and a family of her own. All such dreams were shattered with Sarah's well-laid plan, and Hagar resolved to make the best out of her given situation.

Hagar was touched by the gentleness and kindness of Abraham. He did not treat her as an object of pleasure; rather, he showed her love and understanding. It was the first time Hagar experienced true love from another person. For a change, she was enjoying respect and admiration from others, particularly fellow slaves. As days drifted into months, she announced to Abraham and Sarah the good news of her pregnancy. The news brought great rejoicing for Abraham and Sarah. All who were part of Abraham's household rejoiced at this news and showered great appreciation on Hagar. She began to enjoy her elevated position and was determined to retain it forever. She began to act differently, as if she now had a privileged position and power. She justified her disposition by reasoning that she was about to give a child to Abraham, which Sarah, his wife, had failed to do. She now was destined to bring forth the child through whom God's promises would be fulfilled. It was only natural for Hagar to let her maternal pride overshadow her legal status. As a result she no longer gave Sarah the deference she deserved. Hagar had renounced Sarah's position as her mistress and wholeheartedly embraced Abraham as her sole master. She did not want to go back to being a slave.

Sarah was livid at the changes she saw in Hagar. When jealousy and the quest for power begin to dominate human hearts, they result in strife and discord. Sarah's frustration was evident as she bitterly complained to Abraham and blamed him for endorsing such behavior from Hagar. Though Abraham had affection for Hagar, he emphatically asserted that Hagar's status had not changed: "Your maid is in your power. Do to her whatever you would please" (Genesis 16:6). Sarah, who was deeply hurt by Hagar's pride and disdain, decided to make the maid suffer for her vainglory. Sarah abused her maid physically, emotionally, and mentally. Reverting her to the status of a slave, Sarah increased her workload, constantly chastised her with abusive words, and mocked her continuously for her naïveté. Sarah seemed to take great pleasure in making life difficult for Hagar.

Hagar was greatly distressed at the painful treatment she received from her mistress. She felt that the punishment she was enduring was more severe than she ever deserved. She was extremely hurt at the silent treatment she received from Abraham, who apparently preferred peace in the family. The punishment became too overbearing for the young pregnant maid, and she became desperate to escape. Though Hagar knew that it was extremely difficult for her to get back to Egypt, she ran away from Sarah and began her journey through the wilderness to Shur, hoping to end up in Egypt. The journey through the arid wilderness was fearsome and dangerous. Her pregnant status made her travel all the more unbearable and difficult. Yet she demonstrated great tenacity and courage and stepped out with the sole goal of getting back to her homeland.

The journey exhausted her tremendously, physically and emotionally. She was constantly on the lookout for possible dangers, be it from wild animals, reptiles, and worse still, from other cruel human beings. Although she did not have a strong sense of faith, she found herself begging the gods for protection and needed strength to continue her journey. Strangely, she felt no emotional connection to her familiar Egyptian gods. Though she thought about "that God" whom Abraham and Sarah worshipped, she could not bring herself to ask for help. She was hurt and outraged, and had concluded that she wanted nothing from Abraham, Sarah, or their God. Yet her struggles and sufferings were so great she had no choice but to call out to heaven for help.

The sight of a spring with clean water brightened her spirit, and she helped herself with a long drink. She had no knowledge that life was going to change dramatically for her. Though she was physically exhausted and emotionally drained, she began to experience a sense of peace in her soul. The feeling was unlike anything she had ever experienced in her entire life. For the first time she was enveloped by pure love as she experienced the powerful presence of God. The messenger of God commanded her to return to Sarah and submit to her abusive treatment. This was the greatest test of Hagar's life. She did not want to go back to Sarah. Initially she could have thought God was acting on behalf of Sarah, as her return to Sarah could signify victory for her mistress. She had to learn in time that God's ways are different from human ways. God's promises to Hagar were far beyond her imagination, as He promised her a son and a new destiny. She returned to Sarah with a new purpose in life and submitted to Sarah's abusive treatment.

The birth of Hagar's son, Ishmael, brought tremendous joy to all, except for Sarah. Hagar demonstrated her faith in God by her act of obedience as she named her son Ishmael as instructed by God's messenger (Genesis 16:11). Contrary to her expectation, the birth of a baby in the household did not ameliorate the severity of Sarah's treatment of Hagar. She learned to deal with her mistress and drew great comfort and strength from being with her child. She was totally devoted to her son and took great pride in seeing her son with his father, Abraham. She watched him grow from an infant to a toddler and to a handsome adolescent boy. But the destiny of the mother and son was to change dramatically soon.

The whole household of Abraham erupted with joy at the news of Sarah's pregnancy. However, for Hagar the news was an ominous sign. While everyone rejoiced at the birth of Isaac, Hagar was agonizing over the future of her son. When Sarah gave birth to her firstborn son, Hagar clearly instructed Ishmael to keep a safe distance from Sarah and Isaac. However, as the saying goes, "boys will be boys." Ishmael neglected the instruction of his mother and playfully began to tease his infant brother. The innocuous gesture from Ishmael caused unwarranted fury in Sarah, who demanded that Abraham expel Hagar and Ishmael from their household. Hagar, knowing that the inevitable had finally come, began making preparations to leave the household a second time. Unlike the first time when she was eager to run away and escape the cruel treatment of her mistress, she was hesitant to leave the safety of the place on account of her son. She felt that Ishmael was un-lawfully robbed of his rights to be in the house of his father. She was totally aware of her powerlessness and helplessness. Though she was tempted to beg Abraham to permit them to remain in the household, she realized that she would be fighting a losing battle against the arro-gance of Sarah.

Hagar must have spent the last night in Abraham's house with great anxiety and anguish. Repeatedly she must have looked at her son, who appeared to be restless as well. When the dreaded morning arrived, they came out of their tent to find a distraught Abraham getting provi-sions together for their journey. Looking at his face, Hagar could see the pain he was enduring. Abraham held his son in a tight embrace for one last time and assured them that God would provide them the pro-tection that he was unable to give. All three of them had tears in their eyes when they said good-bye to each other.

Their journey became hard and long with each passing hour. Though Ishmael repeatedly asked her about their destination, she was unable to give him a satisfying answer. She thought about returning to Egypt. However, as she was very confused about the direction, it did not take them long before they began to roam around in the wilderness. Ishmael insisted that he was strong enough to endure the hardship and repeatedly urged his mother to drink from their waterskin. As they dragged themselves along, Ishmael became the first victim of exhaus-tion and thirst. The pain in Hagar's heart was so great that she could not bring herself to look at the face of her dying son. The cry of Ishmael penetrated her heart, and she began to sob uncontrollably.

The cries of a helpless child and an agonized mother opened the doors of heaven, and God's messenger once again appeared to Hagar and assured her of God's protection. Once again she experienced the presence and power of God in her life, and she surrendered herself to-tally to the mighty God. She was no longer afraid as she knew that God would protect and provide for them. God provided for their needs and His Spirit was with Ishmael. He grew up to be an expert bowman and made the wilderness of Paran his home. As he grew older and became prosperous, Hagar, his mother, arranged a marriage for him with an Egyptian girl. Hagar constantly reminded Ishmael that he should con-tinue to respect his father, Abraham, and love his brother, Isaac. She had the joy of seeing her son grow and mature to be a well-respected person.

In many ways Hagar's life and destiny are similar to that of Abraham's. Both left their homeland. Both Abraham and Hagar were given the promise of descendants and lands. Both went through moments of uncertainties in life. Both faced the possible death of their beloved son. Yet, in the end, both became recipients of blessings beyond their imagination. The story of Hagar demonstrates the breadth of God's universal love and care. She is the only woman in the Bible to receive God's promise of numerous descendants and lands. Though she is not an Israelite, God appeared to her twice and delivered her from precarious situations.

> *"May God give you...for every storm a rainbow, for every tear a smile, for every care a promise, and blessing in each trial."* —An Irish blessing

## For Further Reflection and Discussion

1.  Hagar became deprived of the safety and security she enjoyed in Egypt. She had to undergo tremendous suffering under Sarah, yet she was blessed beyond her imagination. Discuss.
2.  Both Hagar and Sarah hurt each other by their attitudes and actions. Describe ways in which they could have reconciled with each other.
3.  What are the evil forces that can destroy the unity of a family?
4.  Hagar's story reminds us that God sees the pain and sufferings of people. What has been your experience of God? Do you feel that God answers your painful cry for help?
5.  How does the story of Hagar illustrate God's universal love and gratuitous gift of grace?

# ISHMAEL:

## God Hears at the Most Opportune Time

*"Drive out that slave and her son! No son of that slave is going to share the inheritance with my son Isaac!"* (Genesis 21:10).

Sometimes innocent children have to suffer the consequences of their parents' choices. Some say that it is unfair for a child to face such challenges that were created by others' actions. However, such struggles a child may face are not necessarily the end of his/her future. The story of Ishmael is one of triumph in the midst of trials and tragedies, and shows God's decisive actions in the lives of a single mother and her son, and their resilience against all odds. The episode of Ishmael is tangled with the impatience of the matriarch of the family, Sarah; the helplessness of his mother, Hagar; the indiscretion of his father, Abraham; and the providential care of the Divine.

The impetuous initiative and impatience of Sarah led her to give Hagar, her Egyptian maid, as a concubine to Abraham. Apparently such practices were acceptable in that society, as we see in Genesis 30:1–13. When Hagar became pregnant, her disposition toward Sarah changed and the relationship between the two women became estranged. Although Hagar attempted to run away from the cruel treatment of her mistress, which Abraham silently endorsed, God's messenger commanded her to return and submit herself to Sarah. Though she was hesitant, the assurance and promise of God to make the son in her womb a great nation empowered Hagar to face her trials. It is fascinating to see that God, who heard the cry of an Egyptian in the hands of a Hebrew woman, would also hear and respond to the cries of the Hebrews in the hands of the Egyptians. By assuring His protection of her, God was revealing to Hagar His universal love. Upon her return to Sarah, she endured the cruel punishment and looked forward to that day when she would give birth to her son and hold him in her arms.

The birth of a baby boy brought tremendous joy to his mother, Hagar. She truly believed that God had seen her sufferings, heard her cries, and blessed her with this precious gift. She named the baby boy Ishmael, which means "God hears." Though the birth of a son in the household was an occasion of jubilation for all, there loomed an air of uncertainty due to Sarah's attitude. Abraham was ecstatic to hold the fruit of his flesh in his hands. All male and female slaves rejoiced with Abraham and Hagar. However, from the beginning, Ishmael received indifference and resentment from the mistress of the household, Sarah, who felt that her well-laid plans were going against her.

Ishmael embodied greatness and vulnerability simultaneously. He was the oldest son of Abraham, and by society's standard, the one who was the heir to Abraham's wealth and family name. His beloved mother, Hagar, never left his side and attended to all his needs herself. His father, Abraham, showed tremendous affection and appreciation toward him. But it was Sarah's attitude that baffled him. She was often unkind to him and took great pleasure in punishing and chastising him. She often referred to him as "that slave's son." He knew who his father was. He did not understand why his father did not intervene to make their situation better. He could not initially fathom why his mother let Sarah treat them the way she did. As time went on, he realized that their position in the household was at the mercy of Sarah. As early as his childhood, Ishmael had heard from his mother the promise God had made to Abraham—the promise of new land and children. Initially he did not understand its implications and never imagined there would come a day when he would be forced leave the house and his father.

Ishmael enjoyed his father's undivided attention and love. It was his father who talked to him about God and His care for all people. Abraham encouraged his son to trust in God and believe in His ways even when things were not clear. Ishmael totally believed and trusted his father and hoped that he would have the same special relationship with God. Though Abraham was up in age, he took keen interest in teaching his son skills that would make him a successful youth. It was from Abraham that Ishmael learned the arts of archery and swordsmanship. Ishmael enjoyed every moment he could muster to be in the company of his father. As far as he was concerned, he was the sole son of his father. He also believed that he would inherit his father's name, blessings, lands, and possessions.

When God renewed His covenant with Abraham (Genesis 17), He

also revealed His plans for Ishmael. When God announced that his promises were soon going to be fulfilled through the son who would be born to Sarah, Abraham was anxious about the future of his firstborn son, Ishmael. God's promise to bless Ishmael and make him a great nation (Genesis 17:20) gladdened Abraham. However, Ishmael was too young to understand the implications of God's promise.

God, who acted many times in the life of Abraham, brought in the greatest of surprises when He blessed Sarah with a child. Laughter echoed everywhere, and the child who would be born to Sarah would be given the name Isaac, which means "laughter." While the rest of the household of Abraham rejoiced at this news, Ishmael and his mother were gripped with uncertainty and panic. Ishmael hoped against all hope that the child growing in Sarah's womb would be a girl. He was aware that if Sarah were to give birth to a male child, his hope to inherit Abraham's blessing and family name would be sabotaged. Though Hagar was uncertain about their future, she assured her son of God's promises of triumph in their lives. She urged her son to carry on with the normal affairs of life and not to worry about the future.

Sarah did not abate her maltreatment toward Hagar or Ishmael. Ishmael had learned to avoid Sarah. However, his heart ached at the thought of his mother's trials and tribulations at the hands of their mistress. When Sarah gave birth to a male child, the household of Abraham erupted with jubilation and festivities. For Ishmael, it was the final blow to his wishful thinking that the child born to Sarah might be a girl. He knew that his fate was now sealed, and the birth of his younger brother stripped him of the bright future he had envisioned for himself. Hagar disguised her anguish well and assured him that God had better plans for him. She urged her son to stay away from Sarah and Isaac.

When a feast was held to celebrate the weaning of Isaac, Ishmael forgot the warnings of his mother. Having become caught up in the mood of celebration, Ishmael playfully began to pick on his brother. Initially it was an innocent act. But the more Ishmael played with his younger brother, his feelings of indignation and jealousy began to grow stronger in his heart. There were times when he had been ridiculed by other boys and girls at his status of being a slave's son. He knew that people's attitude toward him had changed since the birth of Isaac. He looked at his brother as the primary reason for his misery and the deprival of his father's name and inheritance. Ishmael increasingly became angrier and began to mock and insult his little brother. He was unaware that the whole ordeal was secretly observed by Sarah, who was waiting for an opportunity to get back at Hagar and Ishmael.

As he heard the fuming voice of Sarah, he ran away from the scene. Though Ishmael knew he would be in trouble, he did not fathom its gravity. Sarah perceived it as an opportune moment to voice her concerns and grievances against her enemies. Unequivocally she demanded Abraham to "drive out that slave and her son! No son of that slave is going to share the inheritance with my son Isaac!" (Genesis 21:10). Obviously Abraham was greatly troubled at the stance of his wife. He also grieved at the conduct of his elder son. Abraham loved him and did not want to see him go. As always Abraham turned to God, seeking His guidance and direction to solve the crisis at hand. God calmed Abraham through these words, "Do not be distressed about the boy or about your slave woman. Heed the demands of Sarah, no matter what she is asking of you; for it is through Isaac that descendants shall bear your name. As for the son of the slave woman, I will make a great nation of him also, since he too is your offspring" (Genesis 21:12–13). Abraham trusted in the promises of God and decided to act according to God's instruction. Yet, he knew the absence of his older son from his life would grieve him gravely.

Ishmael was distraught as the events began to unfold before him. His failure to heed the warning of his beloved mother had put them both in great peril. He vainly wished he could turn time back and act differently. Upon learning the painful news of their expulsion from their home, he spent the last night in great agony. Repeatedly he asked his mother to forgive him for his actions. Though she tried to comfort him, he could see great anguish and pain in her heart.

Every morning Ishmael was joyfully greeted and received a warm embrace and kiss from his father. This morning was strangely different. Ishmael noticed that his father had already gathered provisions for the journey. Both stood in silence, with tears in their eyes. When they reached out to each other for one last embrace, each could feel the other person's agony. Abraham whispered into the ears of his son God's promises and urged him to take care of his mother.

Ishmael and his mother began their difficult journey through the wilderness. Though he inquired several times about their destination, she was unable to provide a satisfactory answer. He assumed that they were headed to Egypt, her mother's homeland. He tried to remember all the fascinating things she had told him about Egypt. As they moved deeper and deeper into the wilderness, Ishmael knew that they were lost and were merely roaming through the arid desert. Their provisions were increasingly becoming smaller, and they were growing exhausted. Ishmael recalled his father's command to take care of his mother. Ignoring his hunger and thirst, he urged his mother to eat and drink. He was persistent in his persuasion and assured her that as a young man he could endure any hardship. He even tried to demonstrate his strength by carrying her on his shoulders for a while.

With each passing hour, both of them were increasingly becoming weary. Ishmael's young body could no longer take the heat of the scorching sun, and he became the first victim of dehydration, exhaustion, and fatigue. Hagar knelt down beside him and looked at the tired face of her son. Repeatedly she told him of her undying love. With each passing moment, it became clearer to them their death was imminent. She felt totally helpless and moved farther away as she was unable to witness the death of her son. The sobbing of her son penetrated her heart with such agony, she raised her eyes to heaven begging for protection. The cries of the dying son and helpless mother were heard. True to what the name Ishmael means, "God hears," God heard their cry and responded in time to save the dying mother and son. God's messenger appeared a second time and assured them that they were not abandoned by God. He reminded her of God's plan for Ishmael, and directed her to the well where she could find water for their journey.

God's promise always comes to fruition in its appropriate time. His Spirit remained with Ishmael, and he grew up to be an expert bowman. His mother continually reminded him to remain faithful to God and His ways. When he became an adult, Hagar arranged his marriage to a young Egyptian woman. God blessed him with lands and dependents. In time Hagar and Ishmael realized God's plan for them was better than they had ever imagined. With each passing year, bitterness and anger dissipated from their hearts. Both grieved bitterly when they heard the news of the death of Abraham. With the blessing of Hagar,

Ishmael returned to his father's home, from where he was once expelled, and joined his brother, Isaac, in providing a dignified burial for their father. Their father's death became a moment of unity for these two brothers. God was smiling as He watched the two brothers embrace in love and was preparing to bless them even more abundantly.

How often we find people who blame external situations for their miserable status. There are many who become powerless victims of circumstances and situations. However, we also come across people who rise to the challenge and do not let situations and circumstances determine the quality of their lives. Ishmael could have blamed the situation and circumstances for his plight. He could have blamed his father, Abraham; Isaac, his little brother; Sarah, the mistress of the house; or Hagar, his mother, for all the uncertainties and insecurities that he had to face in life. He could have remained bitter toward any or all of the treatment he had received. He did not allow himself to be a victim. Rather, against all odds, he remained hopeful and became an instrument of peace.

*"Hope is the power of being cheerful in circumstances that we know to be desperate."* —G. K. Chesterton

## For Further Reflection and Discussion

1.   Sometimes an innocent child suffers the consequences of his/her parents' choices. Discuss.
2.   The fundamental dignity of a child is not affected by the status of his or her parents. Do you agree? Why or why not?
3.   Did Hagar and Ishmael deserve the punishment given to them?
4.   Ishmael and Isaac joined together to bury their father. Should we wait until disaster strikes for harmony?
5.   The most hopeless situation can become a wellspring of God's blessings. Discuss.

# ISAAC:

## Courageous Even in the Face of Death

*"Father…here are the fire and the wood, but where is the sheep for the holocaust? Abraham replied, 'son, God Himself will provide the sheep for the holocaust'"* (Genesis 22:7-8).

Isaac was the long-awaited and only son of Abraham and Sarah. God had promised to Abraham possession of new land and descendants as numerous as the stars of the sky. God's promises come to pass at His appointed time. However, with each passing month and year, the elderly couple must have wondered when that appointed time would be. Sarah, whose childbearing ability had deserted her long ago, devised a plan and gave the slave girl, Hagar, to Abraham as his concubine. In her mind, God's promises could certainly come to pass through a child Hagar would give birth to. This impatience brought about painful consequences for the whole family. Yet, the imprudence of human judgment was not going to deter God's plan for this particular family and the human race. In the appointed time, God looked favorably upon Sarah and she became pregnant. The news of Sarah's pregnancy brought tremendous joy to all in the household of Abraham, except Hagar, the Egyptian maid, and her son, Ishmael.

When God entered into this covenantal relationship, He assured Abraham and his descendants of His faithfulness and protection. He instructed Abraham to have every male child born into the family circumcised as the sign of the covenant: "This is my covenant with you and your descendants that you must keep—every male among you shall be circumcised…Throughout the ages, every male among you, when he is eight days old, shall be circumcised" (Genesis 17:10–12). Circumcision became a definite sign that set the descendants of Abraham as the chosen people. Fulfilling this command, Abraham circumcised Isaac, his newborn son, on the eighth day.

There was great joy and laughter in the household of Abraham after the birth of Isaac. In fact, his name itself, Isaac, meant "laughter." His mother, Sarah, was ecstatic as she held her newborn in her arms, and laughter echoed in the house. On the day when Isaac was weaned, Abraham gave a great feast for all in the land. All was well for Abraham, Sarah, and Isaac until Sarah began to think seriously about the future of Isaac. Although Isaac was their only legitimate son, she could not deny the fact that Ishmael was the firstborn son of Abraham. The presence of Hagar and Ishmael continually reminded Sarah of her impatience. She knew that Ishmael had a legitimate claim on a portion of Abraham's inheritance. She was perturbed to see that Abraham loved Ishmael and showed no partiality between his sons. She desperately wanted Isaac to be the bearer of God's promises and the sole heir of all Abraham's possessions.

Her opportune moment arrived when she saw Ishmael playfully picking on his little brother, Isaac. She viewed Ishmael's actions as ridiculing Isaac and demanded that Ishmael and his slave mother be driven out of the house. Though Abraham was reluctant to comply with the demand of his wife, God assured Abraham that the plans He had for Ishmael and Isaac were different. When the dejected mother and son left the household, Sarah was jubilant on account of the secured future of her son, Isaac. She dedicated herself totally to the well-being of her son.

Of all the three patriarchs—Abraham, Isaac, and Jacob—the only one whose name is not changed in the Bible is Isaac. Abram's name was changed to Abraham and Jacob's name was changed to Israel. However, God did not change the name of Isaac, which meant "laughter." Probably, Isaac continued to bring joy and laughter to God and everyone around him. Certainly the unconditional faith and trust of Abraham had brought joy to God. Isaac, who was privileged to be the bearer of promises, loved God and placed great trust in God. The faith and trust of anyone brought great joy and "laughter" to God.

The greatest test that proved Abraham's faith involved Isaac when God asked Abraham to offer his son as a sacrifice. Abraham obviously was shocked at this strange command from God; nevertheless he set off on a journey to Mount Moriah, where he had to offer his son. Isaac was thrilled to hear about his journey with his father to offer a sacrifice to God. Hearing the word "God" always brought joy to Isaac's heart. Abraham and Sarah had constantly told him of God's ways and taught him to obey God in all situations. Though it was difficult for Isaac to leave his mother, he was excited at the prospect of journeying with his father. Along with two servants, Abraham and Isaac set off early in the morning. His mother held him in a tight embrace and assured her love for him. As he did not know the true purpose of this journey, he was not able to fathom the thoughts of his father, Abraham. He felt that his father was preoccupied and he attributed that to his father's concern over leaving his mother alone at home.

After three days of traveling they caught sight of the mountain and Isaac was truly excited. Abraham told Isaac that they would continue the journey by themselves and asked the servants to wait there until they returned from the mountain. Abraham took the wood for the holocaust and laid it on his son's shoulder. Isaac was a strongly built young lad and he showed no signs of weariness after three days of their travel. As he walked along with his father, his heart was overjoyed at the thought of the special moment when they would be offering the sacrifice. As he had witnessed many holocausts that his father had offered before, he thought about the sacrificial victim. He called out to his father and asked, "Father, here are the fire and wood, but where is the sheep for the holocaust?" (Genesis 22:7). Abraham assured his son that God would provide the sheep. Though he could sense sadness in his father's voice, he did not dwell on it.

Isaac helped his father build the altar and paid close attention to his father, who was very meticulous about this sacred task. Isaac asked numerous questions about God, sacrifice, and building the altar. When they completed building the altar, his father held him for a long moment. He felt so safe and secure in father's arms. When he looked up, he saw tears in his father's eyes, and he was surprised at this sudden show of emotions. He was totally unprepared for what was to come. Isaac felt his father holding his hands firmly, and within seconds he was bound and placed on the altar. It took a few moments for Isaac to comprehend what was happening to him. As he lay still on the altar he had helped his father construct, he began to realize that he was going to be that "sheep" God was to provide. He had heard about human sacrifices offered to appease gods in different cultures. He had never imagined that the God whom he had come to know and love would ever make such a demand. Looking at his father's troubled, yet determined face, he knew that his father was obeying God's command. He attempted to smile and reassure his father that he, too, was willing to sur-render to God's will.

He was watching intently at his father and the raised knife. He knew that the knife would come down in a moment and everything would be over. Though there was every reason to resist and cry out at this cruelty, Isaac stayed still. He wanted to face his death with courage. He trusted that surrendering his life to God would bring about greater blessings for his father. As Abraham was about to bring the knife down on to Isaac, they heard the powerful voice, "Do not harm the boy…I know how devoted you are, since you did not withhold from me your own beloved son" (Genesis 22:12). Abraham and Isaac realized then that it was a test from God, a painful one indeed, and they had succeeded in it as they were able to focus on God, not on them-selves and their losses.

Abraham must have thrown the knife away, scooped up his son from the altar, and held him in a tight embrace. The bleat of a sheep broke their embrace, and as they looked around they found a sheep, caught between bushes. Isaac remembered the words of his father, "Son, God will provide." With grateful hearts, the son and the father of-fered the holocaust to God. The unwavering faith of the father, Abraham, and the courage of the son, Isaac, was greatly pleasing to God and He assured them of His blessings: "I will bless you abun-dantly and make your descendants as countless as the stars of the sky and sand of the seashore; your descendants shall take possessions of the gates of their enemies, and in your descendants all the nations of the earth shall find blessing—all this because you obeyed my com-mand" (Genesis 22:17–18).

This challenging and painful experience deepened Isaac's love for God. He marveled at his father's unwavering faith as he had been willing to give up the life of his beloved son in order to obey God. He earnestly prayed for the grace to be faithful and was determined to re-main loyal to God in all circumstances. His faithfulness to God was best demonstrated in his loyalty to his parents and his family duties. Although he had heard of the cruel things Sarah had done to his brother, Ishmael, and his mother, Hagar, Isaac knew of the undying love of his mother toward him. He trusted and believed in his heart that there would come a time when he would meet his brother and the two would be reconciled.

When Sarah, his mother, died, Isaac was truly grief-stricken. Abraham comforted his son and asked him to turn his thoughts to God. Isaac obeyed his father, Abraham, when the marriage with Rebekah was arranged. Isaac loved his wife dearly and she was successful in easing the pain in his heart that he had experienced ever since he had lost his mother: "In his love for her Isaac found solace after the death of his mother Sarah" (Genesis 24:67). The couple waited in anticipation for the day when they would be blessed to have a child in the family to carry on the blessings promised to his father, Abraham. Isaac knew that now he was the bearer of his father's blessings. As the years rolled by, Isaac and Rebekah painfully realized their predicament, that they would not have a child as Rebecca was sterile. Isaac, who knew about his mother's barren condition and how God had miraculously intervened on her behalf, assured Rebekah with the comforting words, "God will provide." He poured out his heart to God in prayer asking for the blessing to have a son, who would carry on the name of the family. God graciously heard the entreaty of Isaac and soon Rebekah announced the good news of her pregnancy to Isaac. Isaac was pleased to know that God had blessed them with not with one son but two, as Rebekah was pregnant with twins. Though he loved them both, soon he began to favor Esau, the older one of the two.

When Abraham died, Isaac joined his brother, Ishmael, in giving their father a proper burial. The two brothers reconciled and blessed each other, invoking the name of the almighty God. After the death of Abraham, Isaac settled down in Gerar. God blessed the work of his hands, and he soon became a prosperous farmer and possessed large number of sheep and other animals. Isaac, who was in possession of such great wealth, was grateful to have the help of his son Esau, who assisted his father in the land and with the sheep. Esau was an outdoor man and a skillful hunter, and Isaac was convinced that his older son would carry on the family name. He was greatly disappointed at Jacob, whom he viewed as a weakling as Jacob preferred to stay at home. Although Rebekah continually told Isaac that Jacob had the right qualities to be the bearer of his father's blessings, Isaac did not budge. She reminded Isaac that he was getting older and the clan now needed a leader who would be prudent and wise like Jacob, not careless as Esau, who had demonstrated his carefree attitude by selling his birthright for a bowl of soup. Isaac, who preferred Esau, was totally blind to his son's weaknesses and made it clear that Esau would succeed him and he would pass his blessings to Esau. As Rebekah and Jacob were unable to challenge Isaac's decision, they waited patiently for the opportune time to act.

The right moment came when the old and blind Isaac asked Esau to prepare his favorite dish before he granted his blessing. While Esau went off to make the preparations, Rebekah acted quickly, prepared Isaac's favorite dish, then had Jacob change into Esau's clothes and go to Isaac. When Jacob expressed his reservations about his plain physical appearance as opposed to the hairy Esau, she covered the exposed parts of Jacob's body with a sheep's skin. Isaac contently ate the food, unaware of the deception of Rebekah and Jacob, and gave Jacob the irrevocable blessing. When Esau returned, he was both distraught and furious at uncovering his brother's deception. Though Isaac was very disturbed by the whole development, he eventually came to understand God's plans and began to realize that Jacob was the right person to bear the blessings. Isaac lived to see his sons becoming prosperous and died as a contented man. When he died, his sons, Esau and Jacob, came together and gave him a proper burial.

Isaac goes down in the history of the Bible as a courageous young man who did not resist his father's decision to offer him as a sacrifice. It was intended to be an ultimate test of Abraham's faith. Abraham came to know about this painful test three days before the actual sacrifice and Isaac came to know about it minutes before his impending death. God, who knew the real purpose of this test, rejoiced at the faith of his servant Abraham and the courage of Isaac, who was willing to give up his life in obedience to his father. Though God spared Abraham and Isaac from tremendous agony, He did not spare the agony for Himself or for his Son, Jesus.

*"Have courage for the greatest sorrows of life and patience for the small ones. And when you have finished your daily task, go to sleep in peace. God is awake."* —Victor Hugo

## For Further Reflection and Discussion

1.   What must have gone on in the mind of Isaac as he lay on the altar, bound and ready for death?

2.   The greatest test of Abraham and Isaac became moments to demonstrate Abraham's faith and Isaac's courage. Discuss.

3.   What are the deeper implications of Abraham's test?

4.   Isaac preferred Esau, and Rebekah preferred Jacob. What are the dangers of parental partiality?

5.   What must have gone on in Isaac's heart when he came to know the deception of Rebekah and Jacob?

# REBEKAH:
## Beautiful, Courageous, Yet Deceptive

*"Rebekah had been listening while Isaac was speaking to his son Esau...I overheard your father tell your brother...prepare an appetizing dish for me to eat, that I may give you my blessing...bring it your father to eat, that he may bless you before he dies...let any curse against you, so fall on me"* (Genesis 27:5–13).

Rebekah is introduced in the Bible as a beautiful young virgin. She was not only beautiful in the physical sense of the word, but she possessed godly characteristics that set her apart from other virgins. She was generous, caring, kind, courageous, and hospitable. She was chosen to be the wife of Isaac, the sole heir of Abraham's inheritance and promise of blessings. She played a great role in assuring that God's promises were passed on to her younger son, Jacob, who had the aspirations and perseverance to fulfill the demands God's promises entailed.

When Abraham realized that it was time for his son Isaac to choose a wife and begin a family, Abraham called his trusted servant and sent him back to his country of Ur, also known as Aram-Nahariam. Abraham did not wish for Isaac to marry a girl from the land of Canaan. The Canaanites were known for idolatry and cult worship. Abraham, being privileged to be a friend of the living God, did not want his son to be lured away into idolatry. After assuring his master that he would go and search diligently for the right bride, the servant set off with ten camels and gifts to complete his mission. The servant had witnessed his master's faithfulness, and prayed to God that his mission would be successful. As he approached the city of Nahor in Ur, he came to know that women normally came out in the evening to draw water from a spring. The servant, whose faith was influenced by the example of Abraham, asked God for a sign—the first woman to give water to him and his camels would be the right future bride for Isaac.

As he finished praying, he looked up and found a very beautiful girl approaching the spring with a jar on her shoulder. He intently watched her and asked for a drink. Graciously she responded to his request and ran to the spring and brought water for both him and his animals. The servant believed that God was answering his prayers and was providing him with the sign he had asked for. After providing Abraham's messenger with water, she assured him that there was enough room in her parents' house to accommodate him for the night. Her parents had taught her the virtue of hospitality to strangers. She demonstrated her caring spirit and generosity when she invited him to her house. At that time she did not know that her simple gesture of kindness and hospitality would alter the destiny of her life.

Rebekah's parents graciously accepted the visitor to their home and made him feel comfortable. The servant knew then that the girl was from a respectable family, one that welcomed strangers and offered hospitality to the needy. He was delighted to know that the family God brought him to was in fact related to Abraham, and Rebekah was the granddaughter of Abraham's brother (Genesis 24:15). When the servant conveyed the purpose of his visit to Rebekah's parents and her brother, Laban, they wholeheartedly accepted the proposal. They were glad to learn that Abraham had become prosperous in a foreign land. Rebekah's parents considered the proposal to be a great blessing for their beloved daughter. They had taught her to love God and surrender to His plans. The whole family rejoiced at the favor God was bestowing upon them. They were very thankful for the generous gifts they received from Abraham.

However, it was indeed difficult for everyone to part with Rebekah, who was the joy of their family life. In the morning, her mother and her brother requested that Rebekah be allowed to stay for ten more days. Hearing this, the servant was disappointed, and he tried to convince them to let Rebekah go with him. The decision then was left for Rebekah to make, whether to remain for an additional ten days with her family or to leave immediately. She had to make a very serious decision in her life—whether to leave her home and family without knowing if she would ever see them again, and travel hundreds of miles with a total stranger to marry a man she had never met. She turned to God and asked Him for guidance. Her affirmative response indicated that she was at peace with her decision. Courageously she stepped out in faith to begin her new life in the new land.

During her journey Rebekah received quite of bit of information about Isaac and his family. She was pleased to know that Isaac was a gentle, peace-loving, and God-fearing person. She had heard many stories about the goodness of Abraham and Sarah. She was sad to hear that Sarah was dead and Isaac was still grieving his mother's death. She prayed that she would be able to bring comfort and consolation to Isaac.

When they arrived at Abraham's place, they found Isaac in the field. When she was told that he was her future bridegroom, Rebekah covered her face with the veil. Abraham welcomed her with great joy and thanked God for bringing such a lovely girl into his home as his daughter-in-law. Isaac stood in awe at seeing his beautiful bride, Rebekah. God had blessed these young people with each other, who were beautiful both inside and outside. Overjoyed at the precious gift God had given him, "Isaac took Rebekah into his tent; he married her, and thus she became his wife. In his love for her Isaac found solace after the death of his mother Sarah" (Genesis 24:67). There was a deep bond between Isaac and his mother, Sarah, and her death had brought great agony to Isaac's heart. The deep bond that Isaac had with Sarah was replaced by his love for Rebekah as she loved and comforted him.

Isaac and Rebekah truly loved one another as husband and wife. He communicated to her the promise God had made to Abraham. Rebekah learned that it was through them and the son that would be born to her that the promise would be carried out. As years rolled by, they were distraught to realize that Rebekah was barren. It was indeed painful for both of them. Rebekah felt that she had failed Isaac as she was unable to give him a child. Isaac, who knew of his mother's prolonged barren condition, comforted Rebekah and assured her that God was capable of remedying the situation. Rebekah had come to know about Sarah's predicament and the impatient decisions she had made when she gave Hagar as a concubine to Abraham. Rebekah was prudent enough to wait patiently and allow God to answer their prayers in His time. She did not complain as months rolled into years and they patiently waited God to be kind to them.

People say, "Be careful about what you pray for!" God heard the prayer of this faithful couple. He looked kindly upon Rebekah and, after twenty years of marriage, she became pregnant. However, it was not the sort of pregnancy that she ever hoped for. It was extremely difficult as she was pregnant with twins and they jostled in her womb. It was unlike any normal morning sickness or fetal movement women endure during their pregnancies. She was experiencing something similar to a wrestling match within her womb. Although Isaac shared her concern, he was unable to help her in any way. Rebekah turned to God and sought His guidance. She was a woman of prayer and had the same access to God as Isaac did. She became the first woman in biblical history to seek an explanation for the struggle she was facing. God communicated lovingly to her that she was carrying "two nations" within her, "two nations are in your womb, and two peoples are quarrelling while still within you. But the one shall surpass the other, and the older shall serve the younger" (Genesis 25:23). She was both comforted and appalled at the revelation that she received. She was comforted to know that the children in her womb were healthy, but she was appalled to realize that they were already fighting for supremacy. She wondered what the future would hold for them and how she would deal with them.

It was very evident to her that Isaac would choose the one who would be born first to be the successor of his inheritance and the bearer of God's promises. She was not sure how Isaac would react to the knowledge God had given her about the destiny of the children. She decided to keep the matter to herself and hoped that she would be able to love and support both of her children. She gave birth and named the firstborn twin Esau and the second Jacob. Immediately after birth, Esau became Isaac's favorite and he spent a lot of time with him, while Jacob was left alone with his mother. Esau became very fond of hunting and exhibited exceptional physical abilities. Jacob, however, was very plain in appearance and was content to keep himself at home around Rebekah.

It was only a matter of time before each parent had their own favorite child. Each parent began to recognize the strengths of their favorite child and identify the weaknesses of the other one. Isaac considered Esau to be a true man who could become the head of the household, as he had all the masculine qualities that were needed to take on the responsibility. He saw Jacob as too weak and unable to carry out a man's responsibilities. On the other hand, Rebekah found in

Jacob a drive to achieve what was important in life, and she found Esau to be too carefree and unconcerned about matters of great importance. Rebekah had come to realize why Esau would serve Jacob and why Jacob would be the bearer of God's promises. While Isaac and Rebekah increasingly became fond of Esau and Jacob respectively, they were slowly drifting apart in their love relationship as husband and wife. Both of them were growing older, but they were not becoming wiser. Isaac steadfastly remained blind in his love for Esau. Rebekah, on the other hand, was looking for opportunities to manipulate Isaac and obtain his blessings for Jacob.

Along the way, Rebekah seemed to have lost many of her godly virtues. She became obsessed with making sure that Jacob became the bearer of God's promises. Indeed God had revealed to her that Jacob would succeed Isaac, but He had not revealed to her how it was going to happen. This uncertainty should have been an opportune moment to turn to God for wisdom and guidance. However, she took matters into her own hands and decided to deal with them in her own way. Unfortunately, her way entailed deception that would bring about division in the family. Jacob had already tricked his brother and obtained the birthright in exchange for a pot of soup. Rebekah knew that it was very important for Jacob to receive his father's blessing, and she was determined to obtain it for her favorite son.

Consequently she was constantly eavesdropping on conversations between Isaac and Esau. Her opportune moment arrived when the old and blind Isaac called Esau and asked him to prepare his favorite meal and receive the special blessing. She quickly prepared the meal, had Jacob change into Esau's clothes, and sent Jacob to Isaac to receive the blessing. She was successful in deceiving her husband and depriving her older son. She justified her actions as she believed in her heart that her favorite son was the right person to be the bearer of God's blessings. When she came to know that Esau was enraged at the deception and had vowed to kill Jacob, she stepped in again and helped him to escape. With the consent of Isaac, she sent Jacob to her brother, Laban.

Many might be quick to condemn Rebekah's shrewdness and deceptive actions. However, she had the opportunity to know what the future was going to be for her sons. She also saw the qualities of her sons. Rebekah felt that it was necessary that she act promptly to fulfill the revelation God had given her. Given the fact of Esau's impetuous nature and lack of interest in things of spiritual nature, she was convinced that she was acting in the best interest of the whole family. She was a courageous woman in a man's world, and her deeds eventually ensured that God's promises were passed on through the right person.

*"You can fool some of the people all the time, and all of the people some of the time, but you cannot fool all of the people all the time."* —Abraham Lincoln

## For Further Reflection and Discussion

1.   The dedicated servant of Abraham had great faith in God. How did Abraham influence his servant's faith?

2.   What were the virtues that Rebekah exhibited?

3.   Rebekah and Isaac had a great beginning as husband and wife. Were they able to sustain their love and devotion to one another? Based on the story, identify factors that can lead couples to drift apart.

4.   Your favoritism can make you blind to the obvious weaknesses of the one whom you favor. Discuss.

5.   Is it correct to say that Rebekah seemed to have lost some of her godly qualities along the way? Was her reasoning for her actions justified?

# ESAU:

## Use It or Lose It

*"So Esau sold Jacob his birthright under oath. Jacob then gave him some bread and the lentil stew; and Esau ate, drank, got up and went his way. Esau cared little for his birthright"* (Genesis 25:33–34).

Often people have lost their focus when they began to take things for granted. It is said, "Only when you lose something do you begin to appreciate its true value." That is the story of Esau, whose carelessness and lack of quest for the important matters in life led to his downfall from potential greatness. He would have been hailed as one of the patriarchs of our faith in the line of Abraham and Isaac. Being the first-born, he was entitled to the inheritance of his father, the special blessings that were passed down from generation to generation. However, his carelessness deprived him of this special status and eventually he was reduced to a subordinate position.

The birth of the twins was miraculous. Isaac had married Rebekah at the age of forty (Genesis 25:20) and waited in expectation for years for a son through whom the blessing promised to Abraham would be handed down. The news of Rebekah's sterility must have been a shock to the couple, who wondered how God's promises would come to pass. When Abraham came to know about this predicament, he hoped and prayed that Rebekah would not follow the example of her mother-in-law, Sarah, and invite trouble into the family. Abraham could never forget the whole episode centered on Hagar and his oldest son, Ishmael. However, neither Isaac nor Rebekah attempted to solve the problem on their own. Rather, they turned to God for help as this crisis only deepened their faith in God and His power. Isaac, who knew about his mother's condition and God's hand in his own birth, knew God was capable of remedying the situation. He encouraged Rebekah to trust in God and wait on His time.

The prayer of the faithful couple was answered, and Rebekah became pregnant with twins after about twenty years of their marriage (Genesis 25:26b). It was indeed a long wait for this faithful couple.

Eventually their persistence and perseverance were rewarded. Rebekah's pregnancy was a difficult one, as the twins jostled in the womb, suggesting greater struggle between them in the future. It was unlike any normal morning sickness or fetal movement women endured during the period of their pregnancies. She was experiencing something similar to a wrestling match within her womb. Rebekah turned to God for an answer and His answer amazed her greatly. God said, "Two nations are in your womb, two peoples are quarreling while still within you; but one shall surpass the other, and the older shall serve the younger" (Genesis 25:23). Rebekah knew that Isaac would prefer the firstborn as the normal tradition of the time warranted. She hoped that she would be able to love and care for them equally.

Esau was born first, and Jacob, the one who came second, was gripping on his heel. This was seen as an indication that either Jacob wanted to be born first or that he was not going to let Esau take precedence over him. Their names summed up their physical features and the types of individuals they eventually became. Esau was red and hairy as his name suggested. The second child was named Jacob, which means "independent" and "supplanter." As Rebekah expected, Isaac preferred Esau and pronounced him to be the heir of his inheritance and blessings. Contrary to her initial hope, Rebekah was drawn closely to Jacob and she began to develop a special love for the younger son.

Esau grew strong and muscular and became an expert hunter. He was the favorite of his father and knew he would inherit the blessing as he was the firstborn and possessed the birthright. He loved the company of his father and listened to the stories his father shared while eating the food he prepared. He fancied himself to be the bearer of God's promises and that his descendants would become a great nation. However, he didn't have in him the desire to develop a right relationship with God. He wanted the promised blessings, but he was not willing to make any sacrifices to make it a reality.

One day when Esau returned from the open fields, he was taken aback by the delicious smell of his brother's cooking. He was famished, and the fact that he had worked long and hard for no catch had made him angry as well. He asked for some of the stew his brother was cooking. At first, Esau felt that Jacob was ignoring him. There was not much communication between the brothers. Esau often looked down upon Jacob as a weakling for his plain appearance and overattachment to his mother. On the other hand, he considered himself to be the man, due to his strong physique and exceptional hunting abilities.

Jacob looked up from his cooking and promised to give him a bowl of stew under one condition. What Jacob wanted was the birthright, something that was the privilege of the elder son. Just giving the word did not seem to satisfy Jacob as he demanded it under an oath. Esau's hunger was really taking control of his thinking, and he felt that he needed to satisfy his physical need by all means. He exaggerated when he stated, "I am on the point of dying. What good will any birthright do me?" (Genesis 25:32). His shrewd brother would not give in to him until he denounced his birthright under oath. Esau ate and drank and walked away fully satisfied. He reassured himself that it did not matter, for he could make more fortunes by his hard work than what the birthright could give. He failed to recognize God's favor and blessings that were attached to the birthright. By his casual treatment Esau demonstrated the shallowness and carelessness he had for matters of importance.

Though he had lost his birthright, he believed that since he was his father's favorite he would still be able to obtain the special blessing. The blessing was the gift of a dying father to his firstborn son that covered different aspects of life: peace, prosperity, wisdom, fertility, long life, victory in battles, and success in life. It was like a legal pronouncement—irrevocable, honored by God, and passed down from generation to generation.

As the events unfolded, Jacob deceived Esau once again at the prompting of their mother, and this time Esau lost his father's blessing as well. As Isaac was advancing in years and his eyesight had failed; he called his oldest son, Esau, and asked him to go out to the country to hunt and prepare a delicious meal. Isaac knew it was time to impart his final blessing to his favorite son. Esau departed quickly to carry out his father's orders. Rebekah, who was eavesdropping on their conversation, acted quickly. She called in Jacob and ordered him to slaughter two young kids from the flock. She prepared a delicious meal that she knew Isaac savored and sent the dish with Jacob, who was dressed in Esau's clothes. When Jacob protested about how plain his body was in comparison to the hairy Esau, Rebekah carefully used the skins of the animals and covered any exposed parts of Jacob's body. Jacob successfully carried out their deceptive plan and obtained his father's blessing.

In the meantime Esau was searching for the best available animal. He wanted the dish to be the best he had ever prepared for his father. He knew his day had finally arrived to lead his father's household. As he approached Isaac with his favorite dish, he noticed something totally strange. Isaac appeared to be totally satiated and content. When he announced his arrival and invited his father to enjoy the appetizing meal he had prepared, Isaac realized that he had been tricked and was stricken with sorrow. He knew that the blessing was irrevocable and hence once imparted could never be withheld. At this Esau became both distraught and angry. His desperation was evident as he begged his father, "Father, bless me too!...Haven't you saved a blessing for me?"; "Have you only that one blessing, Father? Bless me too!" (Genesis 27:35-36).

Esau was livid with rage. He had been tricked twice by this shrewd brother. Not only were these severe blows to his manhood, but also Jacob's tricks deprived him of the family legacy. He realized with grief that it would not be through him that the blessings promised to Abraham and Isaac would be passed on. It was too late now, as Jacob possessed the birthright and his father's blessings. However, Esau did not take responsibility for his failures but rather blamed his brother's cunningness and his mother's partiality for his miserable condition.

Esau's bruised ego found a solution to end his misery: get rid of Jacob forever. He did not feel himself to be guilty of any misgivings. He failed to recognize that he had not been careful and forthright in his relationship with God and his parents. He had displeased the Lord by selling his birthright. By his marriages to Canaanite women, he had brought great pain and misery to his parents (Genesis 26:34–35). By his actions he had proven himself unworthy to be the successor of the blessings promised to Abraham. Esau was in no mood to recognize his failures and mistakes. Rather, overcome by rage, he sought to kill Jacob and possibly redeem the lost privileges.

Once again Rebekah came to the rescue of Jacob, who now had the support of Isaac as well—eventually Isaac was convinced that Jacob was the right person to be the recipient of God's blessings (Genesis

27:35-36)—and they sent him to his uncle, Laban, Rebekah's brother. They also instructed him not to follow the example of Esau and marry a Canaanite woman. Jacob obeyed his parents and went off to meet Laban, while Esau went ahead and married Mahalath, the daughter of Ishmael. Even Esau's determination to seek revenge seemed to vanish in the course of time, and he settled down beyond the Jordan in Edom. Though his lack of enthusiasm in seeking revenge was advantageous to Jacob, Esau proved once again his lack of persistence and perseverance.

Esau seemed to be living for the present without any inclination toward the future. He lost his privileged place as a patriarch of our faith because of his shortsightedness. Esau is remembered for his carelessness and shallowness. But Jacob, despite his cunningness, stands before us a towering example of perseverance.

Similarly, two men were called by Jesus to be His disciples. Initially, they followed the Lord faithfully. In the end, both committed serious crimes: the first one betrayed the Master and the other denied the Master three times. One looked at himself and found hopelessness; the other eventually looked into the eyes of the Master and found forgiveness. Judas, who betrayed the Master, found only hopelessness within, and killed himself. Peter, who denied the Master three times, was able to look at Jesus. He found forgiveness and reaffirmed his love and recommitted his life.

How often can carelessness and lack of perseverance deprive us from reaching the heights of life that God wants us to reach? How often can short-term goals and the need for immediate gratification blind us from having a true vision for the future?

*"The scoundrel suffers the consequences of his ways, and the good man reaps the fruit of his paths."* —Proverbs 14:14

## For Further Reflection and Discussion

1.   Isaac preferred Esau and Rebekah preferred Jacob. What danger does parental partiality cause?

2.   Esau sold his birthright for a meal. He was concerned about his immediate need and instant gratification. As a result he was deprived of a possible future greatness. Discuss.

3.   Rebekah helped Jacob to obtain his father's blessings. Was Rebekah's role in the deceptive act justifiable?

4.   "Was not Esau Jacob's brother? Says the Lord: yet I loved Jacob, but hated Esau" (Malachi 1:3). Why did God "hate" Esau? Is this compatible with the idea of God's unconditional love?

5.   Esau's marriages to foreign women caused great misery to Isaac and Rebekah (Genesis 26:35). Discuss scenarios where children can cause great misery to their parents.

# JACOB:

## Towering Example of Perseverance

*"Jacob said, 'I will not let you go until you bless me'...The angel said, 'You shall no longer be spoken of as Jacob, but as Israel, because you have contended with divine and human beings and have prevailed'"* (Genesis 32:27–29).

Human beings are destined for greatness. But one should have a deep aspiration to want it desperately. Jacob wanted it so badly that it separated him from his brother, Esau. From the beginning, Jacob tried to develop a relationship with God. Once he knew there was a special purpose for him in life, nothing could stop him from obtaining it.

Esau, Jacob's older brother, proved in time that he was unfit to carry on the responsibilities entailed in the covenant God had made with Abraham and Isaac. He lived for the moment, with little consideration for the future. God's purposes then would unfold through the younger son, Jacob. One might frown upon the deceitful tactics Jacob employed to accomplish his goals. *How could God let him get away with his shrewdness?* we might wonder. It could be that Jacob had his heart in the right place, and his ultimate goal was to carry on the responsibilities entailed in the covenant through his life.

God had revealed to Rebekah the future outcome of these two sons: they would represent two nations, the younger one stronger than the older one. Esau was born first and was red in complexion and extremely hairy. Jacob was smooth skinned, born immediately after Esau. The younger one was grasping the heel of his brother, indicating already that he was going to be a hustler for greatness. The two sons grew to be opposites. Esau was a hunter and an outdoorsman who won over the heart of his father, Isaac. Jacob was a quiet person who loved his mother. It was from his mother that he learned about what God had in store for him and planned to achieve it somehow.

Abraham, the grandfather, was one hundred and sixty years old when the twins were born (Abraham was a hundred years old when Isaac was born—Genesis 21:5; Isaac was forty years old when he married Rebekah—25:20; Isaac was sixty years old when they were born—25:26; and the whole span of Abraham's life was one hundred and seventy-five years—25:7). It was only natural for Abraham to have special love for his grandchildren. He must have found a marked difference in his grandsons. While Jacob was eager to listen to Abraham and his experience of God, Esau paid little attention to his grandfather. Abraham must have played a great role in helping Jacob to be a "plain and simple" man. In the Hebrew culture, a "plain" person embodied wholeness and totality. Certainly Jacob did not possess the same trust and faith his grandfather had. Initially he was able to achieve many things because of his shrewdness. However, in time Jacob (the name represents "independence") would learn to trust God and surrender totally. The name Jacob would eventually be changed to Israel, indicating total dependence on God.

Though God had chosen Jacob to inherit the birthright and blessings, He did not automatically bring about any change in Jacob. Jacob had to struggle with his own limitations, face the consequences, and eventually look beyond himself to God with whom all things are possible. For Jacob's part, he wanted the birthright so desperately that he was determined to obtain it by any means. The appropriate moment of bargaining arrived when Esau came home hungry one day. The delicious smell of Jacob's cooking made the famished Esau forget about the significance of his birthright, and he exchanged it for a pot of soup. This contrasting attitude separated these two brothers' destinies. Esau did not care about his dedication to God. His present dire need had such a strong grip on him that he forgot about the significance of his birthright: "The firstborn shall receive a double portion of the inheritance" (Deuteronomy 21:17). Esau seemed to be a shallow person, lacking a vision for the future and attaining success. He was not willing to be totally committed to God, as it required deep faith and great sacrifice on his part.

Jacob, who had a vision for the future, cashed in on the opportunity that was presented to him. He now had the birthright, but that was not enough. His mother reminded Jacob that he also needed the blessing from his father, Isaac, which would be irrevocable. Isaac, who was old and blind, had intended to give the blessing to the older son, Esau. Rebekah carefully laid out a scheme and, with shrewdness, succeeded in obtaining Isaac's blessing for Jacob. Having known God's plan for Jacob, she stood by him courageously and acted shrewdly to ensure that God's plan would unfold through Jacob. She knew that Jacob took important matters in life seriously. Unlike Esau, who lacked appreciation for God and His covenant, Jacob had an appreciation of God's ways.

However, their deceptive act was accompanied by a heavy price. Consumed with fury, Esau sought to kill Jacob, who had deprived him of his privileges. It was indeed painful for Rebekah to part with Jacob, to whom she had devoted her life. Jacob felt that he was abandoning his mother and elderly father for his own safety. He had to rely on God's providential care.

God, who had chosen Jacob to be the bearer of His promises, did not stop Jacob from making decisions, even those that included acts of deception. Though Jacob faced the painful consequences of his actions, God never abandoned him. He was greatly strengthened by two wonderful experiences of God, and both of these became moments of blessings for him. One was his powerful dream at Bethel where he saw the ladder, with its foot resting on the ground and the top reaching to the heavens and God's angels were ascending and descending on it. It gave him the awareness of God's constant presence in the world and how his life was continually influenced by God's principles. The Lord renewed His promises once again with Jacob that involved land, descendants, peace, prosperity and, above all, His constant presence. Jacob would make a vow to be faithful to God always. As a sign of his vow, he made a shrine and promised to give a tenth of everything to God. Jacob was acknowledging through his actions the essential truth that all that he was and all that he had originated from God. This was the foundation for Jacob's constant prospering.

The second encounter with the Lord at Jabbok would give Jacob a new identity and greater awareness of God and himself. Jacob, being an independent man, had faced many challenges in life. He was so determined to deal with them and be victorious in every situation. Although he knew God and His ways, he thought of himself as a self-made man. He did not care or worry about the means he used to achieve his goals. He was shrewd in his dealings with his brother, and he justified his actions by ascribing them to God's purpose. He did not

71

seek to see if they were in conformity with God's nature and will. Jacob clearly gave the impression that he wanted to handle life's problems with his own abilities and strengths. He did not think about the morality of the means he employed to accomplish his purposes. However, God, who wanted Jacob to be the bearer of His promises, intended to change Jacob's view of himself as a self-made man.

At Jabbok, Jacob encountered an Angel (or God Himself) and wrestled with him the whole night. The struggle with the Angel proved once again the resilience and persistence of Jacob. Even after dislocating his hips, he would not let the "Man" go until he received a blessing. Something must have happened to Jacob when he experienced the dislocation of his hip joint. Suddenly he must not have been fighting to win but just clasping tightly to the Angel. When the Angel announced his decision to go, Jacob did the unthinkable. In all of his life's battles he had never sought a blessing from his opponent. However, at this juncture, Jacob humbled himself before the Angel when he said, "I will not let you go until you bless me" (Genesis 32:27). The fight had instilled in Jacob a realization that he needed a blessing to go on with his life.

Jacob was not given a blessing but a new name: "You shall no longer be spoken of as Jacob, but as Israel, because you have contended with divine and human beings and have prevailed" (Genesis 32:29). The new name, Israel, which can mean "my master or dependent," would be a constant reminder to Jacob that he could not gain success by deception but only by being the humble servant before God the Almighty.

Jacob attained greatness because, unlike his brother, Esau, he had a spiritual inclination and vision for the future. Though initially he attempted to achieve his goals by his own efforts, eventually he surrendered himself to God and was dependent on Him for his life. Being entirely devoted to God, Jacob decided to serve Him faithfully. His gratitude to God was seen by his promise to be always loyal and return a portion of his blessings back to God. He was always humble and yielded to God's commands. Above all, he was a man of persistence who sought God's will and blessings and would not give up until he received them.

At the end of Jacob's struggle with the angel, he was left with a dislocated hip and walked with a limp. As time went on, Jacob must have realized that he could walk upright only with the help of God. Centuries later, another zealous and persistent person would struggle with God on his way to Damascus. Saul, the ardent Pharisee and persecutor of the church, was very determined to destroy the followers of Jesus. As he was knocked down from his horse, he would hear these words, "Saul, Saul, why are you persecuting me?" (Acts 9:4) After that powerful encounter with Jesus, Saul would emerge blind (wounded). His physical blindness would become the first step in curing his spiritual blindness, and he would realize the futility of his efforts to destroy the truth. He would receive a new name, "Paul." He would commit totally to Jesus and proclaim, "It is no longer I who live, but Christ who lives in me" (Galatians 2:20). He would acknowledge his total dependence on God as he lived out the words of his Master, "My grace is sufficient for you, for power is made perfect in weakness" (2 Corinthians 12:9).

Although Jacob obtained his birthright and succeeded in receiving the blessing of his father and would become the master of the Promised Land, his acts of deception would catch up with him in different times: twice from his uncle and father-in-law, Laban, and from his own children (who would sell Joseph as a slave and convince their father that Joseph was killed by the wild animals, and Jacob grieved over this alleged death until their reunion in Egypt). Those experiences would remind Jacob that human actions do have consequences. Jacob would learn the hard way the meaning of the statement, "What goes around comes around." Despite the greatness he achieved through perseverance, he is remembered for his trickery and deception. Ends, however noble they might be, cannot justify means, if they are evil. Ideally then, we have to be conscious of the means we use to achieve our goals.

> *"Consider it all joy by brothers and sisters, when you encounter various trials, for you know that the testing of your faith produces perseverance. And let perseverance be perfect, so that you may be perfect and complete, lacking in nothing."*
> —James 1:2–4

## For Further Reflection and Discussion

1. What is the significance of birthrights and blessings?
2. Rebekah played a vital role in directing Jacob's acts of deception. What were the primary reasons for her actions?
3. Jacob had a spiritual inclination to the future, which his brother lacked. Discuss.
4. The change of his name "Jacob" to "Israel" signifies a change of identity and mission. Discuss.
5. Jacob's struggle with the Angel may represent the spiritual battle of a believer. How?

# JOSEPH:

## Dreams Come True!

*"But now do not be distressed, and do not reproach yourselves for having sold me here. It was really for the sake of saving lives that God sent me here ahead of you"* (Genesis 45:5).

Joseph was awakened in the early morning by a dream in a jail in Egypt. He tried to recollect what it was but could not remember it. "Dreams have given me trouble," he said. "Look where I am. I should be with my loving father and my family." As he said this, he sat down on the filthy floor of the jail and lifted his eyes and heart to God, whose many blessings and favors he had experienced. Joseph felt the loving presence of God with him constantly and had decided that he would not do anything to offend God.

His thoughts began to drift back to his childhood days. He had always felt so special in the presence of his father. His father loved all of his children, but Joseph, being the child of his father's old age, constantly received special attention. Jacob constantly reminded his sons to be totally devoted to God and to depend on His grace. Unlike his brothers, Joseph paid wholehearted attention to his father and decided to commit himself to God. Jacob's special love and partiality toward Joseph aroused jealousy, hatred, and rivalry in the hearts of Joseph's brothers. He remembered the beautiful tunic his father had made for him, and when he tried to show it to his brothers, he could see anger and resentment in their eyes.

He had always had dreams, and at times they gave him trouble. He shared his two dreams with his brothers and father: "There we were, binding sheaves in the field, when suddenly my sheaf rose to an upright position, and your sheaves formed a ring around my sheaf and bowed down to it" (Genesis 37:6–7). His brothers were indignant upon hearing it as they retorted, "Are you really going to make yourself king over us…Or impose your rule on us?" (Genesis 37:8). Joseph did not understand the maliciousness of his brothers. So he shared with them his second dream: "This time, the sun and the moon and eleven stars were bowing down to me" (Genesis 37:9). When he said this, his brothers were outraged, and his father began to ponder what his special son would turn out to be. Joseph did not feel condescending or judgmental when he shared the two dreams with them.

Not even in his wildest imagination did he think about the cruelty he would experience at the hands of his brothers. It was heartbreaking even to think that his own brothers wanted to get rid of him by killing him. His father had asked him to join his brothers at Shechem as they were tending the sheep. Though his brothers harbored resentment against him, Joseph only possessed love and appreciation for his older brothers. In fact, he had looked up to them as they were all grown up and possessed tremendous physical powers and courage. He went in search of them, wearing the special tunic his father had made for him. He did not realize then that it was going to be his last trip from his father's house.

He was clearly surprised by the demeanor of his brothers. He felt as if he were amongst a hostile group of strangers. He was totally surprised when they all attacked him with heavy blows, and he felt totally defenseless against their collective might. They mercilessly tossed his bleeding body into the empty cistern, cursing him to be doomed. When he cried out for help from the cistern, they mocked him by saying, "You can be the king down there, over all the creatures in the well." He frantically searched for any wild reptiles in the dark, and to his relief found none. As he was being drawn out of the well, he hoped that his brothers had come to their senses and would show mercy to him. However, that was not to be case as he noticed caravans of merchants and strange people negotiating with his brothers. He realized with great agony that his brothers had decided to sell him to the Ishmaelites, who were on their way to Egypt. It was like being rescued from deep waters only to be tossed into the flaming fire. *How could they do such a thing?* he wondered. It was frightening to be in that cistern, and no less frightening to be with these strange merchants. He began to think of his father: *Oh, how grief-stricken he will be! Will I ever see him again?* Though these thoughts were racing in his mind, he felt a sense of protection, like a shield covering him and a sense of peace began to envelop his whole being. "Oh yes, God is with me and I can feel His presence right here. He is not just present in the land of Canaan. He is everywhere." As he said this aloud, he resolved once again to be devoted to God.

God acted mysteriously in his life. He was able to rise in power and gain many privileges with his Egyptian master, Potiphar. However, when he was enticed by his master's beautiful wife, he was both sad and frightened. Never did he think that she would be so evil as to spread false stories and punish him for his loyalty to his master and above all his faithfulness to God. He thanked God for giving him the strength to resist the temptation, because she was a beautiful woman after all. He had no regrets for being in jail as a result of living out his faithfulness to God. It was better to be in jail and be at peace with God than to be in bed with his master's wife and be tormented by the misery of sin. Once again a feeling of peace began to flow through him. He knew God's hands protected him from harm. His master could have put him to death for the alleged crime against his wife. As he sat there on the prison floor, he repeatedly thanked God for His protection.

"But even while he was in prison, the Lord remained with Joseph; He showed him kindness by making the chief jailer well-disposed toward him" (Genesis 39:21). God was a using a foreigner to protect His chosen one from danger and harm. Soon Joseph became in charge of all the prisoners in the jail. Dreams that had once caused him problems now became part of his solution. He won great favors from Pharaoh when he interpreted the strange dreams of Pharaoh about seven years of abundance and seven years of famine. It was very tricky, because he knew if his interpretations were incorrect, he could even lose his life. Joseph trusted in God and interpreted the dreams clearly to Pharaoh. As Pharaoh acted upon Joseph's interpretation, Egypt became the only place where food was available when famine hit the whole world after seven years of abundance.

Joseph was made second in command after Pharaoh, and he felt great joy in being part of alleviating sufferings in these tough times. He began to be hopeful of seeing his family when he saw people from other lands coming to Egypt for food. He believed in his heart that one day they would come to Egypt in search of food. *How am I going to react if and when God brings them to Egypt?* he thought several times. He now had the power and authority that he could deal with them in any way he wanted. He could make them pay for their cruelties, punish them, put them in jail, or even put them to death. God had given them over to his mercy. But Joseph, having experienced the immeasurable love and kindness of God, knew exactly how he was going to act. He knew this was the best opportunity to show them the mercy and the compassion of God and bring them to a greater awareness of God's ways. He only hoped and prayed that they were safe and that his father was still in good health.

Then he saw them one day and immediately recognized them. None of his brothers were aware of his identity. Not even in their wildest dreams could they ever have imagined him in his current position of power and prestige. Joseph played along for some time before revealing his identity. When his brothers realized who he was, they were dumbfounded and startled at the same time. They were afraid of revenge and punishment, and they knew they deserved it.

Joseph assured them that everything happened for a reason. From the evil and wickedness of his brothers, God had brought forth something good. He told them that the God whom their father had taught them to love and obey was able to bring good out of evil. God had clearly used Joseph's innocence, faithfulness, and dedication to prepare for the security of his family in the time of famine. Joseph would make preparations for all his family to stay comfortably in Egypt. His encounter with his father eased the tremendous pain he was carrying in his heart: "As soon as he saw him, he flung himself on his neck and wept a long time in his arms. And Israel [Jacob] said to Joseph, at last I can die, now that I have seen for myself that Joseph is still alive" (Genesis 46:29–30). His brothers must have hung their heads in shame and guilt over their misgivings. God must have been smiling at this beautiful family reunion. Yes, He was mysteriously acting on their behalf to make them a great nation even in a foreign land.

The innocent Joseph was sold to the Ishmaelites for twenty pieces of silver. His jealous brothers wanted to get rid of Joseph forever. Centuries later, a trusted friend and disciple would betray his Master for thirty pieces of silver. Both actions brought excruciating pain and suffering to the victims. These capricious acts demonstrated the cruelties of human hearts. God, who is able to bring good out of evil, uses these moments for His purpose. Joseph's slavery status in Egypt would eventually be transformed and become instrumental in securing protection and safety for his starving family. The act of betrayal by Judas would initiate the great sacrifice of Jesus, through which humanity would be gifted with redemption and salvation.

Even in modern families there are acts of betrayal, quarrels, disputes, dysfunctions, and divisions. Jealousy, greed, selfish ambition, impatience, and intolerance can cause a breach in relationships and turn relatives and friends into enemies. Personal and family vendettas have caused unwarranted bloodshed, made many parents childless, numerous wives widows, and countless children orphans. The only force that can conquer hate, the root of all violence, is the power of love, demonstrated through mercy and forgiveness. We see that through the life of Joseph. We see that more clearly through the sacrifice of Jesus on the cross.

> *"We know that all things work for good for those who love God, who are called according to His purpose."*
> —Romans 8:28

## For Further Reflection and Discussion

1. Jacob's special love for Joseph caused jealousy and resentment in the hearts of his other sons. What are the dangers of parental favoritism and partiality?

2. Saint Paul says, "All things works for good for those who love God, who are called according to His purpose" (Romans 8:28). How is this statement fulfilled in the life of Joseph?

3. Joseph could have been spared the wrath of Potiphar's wife if he had consented to her invitation to be unfaithful. He paid a price for his faithfulness to God. But succumbing to the temptation could have resulted in a heavier price. Discuss.

4. Joseph eventually gained power and authority in Egypt. He had his cruel brothers at his mercy. He chose to forgive, not to retaliate. Discuss.

5. It is said, "Forgiveness does not change the past, but it enlarges the future." Discuss this in light of Joseph's experience.

# MIRIAM:

## A Woman Who Made a Difference

*"The prophetess Miriam, Aaron's sister, took a tambourine in her hand
...Sing to the Lord, for He is gloriously triumphant; horse and chariot
He has cast into the sea"* (Exodus 15:20–21).

We all know the old adage, "Behind every successful man, there is
a woman." In the case of Moses, who led the Hebrew people out of
slavery in Egypt, there were five women who were instrumental in
saving his life, and by extension, his success. One of them was Miriam,
his older sister.

Miriam is introduced in the Bible as the anxious, yet courageous
little girl, hiding in the reeds to see what would happen to her little
brother. In Exodus 2, we have the account of the birth of a Hebrew boy
who would eventually transform the destiny of the people. However,
his birth took place in the most unfortunate situation, when all odds
were against him to have an opportunity to live. But God had special
plans for this infant, and no power on earth could alter the plan of God.

The little boy, who would be named Moses, was born at a time
when every pregnant Hebrew woman prayed and hoped that the child
in her womb would be a girl. For a society that placed great importance
on the birth of sons, it was clearly unusual. However, for the Hebrew
people who were the victims of the wrath, fear, and jealousy of the new
Pharaoh, the birth of male children meant pain and heartache for the
families, in particular for all mothers. The fate of the Jewish people had
drastically changed between the time of Joseph and Moses.

With the help of Joseph, who was a powerful official in Egypt, his
father and all of his brothers and their families had settled in Egypt.
These hardworking and zealous people were successful in the new land
and grew in number, influence, and power. Their unprecedented growth
evoked fear among the Egyptians, particularly in the mind of the new
Pharaoh (presumed to be Ramses II), who knew nothing about Joseph
(Exodus 1:8). He was paranoid that the Hebrews might form an alliance with the enemies of Egypt and take over the nation. His strategy

to oppress the Hebrews involved forced labor (in effect, slavery) and the killing of all newborn male children by throwing them into the river Nile.

Indeed it was an unfortunate time for a male child to be born in a Hebrew family. The whole land of Egypt echoed with the cries of the Hebrew mothers who were being deprived of the joy of holding their little newborn boy to their bosom. The newborn male children were mercilessly snatched away from their hands and flung into the river. Against all odds, one Hebrew baby boy survived! The unusual circumstances that led to his survival in some way were an indication that he had an unusual mission to accomplish in his life. However, it would not be an exaggeration to say that this little boy Moses, the future leader of the people, owed his survival to five different women who acted with courage and determination.

The two midwives, Shiprah and Puah, who feared God and were dedicated to life rather than death, chose to disobey the order of Pharaoh for the midwives to kill every male child born to Hebrew women. They claimed innocence as they falsely reported that the Hebrew women needed no assistance from them: "The Hebrew women are not like the Egyptian women. They are robust and give birth before the midwife arrives" (Exodus 1:19).

The third courageous woman was Jochebed, the mother of Moses. She was assisted by the midwives at the time she gave birth to Moses. She knew that she could trust the midwives not to let anyone know about the birth of her son. Jochebed demonstrated such courage when she decided to hide and protect her child. Looking at the lovely face of Moses, she convinced herself that she would do everything in her power to save this child. She knew she could face death for disobeying the order of the Pharaoh. Indeed she would have been willing to die if that would give an opportunity for her son to be alive. She ardently prayed for his protection and hatched a plan that could help him stay alive.

The fourth person who played a vital role in saving the life of Moses was Miriam, the older sister of Moses. Although Miriam was very young, she was unusually intelligent. When she learned that her mother had given birth to a boy, her heart leapt for joy and wept for grief at the same time. She cherished the thought of having a little

81

brother in her life. At the same time, she was horrified at the thought of what was awaiting her brother. Her innocent heart cried out to God to show her a way to protect her little brother. When she saw how determined her mother was to save the life of the innocent baby, she rallied behind her.

It became evident in a few weeks that they would not be able to hide the child forever. The whole family prayed ardently to be shown a way for them to save the life of this precious baby. Jochebed said that if she could somehow attract the attention of Pharoah's daughter to her precious baby, there could be a possibility for him to live. Though her husband was skeptical about the whole plan, Miriam wholeheartedly supported her mother and said that she knew the exact time when the princess came down to the river to bathe. She helped her mother make a basket, and they carefully placed the child in it. They did not know if they would ever have the opportunity to see the baby again. Though Miriam was heartbroken, she eagerly agreed to watch for the development. As she hid in the reeds, her eyes darted from the basket, to the road, up to heaven, and back to the basket.

Her heart skipped a few beats when the princess spotted the basket and ordered the maid to bring it to her. Miriam was carefully observing the princess, and she was relieved to find a sense of compassion on her lovely face as the princess lifted the baby into her hands. She was indicating to her maids her desire to have this child in her palace. Overjoyed, Miriam raced toward the princess and asked her if she wanted a Hebrew mother to raise the baby for her. The princess, who possessed enough influence with Pharaoh to change his decision, was the fifth woman to play the vital role in saving the life of the future Hebrew leader. God was using all five of them, whether they knew Him or not, to fulfill the plans He had for this helpless baby and the chosen people.

The princess looked at Miriam with great interest and granted her request to fetch a Hebrew woman to care for the child. Miriam's heart was filled with gratitude and joy, and she ran fast to tell the mother of this good news. As they raced back to the princess, both were uttering words of gratitude to God, who on time acted favorably on their behalf. They no longer feared for the safety of the child as they now had the protection and support of the princess. Their joy was inexplicable as the princess allowed them to take the baby to their home.

Miriam truly loved her brother and attended to all his needs. Her younger brother Aaron often helped her. She was exceedingly sad, and yet profoundly grateful, when it was time for the family to bring the boy to the princess. She truly believed that there would be another time when the entire family would be together again.

Months rolled into years. Miriam missed her brother, who was now called Moses. She was horrified to hear about Moses' crime and Pharaoh's decision to put Moses to death. She sought her comfort in God as she prayed ardently for the safety of her brother. Her fears were relieved when Aaron confided in her that their brother had run away from Egypt to escape the fury of the Pharaoh.

God acts in mysterious ways and uses people who seem unlikely to be His instruments to fulfill His purpose. Moses returned to Egypt, armed with the power of God, to lead the people from slavery to a land of freedom. Aaron, the older brother, became the spokesperson for Moses. Miriam, who had acted valiantly to save the life of Moses, became the leader among all Hebrew women. Her influence grew greater with each passing day as she was called a prophetess among the people. When the chosen people crossed the Red Sea safely and witnessed the drowning of Pharaoh's army, Miriam must have thought about those thousands of Hebrew baby boys who were flung into the water. As she looked at her brother Moses, who was triumphantly singing praise to God, a shiver must have passed through her body. As her heart was welling up with joy and gratitude, she could not contain herself but burst into a song of praise to her God. With tambourine in hand, she led the people in song, "Sing to the Lord, for He is gloriously triumphant; horse and chariot He has cast into the sea" (Exodus 15:21).

Though the Bible does not give details about Miriam's activities, one could easily speculate about the important roles she played among the people. She was acknowledged to be a prophetess (Exodus 15:20). A prophetess is a woman who was either a "spokesperson to the people," or who "spoke on behalf of God," or who "foretold the events that were to unfold." She fulfilled all those roles and much more, particularly among the women and children. They looked up to her when they faced different trials and tribulations. She became their counselor, prayer warrior, confidant, and protector of female rights. She constantly encouraged people to remain faithful to God and trust in His promises. Even when people turned against Moses and Aaron, she tried to challenge them to understand the gravity of their own rebelliousness and sin. She reminded them that they were bringing troubles upon themselves by turning their backs on God.

However, even the best can become victims of jealousy and family rivalry. Aaron and Miriam, who were older than Moses, allowed themselves to be blinded by jealousy over all the favors Moses was enjoying with God and with the people. In Numbers 12:1–2 we read: "Miriam and Aaron spoke against the marriage he had contracted with a Cushite woman. They complained, Is it through Moses alone that the Lord speaks? Does He not speak through us also?" When one is driven by jealousy and power, one becomes careless about the choice of words and what influence they can have on everyone who hears them. Miriam was a person of great influence, especially among the women. By her words and actions she was not only questioning God and her brother Moses but also endorsing in some ways family rifts and rivalries. God, who continually acted on her behalf, called her to task right away for speaking ill of Moses. Though both Aaron and Miriam had equal share in their sin, she was the only one who was smitten with the disease of leprosy.

One might wonder why Aaron was spared. Numbers 12:1 might indicate that she was the instigator behind the whole episode, as she is named first in the narrative. It could be that God had set Aaron apart for priestly tasks and spared him from this horrible illness as priests were the ones who had to certify one to be healed of leprosy (Leviticus 13). Aaron turned right away to Moses, asking him to plead with God to heal her. Although Moses' heart ached at the jealousy of his siblings, he held no grudge against them. Immediately he turned to the Lord for healing, interceding on behalf of Miriam.

This painful experience purified the heart of Miriam. For seven days she stayed outside the camp and sought God's forgiveness. Her heart must have been filled with shame and guilt at her misgiving. She must have thought about all the events of her life, including her role in saving Moses' life. She lifted her aching heart to God, beseeching His compassion and mercy on her. The God of mercy heard the cry of His beloved daughter, and He cleansed and healed her of leprosy as well as the guilt in her heart. Miriam was determined to serve God and His anointed Moses for the rest of her life.

The Bible treats jealousy as a grave sin that can bring about confusion and destruction. Proverbs 27:4 states, "Anger is relentless, and wrath overwhelming. But before jealousy who can stand." St. Paul listed jealousy as one of the works of the flesh (Galatians 5:20). When one's heart is filled with jealousy, one can easily forget the importance of relationship and embrace for oneself a negative outlook on life. It is often a self-seeking person who is engulfed in jealousy. In Galatians, St. Paul urges all to recognize the works of the flesh (which includes jealousy), cast it aside, and live by the fruit of the Spirit (Galatians 5:22–23).

As Miriam cast aside her jealousy, the peace of God engulfed her heart, and she lived the rest of her life totally devoted to God and His chosen leader, Moses. God blessed her abundantly as she continued her marvelous role as a prophetess in the lives of the people. She went on to travel with Moses and Aaron for almost forty years. Like her brothers, she did not enter the Promised Land. Her life was marked with great courage, faith, and firm resolve. Along with Moses and Aaron, Miriam suffered the trials and tribulations of life and rejoiced in the triumphs of the Lord.

*"It is not love that is blind, but jealousy."*—Lawrence Durell

## For Further Reflection and Discussion

1.   Miriam is considered a prophetess in the Bible. What were her positive qualities? What were the roles she played in the community?
2.   Have you ever been accused falsely? Have you ever had to let God vindicate you?
3.   What were the real motivations behind Miriam and Aaron's challenge to Moses' leadership?
4.   Do you feel that Miriam was unjustly punished? What are the implications of Miriam being the singular recipient of God's punishment?
5.   Did Miriam redeem herself?

# AARON:

## The Undetermined Leader

*"When people became aware of Moses' delay in coming down from the mountain, they gathered around Aaron and said to him, "come make us a god who will be our leader"...brought them to Aaron, who accepted their offering and fashioning this gold with a graving tool, made a molten calf"* (Exodus 32:1–4).

Aaron (the brother of Moses and Miriam) was the second child of the Levite couple, Amram and Jochebed. Though Jochebed was Amram's aunt (Exodus 6:20), existing societal regulations at the time allowed such marriage to take place until God's law specifically prohibited such practice (Leviticus 18:12). They lived at a time when Egyptians unleashed severe persecutions on the Hebrews. The Egyptians, who saw the Hebrews as a great threat to their safety, unleashed severe oppression. Aaron's life was spared as he was fortunate enough to be born at a time when newborn Hebrew boys were allowed to live. Though the Hebrew people were under various forms of oppression from the tyranny of Pharaoh, the king had not yet thought about controlling their growth by exterminating newborn boys.

Aaron looked up to his older sister, Miriam, who was a true friend to him. His happy childhood was affected by the reality of his mother's third pregnancy. Hebrew women viewed pregnancy as a special favor from God and looked forward to the day when they could hold their newborn child in their arms. However, the new, cruel edict of Pharaoh, which ordered the killing of the newborn Hebrew boys, led to tremendous anguish and pain in every Hebrew family with an expectant mother. As the gender of the child could not be determined until birth, these families went through many anxious and fearful moments. The repeated cries of the young mothers, whose children were cruelly snatched away, echoed from many Hebrew homes and reminded everyone else that their turn was just around the corner. Even though as a little child Aaron was unable to understand the struggles and uncertainties his family was going through, he must have been affected by them.

God had in mind a special mission for this particular family. He was not going to let Pharaoh's edict endanger the life of Aaron's brother. Things dramatically improved in the family when the life of the newborn boy was spared by the courageous deeds of several women, particularly Pharaoh's daughter who entrusted Jochebed, the mother, to look after the child. When it was time for Moses to leave the house to go to the palace of Pharaoh, everyone, including Aaron, was grief-stricken. However, they were all grateful to God for sparing Moses' life in such extenuating circumstances. Each day they heard new horror stories of the merciless murder of innocent boys. Aaron was so grateful that his brother was allowed to live. Nevertheless he realized how much he was going to miss his little brother as he was about to depart for Pharaoh's palace. At the same time, he felt happy for Moses as he would not be sharing the suffering and oppression of his fellow Hebrew people, who were under slavery.

Moses' comfortable life in the palace did not last too long. Consumed with anger at the sight of an Egyptian inflicting cruel punishment of a Hebrew, Moses slew the perpetrator and hid him in the sand. As the news of this murder leaked out, Moses knew that he was in a world of trouble. Aaron was alarmed to hear about the murder Moses had committed and the predicament that he was in. Eventually, he was relieved to know that Moses had fled the land to escape punishment from Pharaoh. While Moses was settling down in the land of Midian, Aaron was sharing in the hardships of the people. He had realized that the people who were under tremendous oppression also required greater unity among themselves. Though he was an eloquent speaker and people often listened to him, he felt that he was not the type of leader who could organize and liberate them from Pharaoh's tyranny. He prayed that God would send someone mighty and powerful to deliver them. The groaning and prayers of the people had reached God, and He was ready to act on behalf of His people (Exodus 2:24). Aaron had no knowledge that he and his siblings would play significant roles in God's plan of redemption.

He was constantly thinking about his brother, and there arose an irresistible desire in his heart to search and find him. Aaron confided his thoughts with his sister, Miriam, and she affirmed his desire. As Aaron set off to find his brother, he had a serene feeling in his heart that his journey and its purpose were guided by God.

In the meantime God was setting the stage for the liberation of the people through the call of Moses. Moses, on the other hand, was frustrating God through his litany of excuses as to why he was not the right person for this mission. When Moses voiced his concern that he was slow of speech and lacked eloquence to communicate and convince people, God mentioned the name of Aaron and appointed him to be the spokesperson for Moses. God made it clear to Moses that his brother, Aaron, whom he had not seen for many years, was indeed an eloquent speaker and he would serve Moses well. God's plans were coming together as He had placed in Aaron's heart the desire to seek and find Moses. The announcement of Aaron's imminent arrival was a pleasant surprise for Moses.

At God's instruction, Aaron went to the desert to meet Moses. The two brothers must have held each other in a tight embrace for a long time. Aaron was looking tenderly at his brother with tears in his eyes. He knew that it was God's special protection that had saved the life of his brother on multiple occasions. When Moses conveyed God's message to Aaron, he had no hesitation whatsoever to believe and accept it. He was only proud to be the spokesperson for his younger brother. He had no difficulty in accepting his younger brother's elevated status. He believed that his brother had the right qualities to unite the people to fight for their freedom and liberation. He had not fully understood at that time that God would be the One who would fight the battle for them.

Aaron knew that he had a difficult job in his hands. He was accompanying his brother back to Egypt, the same place where Moses was considered a criminal and an outlaw. The brothers had agreed that they would first approach the Hebrew people and communicate God's mission to them. Aaron, having understood the people better than Moses did, knew that it would take great persuasion and special intervention from God's part to convince them to accept Moses as their leader. However, all his fears were calmed when they gathered the elders of the people and announced to them the mission God had entrusted to them. The elders and eventually all the Israelites believed the words of Aaron and Moses, and they accepted Moses as their leader. The people were exceedingly joyful to hear about God's concern for them in the time of their distress. Their response to God's mercy was adoration and worship.

Aaron accompanied Moses to Pharaoh's palace to make the bold request. Aaron, who was the spokesperson for Moses, possessed the tough task of communicating God's message to Pharaoh. He knew that he was placing himself in a precarious situation. Yet, faith in God's providential care and the support he received from Moses gave him strength and courage. When Pharaoh heard their courageous request, "Let my people go" (Exodus 5:1), he became livid with anger. He was indignant at their audacity, but strangely he felt powerless to inflict punishment upon them. No power on earth could have stopped Pharaoh if he had wanted to inflict physical punishment or throw these two in-surgents into the dungeon. However, unknown to anyone, God was shielding His servants from the wrath of Pharaoh. At Moses' instruction, Aaron demanded that Pharaoh grant freedom to the people. Aaron performed many signs before the Egyptians, which confounded Pharaoh and his magicians. At God's commands, Moses asked Aaron to stretch out the staff he received from God, and the action of Aaron brought in different plagues upon the Egyptians. Yet the obduracy of Pharaoh prevented him from releasing the people.

The Tenth Plague, which resulted in the death of the firstborn of the Egyptians, finally changed the mind of Pharaoh, and he let the people go. Moses and Aaron led a group of six hundred thousand people, not counting children, along with a crowd of mixed ancestry, and their large number of livestock (Exodus 12:37–38). Aaron led the people in constant prayer and praise to Yahweh, whose mighty deeds had secured them freedom and a new destiny. The crossing of the Red Sea was a profound experience for Aaron, as he witnessed once again the power and protection of God.

Although Aaron possessed several beautiful qualities, he had his share of weaknesses in him. The main weakness he demonstrated was indecisiveness. Though he was an eloquent speaker, when pressures came from different quarters, he would succumb to them. Having seen the mighty deeds of God and having experienced special favors from God, he should have been able to portray unconditional trust and faith in God. However, under pressure from the people, Aaron gave up his convictions and lived out the meaning of his name, "the undetermined one." The decisive moment that tested his character came when Moses was away from the people, at Mount Sinai, in the presence of God, receiving the Ten Commandments. The people, who were impatient with Moses' delay, approached Aaron and asked him to make a tangible god whom they could worship. Though Aaron initially resisted the idea, he succumbed to their persuasion, and molded for them a golden calf, thereby leading people to commit the horrible sin of idolatry.

When Moses realized the abominable sin the people had committed and the role his brother had played in their act of wickedness, he called his older brother to task. Aaron realized his failure, and yet he provided lame excuses: "Let not my lord be angry. You know well enough how prone the people are to evil" (Exodus 32:21–22). First he blamed the people for being prone to evil. Second he claimed to have thrown all the jewelry into the fire and out came the molten calf, as if caused by a miracle (Exodus 32:24). Aaron was admitting to his brother that he was unable to withstand the persuasions of the people.

Though Moses was the unquestioned leader of the people, Aaron and Miriam had shared great privileges of leadership among the people. However, jealousy began to creep in the hearts of Aaron and Miriam, the older siblings, due to the special privileges Moses enjoyed with God. When jealousy is part of a family, relationship is often forgotten and there will be division. When they questioned, "Is it through Moses alone the Lord speaks? Does He not speak also through us?" (Numbers 12:2), they were not only questioning the leadership of Moses but also the authority of God. Aaron, who should have been an example to other people by his obedience to God and Moses, failed miserably when he acted upon his jealous feelings. Yet the mercy of God surpasses the gravity of human sin.

Aaron experienced the mercy and goodness of God in his life when God chose Aaron and his sons to be responsible for the sanctuary and solely vested Aaron's family with the institution of the priesthood. Leviticus 8 and 9 provide a detailed description of the priestly ordination of Aaron and his sons, through which they were elevated to a special status for serving God and His people. Though this must have been a profoundly satisfying moment for Aaron, it became a personal tragedy as well. Two of Aaron's sons, Nadab and Abihu, overstepped their authority and on their own offered incense to God. As God had not instructed them with such a task, fire came forth and consumed them. Though the unfortunate event caused great agony for Aaron, he and his remaining sons were forbidden from mourning. Rather they were to focus on their priestly responsibilities (Leviticus 21:10-11). This became a great moment of realization for Aaron that his priestly office required total personal commitment and wholehearted dedication.

Though he was not permitted to enter the Promised Land, he died as a happy man, passing on the right of priesthood to his son, Eleazar (Numbers 20:22–29).

The different events in Aaron's life clearly show that despite his vulnerabilities and weaknesses, God used him to accomplish His purpose. Clearly Aaron was unworthy to be elevated to the position of high priest. However, through the choice of Aaron, God makes it clear for all that it is He who makes a person worthy to this special calling. Standing before God, who is absolutely holy, no human being can legitimately claim that they are truly worthy. Yet God continues to choose the weak and vulnerable to accomplish extraordinary things. The dictum "God does not call the qualified; rather He qualifies those whom He calls," could very well be applied to Aaron and anyone who humbly accepts God's invitation to serve.

*"If your life is swayed by everyone's opinion, you will find yourself short of your ultimate goal."*

## For Further Reflection and Discussion

1. Aaron, the older brother, became a spokesperson for his younger brother, Moses. What does this reveal about Aaron?

2. Compared to Moses, Aaron faced a greater challenge when they were in Pharaoh's presence. Discuss.

3. Aaron and Miriam complained against Moses. Miriam was inflicted with leprosy, not Aaron. Why was Aaron spared the punishment?

4. Why did Aaron succumb to the pressures of the people and fashion the golden calf?

5. The office of priesthood demanded total commitment and great sacrifice on Aaron's part. Discuss.

# MOSES:

## The Struggle of a Leader

*"I cannot carry all these people by myself, for they are too heavy for me. If this is the way you will lead with me, then please do me the favor of killing me at once, so that I need no longer face this distress"* (Numbers 11:14–15).

With the help of Joseph, the whole household of Jacob had settled down in Egypt. God blessed them, and they multiplied in large numbers and became prosperous. Things were going pretty well for them until fear and insecurity got the best of the new Pharaoh who knew nothing about Joseph and the history of the Hebrews. His fear was clear in his statement: "Look how numerous and powerful the Israelite people are growing, more so than we ourselves! Come, let us deal shrewdly with them to stop their increase; otherwise, in time of war they too may join our enemies to fight against us" (Exodus 1:9–10). He sought to suppress them through various forms of oppression that included forced labor and the killing of the newborn Hebrew male infants. Their cry reached God, and He remembered His covenant with Abraham and his descendants. The appropriate divine time was at hand for God to act upon His promises.

A young Hebrew woman kept her newborn baby boy hidden for some time before placing him in the path of Pharaoh's daughter. God touched the heart of the princess and guided her actions. She took the boy and gave it to a Hebrew woman, his own mother, for nursing. When he grew up, she brought him to Pharaoh's daughter, who adopted him and gave him the name Moses. He grew up as an Egyptian and led a comfortable life in the palace of the Pharaoh.

As time went on, Moses became aware of his identity and family origins. The visit to his kinsmen reassured him that he had to help his people even if it meant leaving his familiar and comfortable life in the palace. Life was never the same for Moses since his visit to his family. He began to be enraged at the forced labor and cruel punishment that were inflicted upon the Hebrews. Right before his eyes was an

Egyptian kicking a Hebrew slave with great force and flogging him mercilessly with a whip that had many pieces of tiny, sharp bones strapped to it. The agonizing cry of the Hebrew as the whip tore into his flesh sent Moses into a frenzy, and drawing his sword, he slew the Egyptian instantly. When reality set in, he quickly hid the body of his victim. He was surprised to witness the next day the quarrel of two Hebrews. He thought to himself, *How can these people fight among themselves when they have a common enemy inflicting constant punishment?* He was horrified at their sneer, "Who has appointed you ruler and judge over us? Are you thinking of killing me as you killed the Egyptian?" (Exodus 2:14). For a moment, fear gripped Moses' heart, and he knew fleeing Egypt was the only form of escape.

Running away from Egypt, he went to Midian, where he found a home and began a new life. He tried hard to put all the events of his past out of his mind. He married Zipporah, the daughter of Jethro, who was a priest in Midian. Though he was content with his new life with Zipporah and their son, Gershom, he often thought about his people in Egypt. His heart ached whenever he remembered their suffering and slavery under the ruthless Egyptians.

Moses was tending the flock of his father-in-law, Jethro, when he encountered the Lord at the burning bush at Horeb. As he witnessed the amazing sight, Moses had no idea that his destiny was about to change forever. The Lord revealed His identity as the God of Abraham, Isaac, and Jacob, and the mission He had in store for Moses: "Bring my afflicted people from the land of slavery to the land of freedom, a land flowing with milk and honey" (Exodus 3:4–10). Moses, overwhelmed by this powerful experience and insurmountable task, frantically searched for excuses as to why he was not the right person. Moses was afraid to go back to Egypt. He felt that he was inadequate and incompetent for such a noble task. God turned down all his excuses and gave him an assistant, Aaron, Moses' own brother. Upon Moses' request, God revealed His divine name as "I AM WHO AM" (Exodus 3:14) and assured him of His constant presence, protection, and the success of his mission.

The reunion of Moses and his older brother, Aaron, was an emotional one. They wasted no time in engaging in their new mission. Moses and Aaron stood boldly before Pharaoh and demanded, "Let my people go" (Exodus 5:1). The angered Pharaoh made a mockery of the demand and inflicted added punishment upon the Hebrews, as if to show Moses that he was in command, not some unknown God. God's power was manifested through Moses through many signs and wonders, but still Pharaoh did not budge. The plagues became intolerable for Pharaoh and the Egyptians, but they left the household of the Hebrews unharmed. At the end of the tenth plague, which caused the death of all the firstborn in Egypt, Pharaoh reluctantly released the Hebrews to be on their way. Jubilant in their state of freedom, the Hebrews celebrated the Passover and set out on their journey to the Promised Land.

The overjoyed Israelites were on their way to the Promised Land singing songs of praise to the almighty God who liberated them from slavery and gave them freedom. They rejoiced at the thought that God was their deliverer and protector from all dangers. The galloping sound of the horses and war cries disrupted their festive mood as they saw in horror the army of Pharaoh closing in on them! Alas, they were by then at the banks of the Red Sea. Ahead of them were the deep waters and behind them was the cruel army of Pharaoh. Moses began to hear the complaints of the people, who seemed to have forgotten God's power. "Why have you brought us out? We want to go back, so we won't be killed. It is better to be a slave than a corpse."

Moses assured them of God's mighty power. God would be with them in this battle and give them victory. The power of God was revealed as Moses, at God's word, lifted his staff and stretched his hands over the sea until it parted. The people crossed over through the parted sea, and once they reached the other side, they witnessed the destruction and drowning of Pharaoh's army right before them. "This will convince the people, and they will trust in God's power," Aaron told Moses, who looked very skeptical.

They reached Mount Sinai and God revealed Himself to all the people: "Moses led the people out of the camp to meet God, and they stationed at the foot of the mountain. Mount Sinai was wrapped in smoke, for the Lord came down upon it in fire" (Exodus 19:17–18). God was set to give them the Ten Commandments that would help them become the holy people through whom the promised Messiah would come into the world. God ratified His covenant with the people, and they said in one accord, "We will do everything that the Lord has told us" (Exodus 24:3).

God commanded Moses to go up the mountain to receive the stone tablets on which He had lovingly written the Ten Commandments. The forty days and nights that Moses spent with the Lord intensified his love for Him. It was like two friends sharing their ideas, dreams, and hopes for people entrusted to their care. While God and Moses were engrossed in planning a peaceful life for the people, there were strange things happening among the people. How short-lived was their memory! How quick were they to forget about the power of God and, to their shame, give themselves over to idolatry! They had persuaded Aaron to mold for them a god whom they could worship. The breaking of the first commandment by worshiping the golden calf was just the beginning of their constant struggle with God and Moses.

Troubles were endless for Moses. The disbelief of the people in God became severe when they were thirsty, hungry, or longing for bread and meat. Constantly they rebelled against God and accused Moses of bringing them out into the wilderness to die. Even though they had witnessed God's power, they failed to trust Him completely to provide for their needs. Instead they constantly murmured, complained, and rebelled. The difficult moments during their journey to the Promised Land should have been an opportune time to renew their dependency on God. Instead, they became moments of rebellion that even led to the abandonment of the true God for other gods.

Even when God's wrath flared up against them to the extent of destroying them (Exodus 32:10; Numbers 21:4–9), Moses found himself constantly pleading for these ungrateful people. He could have let God destroy these stiff-necked and rebellious people, but constantly he pleaded for God's mercy and forgiveness upon them. Even the greatest leader with the best intentions, ideas, motivations, and commitment can become susceptible to discouragement and desperation when he is unjustly criticized and his orders neglected. Overcome by desperation and disappointment over the continuous rebellion and shameful behavior of the people, Moses asked the Lord to take his life: "Please do me the favor of killing me at once, so that I no longer need to face this distress" (Numbers 11:15). Frustration, discouragement, pain, disappointment, anger, and anguish were evident in this plea of Moses. God, who totally understood the turbulent feelings and frustrations of Moses, ignored his request and asked him to select seventy elders as his helpers.

Moses—who enjoyed a very special friendship with God; who led the people out of slavery; who endured tremendous heartaches due to the unfaithfulness of the people—was deprived of the privilege of entering the Promised Land. Numbers 20:2–13 describes the scene of bitter complaints of the people for water, God's specific instruction, and Moses' act of disobedience due to his frustration. God had instructed Moses to speak to the rock to bring out water. Moses, out of frustration, struck the rock twice and water gushed out. This is seen as Moses' sin since it was contrary to God's instruction. As a result, Moses was allowed to view the Promised Land only from the mountaintop.

We might wonder if God was too harsh on Moses. God must have held Moses to a higher standard than anyone else. Moses' act of disobedience was more than a personal sin, as all of his actions had a witness value. God could not allow Moses to set a bad example before the people and let him get away with it. He was allowed to see the Promised Land from the top of a mountain. However, Moses died as a contented man, having accomplished many wonderful things for the people. He was revered as the greatest lawgiver and leader of the people.

Could we also think that while God was stern with Moses, He stored a surprise for him as well? The Promised Land would eventually be seen as a representation of the true home, the heavenly Jerusalem, toward which we all travel in faith to meet God face-to-face. Could it be that God punished Moses by not permitting him to enter the earthly Promised Land but showed the richness of His mercy and compassion by taking him to the true home, the heavenly Jerusalem?

We will see Moses again at the top of a mountain. This time he will be with the prophet Elijah, conversing with Jesus at the scene of the Transfiguration (Mark 9:4).

Despite all his troubles, Moses remained faithful to God. His troubles emanated from the Egyptians, the people he was leading, from some of the leaders of the people, and from his own siblings—Aaron and Miriam. Yet Moses remained steadfast in his faithfulness to God. Moses had painfully realized that in all probability, people would let him down. He believed that God would never abandon him. He constantly sought to follow God's precepts and commandments. God in turn protected Moses from all dangers and harm and eventually took him to his true home.

> *"God gave you a gift of 86,400 seconds today. Have you used one to say 'thank You'?"* —William A. Ward

## For Further Reflection and Discussion

1. The life of Moses was marked with constant twists and turns (birth, Pharaoh's palace, fleeing to Midian, return to Egypt, exodus from Egypt, and wandering through the wilderness). What remained unchanged through it all?

2. Moses presented a myriad of excuses to God as to why he was not the right person for the mission. What are our excuses that can frustrate the plan of God?

3. Several passages show that God wanted to destroy Israel (Exodus 32:10; Numbers 14:12). However, Moses constantly pleaded with Him to forgive them. What are the implications of these passages?

4. No human being could have possibly endured all that Moses endured in leading an ungrateful group of people. What gave Moses motivation and strength to go on against all adversities?

5. Moses was not permitted to enter the Promised Land due to his sin. Do you feel God was unduly harsh on Moses?

# JOSHUA:
## On the Battlefield for the Lord

*"If it does not please you to serve the Lord, decide today whom you will serve, the gods your fathers served beyond the River or the gods of the Amorites in whose country you are dwelling. As for me and my household, we will serve the Lord"* (Joshua 24:15).

While many consider Moses to be the greatest lawgiver of the people, Joshua, his successor, is viewed as one of the greatest military leaders in all Bible history. His parents had named him Hoshea, meaning "salvation." Like many other great personalities in the Bible, his name would later be changed. This change of name in the Bible often indicates a new identity and a new mission. Moses changed Hoshea's name to Joshua, which means "the Lord is salvation" (Numbers 13:16).

Hoshea (Joshua) was born at a time when the Hebrew people endured severe persecution under the Egyptians. Growing up, he must have dreamed of a time when his people would be free of such dreadful oppression. Joshua differed from other young people of his time. He possessed natural leadership skills. Other young people looked up to him and marveled at all the abilities he possessed. He was physically strong and mentally tough. His most important virtue was his devotion to the Lord. Even in the midst of suffering and pain, Joshua believed that God was with them. Many young people were urging Joshua to unite them under his leadership to fight against the Egyptians. Joshua knew that such a venture would only lead to greater persecution and suffering. Sheer audacity was not enough to match the military power of the Egyptians. Joshua urged them to be patient and wait for the sign God would provide in time.

From the beginning, Joshua was determined to serve the Lord. He had heard of the covenant God had made with Abraham, Isaac, and Jacob. He believed that God's covenant extended to all the Hebrews in Egypt, as they were all descendants of Jacob. When Moses burst forth onto the scene with the cry, "Let my people go," he knew God was acting on His promises. Joshua wholeheartedly accepted Moses as the leader. He believed that God would act through Moses and gain freedom and liberation for His people. The events that followed were like a dream come true. He witnessed God's mighty power many times and was convinced that the living and true God would lead the people to the Promised Land by removing all obstacles in their path.

Moses took notice of this young man, and soon Joshua became an active participant in the Exodus event. Within a few months after their departure from Egypt, the Israelites faced their first physical threat from another nation: "At Rephidim, Amalek came and waged war against Israel" (Exodus 17:8). Moses had identified Joshua as the best person to lead the people in battle and made him the military commander. He ordered Joshua to select courageous and able-bodied men for the battle. It was indeed a challenging task as the Israelites neither had any formal military training nor possessed any advanced weapons. Moses urged Joshua to remain unafraid as God Himself would fight for the people and obtain victory for them.

Joshua led his brave men in a fierce battle against the Amalekites. While Joshua was engaging in battle, Moses urged everyone to pray for victory. He stood on the top of a mountain with the staff of God in his raised hands. As long as Moses' hands remained in an upward position, the Israelites had the upper hand. When Moses let his hands fall, the Amalekites began gaining ground. Aaron, the brother of Moses, and Hur, a prominent leader among the people, supported Moses from both sides by holding his hands. Joshua and his warriors succeeded in destroying the Amalekites. When Joshua and his men returned, the people welcomed them with jubilant shouts. Moses built an altar there, offered sacrifice, and called the place "Yahweh-nissi" (Exodus 17:15), which means "The Lord Our Banner," where banner is understood to be a rallying place. This event brought an important realization for Joshua about the power of God and the significance of being under God's protection and rallying behind the chosen leader, Moses.

Moses trusted Joshua unconditionally. When God commanded Moses to come up to the mountain to receive the Ten Commandments, he permitted Joshua to accompany him part of the way up Mount Sinai (Exodus 24:13). Aaron, Hur, and other elders were to take care of the people and settle any disputes among them. However, in the absence of

Moses and Joshua, they succumbed to the pressures of the people and committed the abominable sin of idolatry before the golden calf. Upon his return, Moses exhibited his fierce anger and called both the leaders and the people to task. Joshua grieved over the people's unfaithfulness and made up his mind to serve the only living and true God.

If someone had told him earlier about leading the people to the Promised Land, he would have laughed at it because he knew of only one leader, and that was Moses. He always marveled at the friendship and closeness Moses seemed to enjoy with God. Many a time he was saddened at all the trouble the people gave to Moses. The people seemed to have short memories, like children who often concentrate on their present need, forgetting everything that was done for them in the past. When Moses exhibited anger, Joshua knew that his leader was acting out of frustration because of the ungrateful acts of a stiff-necked people. He vowed to be faithful to God, never straying from His path, and to be always loyal to Moses.

He cried bitterly when he learned Moses would not be with them to take possession of the Promised Land! He never doubted God's ways, but it was only natural for him to feel tremendous sadness at the loss of his beloved leader. God assured Joshua of His protection when He said, "Be brave and steadfast, for it is you who must bring the Israelites into the land which I promised them on oath. I myself will be with you" (Deuteronomy 31:23). Moses accepted the reality that he would not be permitted to enter the Promised Land and wholeheartedly supported the new leader, Joshua, when he imparted his blessings upon him through the laying on of his hands (Deuteronomy 34:9).

The responsibilities at hand made Joshua forget about his personal loss of his beloved leader, Moses. He wanted to be at the service of his Lord and God. He knew that people respected him and believed in his capabilities. Every single person knew Joshua, and he knew many of them by name as they all had set off together from Egypt. A vast majority of the original people had died along the way due to their rebellious actions and unfaithfulness. He knew every single newborn and prayed that they would be different.

He was apprehensive about the task ahead, although he firmly believed that God's hand would guide him. It was the people who gave him anxious moments and sleepless nights. He knew how easily they could turn their backs on God. There were some who constantly complained and murmured about everything, making even the upright ones go astray. For some, the best plans, intentions, and actions of the leader were never good enough. But the task at hand demanded not doubt or self-pity but resolute determination to carry out God's commands. He gathered the crowd and moved on. God's mighty Spirit was with him, enabling him to work signs and wonders like his great predecessor, Moses, did.

Their greatest challenge was ahead of them—to conquer Jericho, a well-established city with a mighty wall and a powerful army. The inhabitants of Jericho believed that no power on earth or in heaven would be able to defeat them. But there was an air of fear when they heard about the Israelites advancing toward them led by the fearsome leader Joshua. What frightened them even more was a rumor that the Hebrew people were led by their living God, who had performed many wondrous signs in Egypt. Consequently they were always on the lookout for any strangers in the city.

God often does extraordinary things and uses unlikely people. In this case, the one who came to the aid of the spies for Joshua was Rahab, the harlot. She protected the Hebrew spies from the king and helped them to complete their mission. Her sole request was for the safety of her family during the battle as a returned favor, which Joshua granted her.

Joshua knew that his military power was not enough to conquer the enemy. The greatest power, he knew, came from God Almighty. The Ark of the Covenant reminded them of the constant presence and power of God. Joshua knew that the only way to capture the city was by following the commands of the Lord. God gave him instructions as to how the people should circle the city with the Ark of the Lord for seven days, which sounded like an unlikely military strategy. But Joshua wholeheartedly trusted in God's commands. He did not reveal to the people God's instructions all at once but little by little. The selected troops marched ahead, followed by seven priests carrying rams' horns, followed by priests carrying the Ark, the rear guard, and finally the people. They were to circle the city once a day for six days. On the seventh day they were to march seven times and then, at a long blast of the rams' horns, they were to shout out loud.

Joshua demanded perfect silence from all. The only noise allowed was the blowing of the horns. Joshua knew that marching once for the six days and seven times on the seventh day would make the people doubt his plans and God's power. It wouldn't be long before someone suggested the futility and insanity of the whole affair. He knew then it would grow from a murmur into shouts of rebellion. He had witnessed the murmuring and complaints of the people several times in his life. He sternly ordered them to keep their mouths shut so that they would not imitate the sins of their fathers.

After a few days of witnessing this strange phenomenon, the inhabitants of Jericho might have been amused. But Joshua knew that God would give them victory if they followed His commands. At the end of the seventh round, there was the horn blast and Joshua urged the people to shout aloud. At the tremendous shout of the people, the walls of Jericho crumbled, and they witnessed the awesome power of God.

The conquest of the Promised Land was not an easy task. A number of times Joshua experienced failures just as Moses did due to the faithlessness of his people. Like Moses, he constantly challenged them to make the Lord their choice. He attributed every military victory to the Lord and the new territories they occupied as God's gifts.

Joshua was convinced that the acquisition of the Promised Land was not the end of God's promises. It was an indication of how serious God was about the covenant He made with their fathers and with the people at Mount Sinai. God had promised Abraham that through him all the nations of the world would be blessed. The newly formed tiny nation was to become a sign of God's plan for the world, as it was through her (Israel) that God was going to unfold His plan of salvation for the whole world. It was through Israel, the newly formed tiny nation, that God would send the promised Savior. It was imperative then for the people to be faithful and loyal to God and His statutes, commandments, and decrees. Joshua challenged them to decide for themselves whom they would serve. He made his intention clear when he said, "As for me and my household, we will serve the Lord" (Joshua 24:15). Joshua remained faithful to the Lord until the end.

Joshua believed in the power of God and relied upon His strength to accomplish his goals. There are times in our lives when even the best-laid plans and preparations might not lead us to success in reaching our goals. Human capabilities, though noble in many ways, are at the same time insignificant when we compare them to the power and might of God. However, when human abilities are guided by the grace and power of the almighty God, we are assured of victory in the battles of life.

*"Trust Him. Ultimately, it is the Lord*
*who wins your battles."*

## For Further Reflection and Discussion

1. What were the greatest qualities of Joshua that set him apart from the rest?

2. Could Joshua have prevented the people from committing the sin of idolatry if he had stayed back?

3. Saint Augustine said, "Pray as if everything depends on God but work as if everything depends on you." Could the battle against the Amalekites (Exodus 17:8–16) substantiate this statement?

4. As the people circled the walls of Jericho, they were ordered to remain silent. What must have been the wisdom behind such an order? What are the dangers of having too many opinions?

5. Joshua said, "As for me and my household, we will serve the Lord" (Joshua 24:15). What significant roles can the head of the family play in fostering faithfulness to the Lord?

# DEBORAH:

## The Spirited Woman of the Lord

*"Be off, for this is the day on which the Lord has delivered Sisera into your power. The Lord marches before you"* (Judges 4:14).

God continuously sends men and women of courage and faith to lead His people. The book of Judges describes the tenacious deeds of twelve leaders who provided leadership for the people during the difficult periods between Joshua and Saul, the first king. They exercised judgment when there were disputes among the people and acted as military leaders when they were threatened by an external enemy.

Deborah rose to prominence after the death of Ehud, who had cunningly murdered Eglon, the wicked king of Moab (Judges 3:21). Ehud had inspired people to turn away from their wickedness and follow the precepts of God. When people abandoned their evil ways and turned to the Lord, they began to enjoy peace and prosperity for the next forty years. However, when people became too comfortable with their lives and daily affairs, they began to forget God, the source of their safety and security. Often the threat of a common enemy unified the people, and on such occasions they turned as one to God, seeking His protection. However, when their land was at peace and they faced no threat from external enemies, they lost their unity and became their own enemies by their wicked ways. The people had not learned their lessons from the experience of their ancestors, and as a result they had to personally experience the familiar cycle: sin, suffering, servitude, supplication, and redemption.

Idolatry was the primary sin through which the Israelites constantly offended God. The people were often wooed away from following the demands of right living by those who embraced for themselves easy ways of life. Believing in the true God entailed discipline, right conduct, caring for others, right relationships, and upholding fairness and justice in worldly affairs. Those who wanted to live their lives according to their whims and fancies as opposed to the ways of God embraced for themselves a way of life that was both self-seeking and hedonistic. When right belief and right living are neglected, society can easily be plagued with chaos and injustice.

As people moved away from the shadow of God's protection, they fell under the control of the Canaanite king, Jabin, and his fierce general, Sisera. The Canaanites, who had no sense of fairness and justice, began to oppress the Israelites. Sisera, who was in command of one of the best armies, exerted his might by forcefully appropriating anything and anyone who might serve his selfish purposes. As people endured the cruelties of their enemy, they began to realize their failures and cried out to God for strength and protection. The grave situation demanded a courageous leader to match the fearsome general, Sisera. Though many people might have expected Shamgar, who singlehandedly slew six hundred Egyptians with an oxgoad, to become the new leader, God chose Deborah to save His people. God's ways are different from human ways, and He chose a courageous woman to rescue the people from their enemies.

Deborah is presented in the Bible as the wife of Lappidoth, a familiar way in which a person is introduced in a patriarchal society. She was chosen by God to be a judge, a prophet, and a military leader. She ranks with Moses and Samuel in possessing these triple duties. Everything she accomplished in her life resulted from her special relationship with God. She trusted and believed in God in all situations. Her faith and devotion to God enabled her to be a faithful wife to Lappidoth and a fair judge among the people. The people of Israel were familiar with the roles their judges played. They viewed them to be God's representatives, and unlike other leaders in the surrounding cultures, these judges did not strive for power and authority. They faithfully communicated God's message to the people and pressed upon the people the need to be faithful to God. They were very successful in settling disputes among people and—when threatened by external enemies—they rallied men to fight their common enemy.

Deborah was exceptionally wise in settling disputes among people and soon won their admiration. Though initially it was unsettling for some to accept a woman as their leader, she won the admiration of her critics through her righteous life and wise judgments. She knew the hardships the people endured under the tyranny of Sisera. She constantly challenged people to abandon their idolatrous behaviors and be faithful to the living God. As a true prophetess, she assured them that in God's time He would deliver them from their enemies. When people expressed skepticism in their ability to win battles against the Canaanites, who were advanced in their military powers and tactics, she assured them that God would manifest His power and lead them to victory. Though some were impatient about the delay, she reminded them that to win a battle against an external enemy, one needs to win the battle that is being waged in one's own life. People had become their own enemies by being unfaithful to God, and it was time for them to conquer their unfaithfulness and surrender themselves to God's will.

Sitting under a palm tree from which she settled disputes among the people, Deborah received a special message from God. Despite their rebelliousness, the patient and compassionate God was about to act favorably in the lives of His chosen people. Deborah summoned Barak, a young warrior, and gave the message she had received from God: "Go, march on Mount Tabor, and take with you ten thousand Naphtalites and Zubulunites. I will lead Sisera, the general of Jabin's army, out to you at the Wadi Kishon, together with his chariots and troops, and will deliver them into your power" (Judges 4:6–7).

Although Barak believed Deborah, he was skeptical about leading ill-trained men against a well-trained army and nine hundred iron chariots. Sisera could easily tear apart the marching troops with his iron chariots and massacre Barak's troops with relative ease. Instead of arguing about the futility of such an endeavor, he requested Deborah to accompany him on the mission. Barak knew that having Deborah on his side would boost confidence among his men. Deborah demonstrated no fear when she consented to his request but made it clear that he would not take credit for the impending victory. Barak was a bit puzzled when she stated that "the Lord will have Sisera fall into the power of a woman" (Judges 4:9). Although it hurt his pride to lose the honor of victory to Deborah, he swallowed his pride and proceeded with his mission.

Barak was surprised at the response he received from the young men of Zebulon and Naphtali. People who were bogged down under the tyranny of Jabin and Sisera were waiting for an opportunity to wage a war against them. They arrived in great numbers, equipped with whatever weapons they could obtain to rally behind Deborah and

Barak. Before they began their march, Deborah challenged the young warriors to put their trust in God and to believe that He would fight the battle for them. She urged them to rely on the might of God, not on their military power or the weapons they possessed. The confident men were jubilant at the thought of victory as they marched down Mount Tabor.

The warriors of Israel were about to see the awesome power of God as Deborah had prophesied. The two opposing forces faced each other and let out a thunderous roar. The shout of the Israelites was the loud praise of God, whom they believed to be the One to fight the war. Suddenly the heavens roared with thunder and there was such a great downpour. The torrential rain made it impossible for the Canaanites to maneuver their chariots, as the wheels of the chariots began to sink in the mud. The warriors of Israel were on foot and made use of this advantageous opportunity as they killed their enemies. When Sisera faced this unexpected scenario, he was quick to run like a coward to save his life. Barak, who was on a rampage mercilessly slaughtering his enemies, failed to notice the quick exit of his opposing general. When Barak realized the escape of Sisera, it was too late as Sisera had taken refuge with a family of the Kenite Heber. Barak remembered the words of Deborah that "Sisera will fall into the power of a woman," and he was convinced that Deborah would find a way to kill their evil opponent.

The family of Kenite Heber was at peace with King Jabin, and Sisera felt safe in taking refuge with the Kenites. However, Sisera was unaware of the kinship that existed between the Kenites and the Israelites: "Kenite Herber had detached himself from his own people, the descendants of Hobab, Moses' brother-in-law" (Judges 4:11). The scene was perfect for the woman that Deborah had prophesied to take the center stage—Jael, the wife of Kenite Herber, allowed Sisera to hide in her tent under a rug. When Sisera asked for some water, she gave him goat milk and ensured him that he was safe at her place.

Sisera was exhausted from the warfare and fell into a deep sleep without realizing that he was never going to wake up. Jael, standing beside the sleeping savage, remembered all the evil things he had done to her kin people. She quietly lifted her heart to God in gratitude for delivering the enemy into her hands. She decided that the vicious man deserved a gruesome death for all his brutal acts, and with a steady hand she approached him with a peg in one hand and a wooden hammer in the other. Positioning the peg on his temple, she swiftly brought down her wooden hammer, driving the peg through his temple into the ground. Sisera, the fearsome general, had no chance even to let out whimper. Barak, who was pursuing Sisera, found the dead man and the courageous woman who had meticulously carried out the murder as foretold by Deborah.

Knowing that God had shown His mighty power and delivered His people from their enemies, Deborah broke into a triumphant song of praise to God. Her faith, devotion, commitment, dependence, and unwavering trust are woven into this majestic song. Jubilantly, she reminded the people that Yahweh is the true and living God and He had brought this great victory against their mighty enemies.

Deborah goes down in the history of God's people as a faithful and courageous Israelite woman. She made herself available to God, and He used her in a powerful way as His true prophetess, fearless warrior, and just judge over people. In calling Deborah as one of the judges, God was reminding His people that He can use anyone to accomplish His purpose. What is expected from our part is faith, devotion, commitment, dependence on God, and unwavering trust.

*"Dependence upon God makes heroes of ordinary people like you and me!"* —Bruce Wilkinson

## For Further Reflection and Discussion

1. What were the most beautiful characteristics of Deborah?
2. What were the possible challenges that Deborah faced as a judge in a patriarchal society?
3. Did Barak fully trust Deborah? What must have gone through his mind when Deborah said, "The Lord will have Sisera fall into the power of a woman"?
4. Did Deborah know how God was going to deliver the enemies into their hands?
5. Deborah called Jael "blessed." Why?

# GIDEON:

## To God Be the Glory

*"The Lord turned to him and said, 'go with the strength you have and save Israel from the power of Midian. It is I who send you'"* (Judges 6:14).

Deborah's decisive victory over the Canaanites had brought about a forty-year period of peace and prosperity in the land of Israel. Often there is a tendency in human beings to forget God in comfortable times of life. People who remained close to God in times of trouble slowly began to retreat into old ways of sin. Their sin of idolatry gravely offended God. People chose to move away from the fortress of protection God had built around His chosen people. They failed to notice that their drifting away from God caused moral erosion in their society and the weakening of their unity.

The Midianites, Amalekites, and Kedemites took advantage of the feeble status of Israel. They employed an unusual tactic to keep the people of Israel in a miserable state. They did not conquer and destroy the people of Israel; they did not occupy their lands. However, when the Israelites toiled in their lands and raised their flocks, the enemies surrounded them from all directions like wolves. The growing crops, the result of the Israelites' hard work, brought great delight to their enemies. However, the Israelites were in distress as they were unable to defend their land. For seven years the enemies plundered the crops of the Israelites, took away all the well-bred animals, and destroyed everything else, leaving the people malnourished and impoverished.

In their misery, people once again began to turn to the source of their strength, God, who seemed to have moved away from their lives. God sent a prophet to remind the people that it was in fact they who had deliberately moved away from His armor of protection by their worship of foreign gods. The classic question, "If God is not in your life, who moved?" painstakingly brought among the people the realization that it was, in fact, they who had deserted God. They were the ones who had moved away from Him and gone after their whims and fancies. Nevertheless, God, the greatest lover and fountain of compassion, heard the cry of His people and decided to act once again in the lives of His chosen people.

The people of Israel, who were continuously exploited by the plundering acts of the Midianites, were driven to live in hiding. Parents who heard the hungry cries of their children and who themselves experienced hunger pangs tried their best to "steal" crops from the lands they owned and the food they had raised. God must have looked around to see whom He would choose to bring hope to the people and put an end to their misery. His eyes fell upon the young Gideon, who was secretly threshing wheat to save it from the Midianites. In the eyes of the society, Gideon should have been an unlikely candidate to be God's instrument, as his own father had led the people to idolatry by building an altar to the Canaanite god Baal. However, God had known the faith of Gideon, who constantly raised his eyes to heaven, beseeching God to end their misery. Though young in age, Gideon had realized in his life that the current status of impoverishment was not a punishment from God but rather the consequences of people's sinful lives.

To this faithful person came the messenger of God with an unusual greeting: "The Lord is with you, O champion" (Judges 6:12). God was acknowledging the audacious nature of Gideon, which Gideon himself had yet to recognize. Taken aback, he raised the popular concern of the people, "If the Lord is with us, why has all this happened to us?" (Judges 6:13) It was as if Gideon were telling the angel, "No, God is no longer in our midst. He has deserted us because of the evils committed by the people. I have tried my best to be faithful to God and encouraged others to turn back to God. I have not been successful as my own father has been leading others astray by his worship of idols. Everyone is paying a heavy price for the sins of some." Though the angel could sense anguish, frustration, and disappointment in the words of Gideon, he conveyed the message from God to Gideon that he had been chosen by God to deliver the people from the power of the Midianites.

Surprised at the words of the angel, Gideon searched for excuses to reject this enormous responsibility. He had tried to convince the people to turn away from their wickedness. There were some who mocked Gideon because he came from a "mean family" in Manasseh. His fa-

110

ther had in fact erected an altar for Baal (Judges 6:25), and it had become a sanctuary for the Canaanite god. When he tried to encourage people to return to God, he was ridiculed for his failure in changing his own family. Sarcastically they advised Gideon to get his house in order before trying to bring order in others' lives. Even his own family rejected his words, as he was seen as a naïve young man by his older brothers.

Gideon did not feel that he was the right man for the task and echoed similar sentiments of biblical heroes like Moses and Jeremiah. Moses was reluctant to accept the mission from God when he said, "Who am I that I should go to Pharaoh and lead the Israelites out of Egypt?" (Exodus 3:11). The young Jeremiah pointed out his lack of speaking skills when he expressed his reservation: "Ah, Lord God! I know not how to speak. I am too young" (Jeremiah 1:6). Gideon had to learn that he had to look beyond his abilities or inabilities and trust in the power of God to accomplish anything worthwhile in life. He was empowered by the words of the messenger from God: "I shall be with you, and you will cut down the Midian to the last man" (Judges 6:16). Gideon was challenged to realize that he would be a failure if he relied on his abilities or focused too much on his own inabilities. He realized that if he turned his attention to God, who would be with him in all circumstances, he would taste victory.

Gideon, who experienced many episodes of rejection from his family (Judges 6:15) and fellow Israelites, wanted to be certain that he was not being tricked into another moment where he would be ridiculed. Understandably he asked for a sign to prove that he was, in fact, hearing God's word. Gideon placed before the angel an offering, knowing well that if it were consumed, he was indeed speaking to God. To his amazement, God accepted the offering and calmed the troubled spirit of Gideon when the angel said, "Be calm, do not fear. You shall not die" (Judges 6:23). Gideon demonstrated his faith when he built an altar to God and called it Yahweh-Shalom, or "the Lord is peace." From that moment Gideon became the powerful spokesperson and warrior of God for His people.

The first challenge Gideon faced was to bring people back to their true faith. Worship of Baal, the Canaanite god, had led many people away from Yahweh. Unfortunately, Gideon's own father had led the people to the worship of Baal. God's command was to destroy the same altar that was built by Gideon's father and to build a true altar to Yahweh and to offer a sacrifice. The task God gave to Gideon was very dangerous, because it could bring upon himself the wrath of his family and townspeople. It was as if God were testing Gideon to see if he would now have the courage to stand up for what was right in God's sight. The hesitant Gideon demonstrated his temerity when he chose to complete the task at night. As God commanded, he destroyed the altar and cut down the wooden pole: the wooden pole was a symbol of fertility associated with the Canaanite goddess Asherah. He built an altar, used the sacred pole as firewood, and offered a bull as a sacrifice to God.

Joash, the father of Gideon, was initially enraged at the realization that his youngest son had destroyed the altar and sanctuary he had built for Baal. Unlike his other children, Gideon had refused to worship Baal and had challenged them to return to Yahweh. Joash knew that other Baal worshippers would be enraged at Gideon's act of desecration in their sacred sanctuary. However, he could not but marvel at the tenacity of his son. He did not know that it was the power of God that had enabled Gideon to accomplish such a dangerous task. With each passing moment, Joash realized the validity of his son's gesture and the severity of his own sin. He was ready to face the outraged crowd, whom he knew would demand a gruesome death for desecrating the altar of Baal.

Joash's realization of his sinful ways and the defense of his son are clear in his words: "If he whose altar has been destroyed is a god, let him act for himself" (Judges 6:31). Gideon was jubilant at the conversion of his father and those in his household, who seemed to acknowledge the power of the living God and the futility of worshipping lifeless idols. Gideon was given a new name "Jerubbaal," which means "Let Baal Contend." It was indeed a constant challenge to Baal, who had failed to defend his own sanctuary and a mockery to the Baal worshippers, who were repeatedly reminded that they were worshipping lifeless images. Gideon was content that he was finally able to put his own house in order, and he was empowered to bring that order into the lives of God's people.

Enveloped by the Spirit of God, Gideon ventured into fulfilling his ultimate mission of freeing the people from the enslavement of the Midianites. When Gideon began his campaign to rally the troops to fight against these enemies, he might not have envisioned the success of his mission. People who had heard of the courageous deeds of Gideon wanted to rally behind him and defend their lands from the plundering acts of their enemies. It appeared that every able-bodied man wanted to be a soldier under the leadership of Gideon. People were convinced that they finally had a courageous leader in Gideon, who was unafraid to face the fury of his father, the townspeople, and the powerful foreign god Baal. In fact, initially Gideon was afraid of all of these. However, he had been empowered by God to overcome all such fears and to fear only the living God.

When Gideon gathered his army of thirty-two thousand men, God made it clear to Gideon that they were too many. God knew that if the sizeable army were to wage war, there was a remote possibility that they could defeat the Midianites on their own. In case of a victory, they would give all credit to themselves and their valor. If victory occurred on account of their warring abilities, people would have added reason to rely on their own abilities rather than on the power of God. God also knew that a war in such great numbers would bring about greater bloodshed among the Israelites, making many women widows and numerous children orphans. Gideon, who believed in giving all credit to God and giving Him the glory, wholeheartedly agreed with God's message. Calling the troops together, he tested their valor and made it clear that if anyone had a trace of fear, that soldier was not fit to fight in his army. He pressed upon them the idea that any case of dishonesty would lead to greater disaster striking them and their families. They were completely free to leave the army if they were afraid. Some were relieved, while others grumbled. However, Gideon thought that he had accomplished his purpose when the number was down to ten thousand.

However, God wanted Gideon to choose only three hundred soldiers for this important mission. Gideon was shocked by the realization that he would have such a small army, one that was less than one percent of its original size of more than thirty thousand men. Gideon, who had seen the power of God, did not complain, but he placed his trust in Him. God had promised to be with Gideon and assured Gideon by giving him an opportunity to hear the conversation between two

Midianites. They were talking about their dreams in which Gideon's sword was envisaged to be the source of downfall for the Midianites. They were afraid now that the God of Israel would deliver them to the power of Gideon. When Gideon heard this, he knew that it was the right time to execute his plans. Calling his small army together, he divided them into three groups and gave them all a horn, a jar, and a torch. They were to blow the horns, break the jars, and let out the battle cry in unison, "For the Lord and for Gideon" (Judges 7:18). The unexpected spectacle brought such panic among the Midianites they began to flee and attack one another. None of Gideon's soldiers had to use any weapon, and yet they succeeded in freeing their lands from their enemies. Gideon and the people knew that God had waged this war for them and given them the victory.

People who were jubilant at the victory now requested that Gideon rule over them. However, Gideon made it clear to them that God alone was their king, and they should give Him all glory and honor. His desire was to see the Israelites constantly giving allegiance to God, their true King. Gideon, who was hesitant and timid initially, demonstrated great obedience and humility before God.

There were times when Gideon allowed his human tendencies of doubt, hesitation, and fear to affect his decisions. However, when God assured him of His constant presence and protection, Gideon gradually grew to place his complete trust and faith in God. A person might be cautious, might have doubts in his or her abilities, and might possibly wonder how things could turn out to be. Those moments of hesitation do not stop God from choosing that person to accomplish His plan. However, the greatest disposition we all need is placing our complete trust in God. The greatest desire we all need to have is giving glory and honor to God.

> *"Faithfulness is not doing something right once, but doing something right over and over and over and over."*
> —Joyce Meyer

## For Further Reflection and Discussion

1. Gideon did not have the credentials to be a leader of the people, yet God chose him. What are the implications of this?

2. Gideon can easily be viewed as a skeptic, yet God used him to accomplish His purpose. Discuss.

3. Gideon was instructed to "clean his own house" first. How important is it to change oneself and one's family before attempting to change others?

4. Gideon was shocked at the size of his army, one percent of its original size! What were the lessons God intended to teach Gideon and the Israelites?

5. Gideon was fortunate enough to receive many signs from God. Where do we look for God's signs today?

# SAMSON:

## The Incredible Hulk of the Bible

*"Samson cried out to the Lord and said, 'O Lord remember me! Strengthen me, oh God, this last time that for my two eyes I may avenge myself once and for all on the Philistines'"* (Judges 16:28).

Samson's story is one of the great dramas in the Bible. His life and work depict heroism, valor, amazing physical strength, sexual escapades, love, betrayal, treachery, revenge, and exoneration. One has to go beyond all these human experiences to discover the psychological and spiritual strengths of Samson. When we do that, we will find this man who was consecrated from the beginning to be a chosen instrument of God.

The familiar story of Israel's sin and redemption continues through the period of Judges. The saying, "People need a strong leader," was very true in the lives of the people. Very often the people remained faithful whenever they were guided by a faithful leader who remained close to God. After the death of Abdon, who had judged Israel for eight years, the people were under weak leaders. In such perilous situations, the people began to go astray and fall into their familiar ways of sin. One theme that was constantly emphasized in the life of Israel was the theme of faithfulness. They were to be faithful to God, their Creator and Redeemer. Time after time God had revealed His power, compassion, and mercy. The first commandment reminded the people that there was only one true God, and they had to worship Him alone. The people were to keep themselves holy from the allure of other cultures that worshipped idols. The sin of idolatry gravely offended but, despite all the warning, the people once again chose to turn their backs on God when they bowed down to worship idols. This time they were delivered unto the mighty Philistines, who were known for their extraordinary physical strength and cruelty. The period of enslavement was for forty years, the same number of years their forefathers wandered in the wilderness on account of their sin against God.

God's hand might occasionally turn against His people but never

His heart. Although there is no reference about the people turning desperately to God for help, the God of compassion reached out to them in mercy. Knowing that He had to deal with an enemy of tremendous physical power, He fashioned someone who would be superior in physical strength and courage.

There are no specific descriptions of the parents of Samson, except the fact that they were without any children. God acted favorably on their behalf when the messenger of God came to the wife of Manoah and announced the good news that she would conceive and bear a son. This special act of favor bestowed upon the lives of this childless couple resonates the familiar theme that the child to be born would be set apart by God for a special mission. The angel revealed to her that the child should be consecrated to God from the womb. The angel stressed that the child would be under the Nazarite vow, and no razor should touch his head. Along with the good news, the angel warned the woman to refrain from all intoxicants and certain foods that were ritually forbidden. She was challenged to live a disciplined life from the moment of conception for the betterment of her child. The angel seemed to be indicating to her that the healthy lifestyle of a mother can greatly contribute to the betterment of her child. It is clear that what modern medicine endorses about the lifestyle of a mother had already been clearly revealed by God.

Samson was totally devoted to his parents and lived under their watchful care. His parents and neighbors marveled at his physical strength and valor. He was fearless in all situations and showed no signs of fear when he faced cruel wild animals or deadly reptiles. There were many young men who wanted to acknowledge Samson as their leader and hoped that he would lead them to fight against the fearsome Philistines. Many young women secretly wished to have the honor of being his wife. However, Samson was unwilling to lead an army or be a family man. He knew his mission was to weaken the power of the Philistines. He must have thought that having a family to care for and followers to lead would distract him from achieving his goal. Unlike other judges of Israel who mobilized people to fight against their enemies and gain victory with the help of God, Samson entered into battle in a singular fashion. He wanted the war against the Philistines to be something personal.

The Spirit of the Lord stirred Samson to begin his mission to end the domination of the Philistines. He insisted to his parents that he wanted to marry a Philistine woman. His parents were shocked at this strange demand from their son. They did not realize that Samson was truly acting in the interest of God to obtain an entry point into the lives of the Philistines. As Samson journeyed with his parents, they were confronted by a fearsome lion. The sight of the lion sent tremors of fear in his parents and they ran away to hide themselves, calling out to Samson to do the same. However, Samson stood his ground, and he felt the strength of the Lord coming upon him. As the young lion leapt upon Samson with its mouth wide open to devour him, Samson moved with lightning speed, took hold of its wide open jaw, and tore it into pieces. When his parents came out from their hiding, Samson joined them in a nonchalant manner, without revealing what he had done. On his next trip he found the skeleton of the lion and to his surprise saw a honeycomb under the hollow rib cage. Scooping off the honey, he ate it as he went to Timnah in Philistia. Samson thanked God for His amazing blessings and vowed to remain faithful to Him.

Although Samson exhibited extraordinary physical strength and courage, he became weak before the seductive love of two women. In the first instance, Samson had challenged the young Philistines to give an answer to the riddle he posed: "Out of the eater came forth food, and out of the strong came forth sweetness." Though he was referring to the lion and honey, no one was able to solve the riddle as they were unaware of such an event. When the young men were unable to find an answer for the riddle, they approached Samson's wife and coaxed her initially, and later threatened her to obtain the right answer from Samson. Playing a game of seduction—"If you love me, you will tell me"; and, "If I am number one in your life, you will trust me"—she was successful in extracting the answer from Samson. When the cunning young men conveyed the answer to Samson, which they had obtained through deception, he went on a rampage. He went to the city of Ashkelon, killed thirty Philistines, ripped off their garments, and gave those thirty garments to the treacherous young Philistines.

Samson must have been heartbroken to realize that the woman whom he had trusted and loved had deliberately betrayed him to support her countrymen. Though she revealed her helplessness and begged forgiveness for her act of treachery, Samson remained unmoved. In anger, he returned to his home. Upon his return to Israel, he tried to be a fair judge over the people. He was the eighth judge since Joshua's time. He knew that God had chosen him to bring about justice in the lives of the people. He was fair and wise when he was to settle disputes among the people. People who had heard of Samson's formidable adventures among the Philistines did not want to bring his wrath upon them. Samson was fearsome when he encountered acts of injustice committed against weak and helpless people. Soon there was peace among the people, and they began to show greater faithfulness to God.

Though the land was at peace, there was a storm raging in Samson's heart. He wanted to get back at the Philistines, whose foul play had ended his marriage abruptly. He began to think about his bride often and knew that he would have no peace until he returned to her. His initial hurt and anger were now replaced by love and longing. However, he did not know that returning to Timnah would result in greater heartache for him. He was crushed when he realized that his wife, whom he had disowned in anger, had become someone else's wife. Samson was not willing to accept the responsibility of the result of his anger and his impetuous gesture. Rather, he thought about the trickery of the Philistines and his anger flared up against them. He was also reminded that the Philistines, who had caused him to lose his wife, were also responsible for bringing great pain and suffering in the lives of God's people. He knew that destroying their wealth would severely hurt these enemies. Samson, who fearlessly moved among the wild animals, got hold of many foxes, tied their tails together with burning torches, and released them into the fields, orchards, and barns of the Philistines, destroying their crops.

However, the Philistines were not accustomed to accepting defeats and setbacks. Upon learning that Samson was the reason behind the loss of their harvest, they vowed to take revenge on him. When they searched for Samson, they realized that he had retreated to the land of Etam. They needed victims to satisfy their anger, and they felt justified in killing the former wife of Samson and her family. Mercilessly they torched them as an act of retaliation against Samson. As their anger still did not subside, three thousand strong men went in search of Samson to the place where he was residing.

The inhabitants of Etam approached Samson and expressed their anguish, as Samson had put them all in a precarious situation. They were afraid that the Philistines would take revenge on them for hiding Samson in their land. Samson asked them to bind his hands in chains and deliver him to the hands of the enemies.

The Philistines were jubilant at having their formidable enemy, Samson, under their control and in chains. They wanted to inflict great pain upon him and make him suffer for all the insults he had heaped upon them previously. However, they had not fully fathomed the power of God that was at work in Samson's life. The Spirit of the Lord came upon Samson, and "the ropes around his arms became as flax that was consumed by fire and his bonds melted away from his hands" (Judges 15:14). Getting hold of the jawbone of an ass, Samson turned to his enemies. The Spirit of the Lord that rushed upon him, and the hostility he had toward the Philistines formed into a dangerous combination of fury, and Samson ravaged the enemy camp and killed over a thousand mighty men. Unable to withstand Samson's rampage, the rest ran away to save themselves. At the end of such a gruesome act, Samson collapsed in thirst and cried out to God for help: "You have granted this great victory by the hand of your servant. Must I now die of thirst or fall into the hands of the uncircumcised?" (Judges 15:18). God miraculously provided Samson with water, and he went away refreshed and renewed. Samson was challenged to realize that ultimately he had to rely on God, not merely on his own amazing physical strength.

When Samson fell in love with Delilah from Philistia, he was scripting his own downfall and eventual demise. The Philistines coerced and bribed her to gain the secret of Samson's strength. She used her beauty, charm, and deception, and after repeated attempts she made him divulge the unique secret. When Samson revealed the secret about his Nazirite vow and his hair—"no razor shall touch his head"—he was trusting her with his life. He should have known her trickery, but his love for her made him blind to any such deception. His love and lust for her overpowered any sense of reason, and he believed that he could trust her. As he was peacefully sleeping on her lap, Delilah called in a man and had Samson's hair completely shaved off. The Philistines rewarded her with the bribe, overpowered Samson, and took him as their captive. As Samson had lost the power of God, he felt helpless to defend himself. Rather than killing him instantly, they preferred to humiliate Samson by gouging out his eyes and subjecting him to hard labor in their prison in Gaza. However, they did not notice that his hair was beginning to grow back. As Samson spent his dark days in prison, his heart once again turned to the Lord and he sought help.

When the Philistines assembled to celebrate the great feast of their god Dagon, they brought out their prized enemy prisoner in chains to entertain the jeering crowd. As Samson was now blind it was easy for them to play different tricks on him and thereby entertain the masses. Eventually they had him stationed between two mighty columns. As Samson stood there, hearing all the ridicule and mockery that were directed against him and his God, Samson's heart was raised up to heaven in humble supplication. As he asked God for forgiveness, he also sought for strength to take revenge on the enemies. As he was braced between two columns that were central support pillars, he pressed his palms against them and pushed them with all his strength. Down came the majestic temple upon Samson and the thousands of enemies that were gathered. This single sacrificial act of Samson accounted for the killing of more enemies than all his previous battles combined.

No doubt, Samson's life and activities often raise more questions and concerns than real inspiration for modern readers. We might even look at Samson's infatuation with Delilah as sheer foolishness. We might be quick to judge Samson as gullible and weak in resisting temptations. However, his life and his failures can teach us powerful lessons. When Samson allowed the love of women to take away his love for the Lord, he was setting himself up for his own downfall. Spiritually Samson lost his calling from God and the power of His Spirit when he was willing to reveal the secret of his strength to capture the affection of Delilah. In the end, he lost everything—his calling, God's strength, his sight, his freedom, his dignity, and finally his life.

Yet the story of Samson is a powerful reminder that it is never too late to turn to God for redemption. Naturally, one will have to face the consequences of one's actions. However, one can be certain of God's forgiveness and mercy when one recognizes one's failures, humbles oneself before God, and begs Him for mercy.

*"Don't trust to hold God's hand; let Him hold yours. Let Him do the holding, and you the trusting."*
—Hammer William Web-Peploe

---

## For Further Reflection and Discussion

1.  When you think of Samson, what qualities or characteristics come to mind?

2.  When Samson had killed a thousand Philistines, he became extremely thirsty and cried to the Lord for help. What are the implications of this?

3.  Why couldn't Samson realize Delilah's deception? Did Delilah really love Samson as she professed?

4.  Samson's life became miserable when the Spirit of the Lord left him. Discuss.

5.  Did Samson die as a person redeemed?

# RUTH:
## Filial Piety Rewarded

*"Boaz took Ruth. When they came together as man and wife, the Lord enabled her to conceive and she bore a son...They called him Obed. He was the father of Jesse, the father of David"* (Ruth 4:13–17).

Sometimes life can take one to places and situations that one can hardly imagine. Could Ruth, a Moabite woman, a Gentile according to the biblical norms, have ever imagined that she would be remembered lovingly and with great admiration centuries after her life? Better still, could she ever have hoped to be connected with the family of the great Israelite King David? Greater still, had she ever realized that she was going to be part of God's plan of salvation for human beings as an ancestress of Jesus, the Savior of the world? She became part of the ancestry of Jesus through her filial piety and devotion. Through her dedication and faithfulness, she communicated the greatest good news to the whole world—God's universal love and gift of salvation.

To understand the person of Ruth better, it is important to pay close attention to different persons who are mentioned in this short book, Ruth, in the Bible. The characters in the book are Elimelech of Bethlehem; Naomi, his wife; their sons, Mahlon and Chilion; two Moabite women, Orpah and Ruth, who became wives of the two sons; and Boaz, the influential kinsman of Elimelech. The names of the characters and the meaning of their names provide significant insights about the book (see *The International Bible Commentary*, 1998, p. 567). Elimelech, which means "my God is king," points to the period when Israel had no king. Naomi means "beautiful or delight": the bearer of the name had a bitter lot in life, but in the end it all turned into great delight. Ruth means "companionship and refreshment," and through her dedicated life she provided companionship to everyone, Naomi in particular. The name Boaz entails "in His strength." Boaz is a man of great wealth, commanding authority, and power; he is a man of moral and spiritual strength, firmly grounded in the strength of the Lord.

Unimaginable things can happen to a person who places absolute trust in the Lord. The story of Ruth bears witness to that. It was only through God's plan that two persons, Naomi and Ruth, born and raised in two different countries and cultures, could come together to accomplish His purpose. Naomi and her husband, Elimelech, and their two sons, Mahlon and Chilion, lived a comfortable life until famine hit the land of Bethlehem. Collecting all their possessions, they departed for the land of Moab, where there was food. According to Genesis 19:37, the Moabites were the ancestors of Lot (the nephew of Abraham) through his incestuous relationship with his older daughter. As a result, the Israelites had often looked down on Moabites. However, in severe moments of crisis such as famine, these feelings are often set aside and people attempt to satisfy their basic needs. Elimelech and Naomi experienced the kindness and hospitality of the Moabites and quickly they cast aside their prejudice against the Moabites. Life was fairly comfortable for this family until disaster struck. Unexpectedly Elimelech died, leaving Naomi a widow with her two sons. Naomi, who had come to appreciate the Moabites, had not resisted the sons' desire to marry foreign women so the sons had married two beautiful women of Moab: Orpah and Ruth.

Tragedies seemed to continue in Naomi's life as both of her sons died unexpectedly, leaving the two beautiful Moabite women widows. There they were—three widows wondering about their future with little support from any man. Naomi knew that she was approaching the sunset of her life, but her young daughters-in-law had long lives ahead of them. Knowing that she would not be able to take care of them, she urged them to return to their people. She really loved them, but she realized that she was helpless in every way to offer the help they needed. She only wished and prayed for their security and happiness. She knew that Orpah and Ruth could return to their homes, probably remarry, and have children and secure lives. She did not want to become a hindrance to their future security and safety.

Orpah unwillingly agreed; however, Ruth refused. The words that immortalized Ruth came from her great love and devotion to Naomi. Ruth said, "Do not ask me to abandon or forsake you! For wherever you go I will go, wherever you lodge, I will lodge, your people shall be my people and your God my God" (Ruth 1:16). What powerful words from Ruth, a young Gentile widow, totally willing to abandon her life and face the unknown! She was willing to give up her homeland, her people, her traditions, and her religion to support her helpless mother-in-law and to serve her God. The words of Ruth would become the hallmark of her pledge of loyalty, which would be favorably rewarded by God beyond her imagination.

Ruth might not have come to this conclusion overnight. She must have considered herself fortunate to have been married to a wonderful person who was devoted to her in every way. She assumed that he had learned this dedication from his parents, who were devoted to one another as well. There was great affection and respect among all the members of this Hebrew family. What touched her the most was their dedication to their God. It was only natural for Ruth to come to the conclusion that their obedience to their God was the reason behind their righteous lives. Even great calamities and misfortunes in life never seemed to shake their trust in Him. It was natural for Ruth then to inquire more and more about their God and slowly come to the realization that the living God would extend His love and mercy even to her. Deep within her, there was a great conviction that there was a purpose in her life and that could be actualized only by her faithfulness to Him. There was a sense of calmness within her when she made her decision known to her mother-in-law.

She was stepping out in faith to face the unknown. Although it was rather painful to leave the familiar shore and set out onto the unknown waters, a sense of God's presence calmed her fears and anxieties. She trusted and believed that everything happened according to God's plan even when the plan was not very clear to her. Naomi informed her that they would be returning to Bethlehem. Ruth had heard many things about Bethlehem from her husband, Chilion, and from Naomi. She had hoped that one day she would visit Bethlehem with her husband. However, she was going to the place of her husband's birth under the most unusual circumstances. Tears must have blinded Ruth several times as she made the long journey with Naomi.

They reached Bethlehem in time for the harvest. When the women asked, "Can this be Naomi?" we can feel the anguish and pain in Naomi's response, "Do not call me Naomi, (beautiful or delight). But call me Mara, for the almighty has made it bitter for me. I went away with an abundance, but the Lord has brought me back destitute" (Ruth 1:20–21). True, Naomi went away with abundance and in the company of her husband and two sons. She came back destitute, only in the company of Ruth, a humble girl whose loyalty now gave her strength.

Even though there was anguish in her heart, she came to the realization that the loyalty of Ruth could open up possibilities of a better life for both of them. Naomi had left Bethlehem at a time of famine (nothingness) but came back at a time of harvest (abundance). The abundance of blessings would be reaped through the dedication of Ruth. She marveled at her daughter-in-law, who possessed great virtues in life. Ruth exhibited great love, compassion, obedience, humility, kindness, wisdom, understanding, and willingness to be at the service of anyone in need.

Ruth made herself available to work with Boaz, a kinsman of Naomi's dead husband, Elimelech. According to the custom of the day, he was one of the people who could marry Ruth and give her an inheritance. Ruth soon gained the attention of Boaz, and this eventually led to their marriage. When Ruth conceived, the women of Bethlehem, who were touched by the goodness and kindness of Ruth, came to Naomi and said, "Blessed is the Lord who has not failed to provide you today with an heir! May he become famous in Israel! He will be your comfort and the support of your old age, for his mother is the daughter-in-law who loves you. She is more worth to you than seven sons" (Ruth 4:14–15). The women were acknowledging the great qualities of Ruth and her devotion to Naomi.

The son, Obed, born to Ruth and Boaz, would become the grandfather of King David. Ruth thus became an ancestress to the King of kings and Lord of lords—Jesus, the promised Savior of humanity. What they hoped for was much less in comparison to what God had in store for both of them. God richly rewarded Ruth's unwavering commitment. Her life clearly proclaimed that God's blessings were not restricted to one nation or to certain people but for all people who would acknowledge Him as their God. To a Moabite woman, God gave the privilege of being part of the ancestry of Jesus, the promised Savior.

Ruth's story is a beautiful portrayal of faithfulness on the part of all the leading characters portrayed in this book. Naomi showed her care and faithfulness when she urged Ruth to return to the safety of her home, remarry, and begin a new life. Ruth, on the other hand, was dedicated to her old and helpless mother-in-law and wanted to serve her and her God. Boaz was willing to redeem the family's land and marry the helpless Moabite widow. God, who saw it all, blessed their faithfulness beyond their imagination: Ruth and Boaz became part of God's covenant and ancestors of Jesus, the Savior of the world.

*"Life presents numerous opportunities to make it sublime. Blessed is the one who sees and holds on to God's hidden hands and makes the best of those opportunities."*

## For Further Reflection and Discussion

1.   Cultural prejudice and bias can often preclude a person from experiencing the goodness of a person from another culture. Discuss this in light of Ruth's story.

2.   Naomi's life shows a very familiar pattern: "up and down." Ultimately God is still in control. Discuss.

3.   Ruth's devotion and filial piety became the hallmark of her personality. Upon this devout and faithful person, God showered His choicest blessings. What are the implications of this story to our lives?

4.   Ruth's life clearly proclaimed that God's blessings were not restricted to one nation or to certain people but for all people who would acknowledge Him as their God. Discuss.

5.   "When one door is closed in life, God opens a window somewhere." Discuss this principle based on Ruth's life. What are the implications for our lives?

# SAMUEL:

## Always Listened and Always Obeyed

*"When Samuel went to sleep in his place, the Lord came and revealed His presence, calling out as before, 'Samuel, Samuel!' Samuel answered, 'Speak Lord, for your servant is listening'"* (1 Samuel 3:10).

Samuel was the last judge of Israel before the onset of the kingship and monarchy in Israel. The period of Judges that began after the death of Joshua described a familiar cycle—sin, slavery, supplication, and salvation. In the absence of a strong leader, people often went astray and committed the abominable sin of idolatry. The sin of idolatry was viewed as the greatest offense against God. As they deliberately chose to worship the false gods of other nations, the living God withheld His armor of protection and they became susceptible to failures. Under slavery and suffering, people remembered God and cried out for His help. God sent a judge to deliver them from bondage and instruct them in His ways. Their freedom and peace in the nation often lasted as long as the judge lived and led them by example. When he died, they would go back to their former way of life, and chaos would set in again. The pattern continued to repeat, and God's mercy continued to manifest itself. The last person to judge the people was Samuel (1 Samuel 7:15–17), who was at the same time a prophet (1 Samuel 3:20).

Samuel's birth was very miraculous, similar to other biblical leaders like Isaac and Samson. His father, Elkanah, was a devout and godly descendant of Levi. He had two wives, Hannah and Peninnah. While Hannah was barren, Peninnah gave birth to many children. In a society that valued the worth of a woman by the number of sons she brought forth, Hannah quietly bore the pain and shame of being a barren woman. Though her husband, Elkanah, loved her dearly, she was constantly ridiculed and reproached by Peninnah. Each year when these three made a pilgrimage to Shiloh, Peninnah would deliberately insult Hannah and prevent her from enjoying the celebration. The upset Hannah then would weep bitterly and refuse to eat and partake in the festivities. Though Elkanah earnestly attempted to ease the hurt by reassuring her of his love and her self-worth, his words could not ease her pain.

On one such trip, Hannah presented herself before the Lord at the temple and poured out her sorrow to Him. When one is in deep distress, one does not follow a set pattern of mourning and weeping. Occasionally Hannah sobbed, sighed, choked on her words, babbled, beat her breast, laughed bitterly, and made a solemn oath. Eli, the priest, who was watching her with great interest, concluded that she was drunk from the festivities. He chastised her for her emotional demonstration when he sternly said, "How long will you make a drunken show of yourself? Sober up from your wine!" (1 Samuel 1:14) When Hannah confided in Eli her painful story, the contrite priest blessed her and assured her that God would grant her request. True to the words of Eli, she conceived and gave birth to a son, whom she named Samuel, which means "name of God." She rejoiced at the favor God had bestowed upon her. Yet, she did not forget the oath she had made to God in her moment of desperation. Although it was painful for her to part with her little child, after he was weaned she brought the boy to Eli and consecrated him to the Lord.

The little Samuel lived with the aging priest Eli and attended to his needs. As a young boy, he could see the pain and hurt of his master, who was grieving over his sons who were living lawless lives. Although two of Eli's sons were priests, they were extremely wicked and did not respect God, the office of the priesthood, or the people. They had become entirely corrupt and were leading the people astray. Time after time Eli made attempts to correct his sons, but they totally ignored his wisdom and guidance. "Meanwhile the young Samuel was growing in stature and in worth in the estimation of the Lord and people" (1 Samuel 2:26). Eli devoted his time to helping the young Samuel to know the ways of God. He earnestly prayed that Samuel would not imitate the example of his corrupt sons.

God called Samuel to give him a special task. Initially Samuel misunderstood God's voice and ran to his master. After a third time, Eli knew that God was calling the young man and prompted him to reply to God's call, "Speak, Lord, for your servant is listening" (1 Samuel 3:9). God revealed to Samuel that He was displeased with Eli's sons and their priestly service. However, God was not going to abandon His people since they needed a godly leader in their midst. His Spirit remained with Samuel, who committed himself to God completely. Eli rejoiced at the way Samuel conducted himself before God and the people. God worked through Samuel, and soon he was regarded as a prophet mighty in word and deed by everyone.

Samuel knew the greatest challenge at hand was to inspire people back to their true covenant relationship with God. As Samuel was attempting to bring people back to God, the children of Israel faced the threat of the mighty Philistines. The elders of the people panicked at the impending doom and were convinced that Samuel could help the people unite and fight against the Philistines. However, the two corrupt sons of Eli, Hophni and Phinehas, boasted that they could defeat the enemies as they were in possession of the Ark of the Covenant. They imprudently believed that they possessed the power to defeat the Philistines as they carried the Ark. They prevented everyone from letting Samuel know what their plans were. However, to the horror of everyone, the Philistines defeated the Israelites, killed the sons of Eli, and carried the Ark away. Eli himself collapsed and died upon hearing the news of this great catastrophe. Samuel was heartbroken at the dual loss he experienced—the loss of the Ark and the demise of his beloved master. For the people, who always believed in the power and might of God that rested with the Ark, such a horrible event totally devastated their lives. Some even began to doubt the power of God and gave themselves to the worship of idols.

Although the loss of the Ark greatly grieved Samuel, he knew God was teaching a valid lesson to the people. Their success against the enemies did not depend on having the Ark in their possession but rather having their hearts right with God. If they had turned to God in repentance, He would have manifested His glory before them. The capture of the Ark was not a defeat of the power of God but a tangible sign of the moral degradation and corruption of the people. Samuel challenged the people to turn back to the Lord in repentance. He vehemently denounced idolatry and confronted the people to give up all idols and false worship of foreign gods. As people heeded and turned to the Lord with contrite hearts, He revealed His mercy and manifested His glory by the defeat of the mighty Philistines. Samuel urged the people to realize the fact that God would fight their battles only when they remained faithful to Him.

The victory over the Philistines brought about a period of peace in the nation. Samuel constantly moved about from place to place, settling disputes among the people and challenging them to live an upright life. He restored true worship of the living God. Samuel knew it was important to have more than one prophet who could serve the people and teach them the statutes and commands of the Lord. He selected godly men and instructed them in the ways of the Lord and formed them as a formidable group—a guild of prophets in Ramah (1 Samuel 19:20). The period of time Samuel judged over Israel was marked with peace, prosperity, and the true worship of Yahweh.

Though Samuel was a godly man, his sons failed to live up to the standard of their father. In his old age Samuel appointed his sons, Joel and Abijah, as judges over Israel. However, his sons did not follow the example of their father. Instead of seeking justice for the people, they began to cater to their selfish needs through acceptance of bribes and acts of partiality. When Samuel came to know about the moral debacle of his sons, he called them to task. However, they ignored him and went on with their corrupt affairs. Samuel painfully realized that as a father, he could only show them the way, and it was ultimately left to his sons to walk on the right path.

The corruption of Samuel's sons attracted public attention, and people were afraid for their future. Samuel was advancing in age and his sons did not possess the right qualities to lead them in the right path. When they looked at their neighboring nations, they found that they were led by kings, who secured peace for people and protected them from enemies. Though the people of Israel had accepted the sovereignty of God over their lives and accepted God as their only King, many felt that it was time for a new beginning. Samuel was heartbroken when he heard of their demand for a king. Samuel knew that their request was wrong and sinful. He felt that they were rejecting his authority and judgment. But God assured Samuel that, in fact, the people were rejecting God as their king, not Samuel. For a man of deep devotion, Samuel's heart ached for God. God reminded Samuel of the continuous rejections He had experienced from the people since He had brought them out of Egypt. God insisted to Samuel that he consent to their demands. At the same time God commanded Samuel to warn them of the right of a king, which could entail forced military recruitment, forced labor, taxation, and annexation of properties. He was reminding them of the cost of kingship. Compared to the "low costs" of judges, who lived with limited means, they were bargaining for "higher costs." However, the people persisted in their demand for a king.

Reluctantly Samuel found himself playing the role of kingmaker for Israel. Samuel once again turned to the source of his strength, God, seeking who could be the right person to be the first king of Israel. God directed Samuel to Saul, who was valiant, handsome, faithful, and humble. Upon seeing Saul, Samuel's turbulent feelings subsided slightly, as he seemed to be the right person to rule the people. Saul was courageous, strongly built, and "he stood head and shoulders above all the people" (1 Samuel 9:2). Samuel anointed Saul's head with oil and pronounced these words: "The Lord anoints you commander over his heritage. You are to govern the Lord's people Israel, and to save them from the grasp of their enemies roundabout" (1 Samuel 10:1). The Spirit of the Lord rushed upon Saul, and he committed himself to the Lord. He enjoyed initial success when he defeated the Amonites (1 Samuel 11) and found acceptance among the people. However, his success was short-lived. His enthusiasm to remain faithful to the Lord did not last very long as he continuously broke the precepts of the Lord by taking upon himself duties of the priests. Saul thought that he was above the law and could do anything he pleased.

Samuel confronted Saul and rebuked him for his foolish act of offering sacrifice. Standing boldly before the king, Samuel prophesied that Saul's kingdom would not last and that God had chosen another person to succeed Saul: "The Lord has sought out a man after His own heart and has appointed him commander of his people, because you broke the Lord's command" (1 Samuel 13:14). In his old age, Samuel was directed to Bethlehem to anoint the new king from the family of Jesse, of the tribe of Judah.

When Samuel anointed Saul as king, God was selecting a person of great physical strength and stature. However, when Saul failed, God looked for a man after His own heart and found David, the youngest son of Jesse. Samuel, however, was looking for someone who would resemble Saul's physical features. At the sight of Jesse's first son, Eliab, who was dignified in appearance, Samuel was quick to conclude that Eliab was the chosen one. But God made it clear to Samuel that He was going to choose someone whose heart would always be with Him. When David, the youngest son, was presented to Samuel, God directed him to anoint the young boy as the next king. God had chosen the youngest and smallest son of Jesse, not the strongest and biggest. As Samuel always obeyed the Lord, he did as he was told and then departed from Bethlehem. He trusted and believed that the young boy whom he had anointed would unite the people and bring them back to God.

Listening and obeying God's word were the greatest qualities of Samuel. He believed that God's plans were ultimately better than human plans. Human beings often look for immediate gratification and short-term benefits. God's plans are enduring, everlasting, and always for the well-being of His people. Samuel observed that, whenever people preferred their plans above God's own, they faced the painful consequences of their choices. Samuel listened and obeyed God's word and as a result became a powerful instrument of God in one of the most trying times in the history of Israel.

*"The third petition of the Lord's Prayer is repeated daily by millions who have not the slightest intention of letting anyone's will be done but their own."* —Aldous Huxley

## For Further Reflection and Discussion

1.   Samuel had the right disposition when he prayed, "Speak, Lord, for Your servant is listening." How often we tend to say, "Listen, Lord, for Your servant is talking." Discuss the importance of "listening" in prayer.

2.   Parents can only show the way. It is left to the children to walk on the path they are shown. Discuss this in the light of the painful experiences of two fathers—Eli and Samuel.

3.   The people were horrified to know that the Philistines carried the Ark of the Covenant away. They believed that the Ark would protect them always. What are the implications of this?

4.   The people demanded a king and Samuel warned them of the consequences of their demand. Discuss.

5.   God said, "Do not judge from his appearance or from his lofty stature, because I have rejected him. Not as man sees does God see, because man sees the appearance but the Lord looks into the heart" (1 Samuel 16:6–7). Discuss.

# SAUL:

## Great Start but Sad End

*"The Spirit of the Lord had departed from Saul, and he was tormented by an evil spirit"* (1 Samuel 16:14).

The people of Israel looked around and found that neighboring nations were ruled by kings. They, on the other hand, had prophets and judges. Though they conceptually believed God to be their king, they were impressed by the organizational structure of neighboring monarchies. The famous judge Samuel had led the people according to God's statutes and decrees. Previously there were many God-fearing prophets and judges who constantly reminded the people that they were people of the covenant, and that God would accomplish His special purpose for humanity through them. Samuel, the holy man of God, had done just that. He was getting old and hoped that his sons would live for the people just as he had dedicated his life to them.

However, human weaknesses and sinful attractions got the best of Samuel's sons, and they strayed from righteous living. "His sons did not follow his example but sought illicit gain and accepted bribes, perverting justice" (1 Samuel 8:3). They were selfish and self-seeking, bringing shame to the noble family. They served the rich and powerful, and their sense of justice was based on their benefit. As a result many innocent people were punished and many culprits were exonerated. It was like the evil corrupting the head and making the whole body ill as a result.

The elders of the people, who had seen the benefits of living according to God's ways, nevertheless experienced injustice under the current judges and approached their favorite old judge, Samuel, with a demand for a king. They were afraid that it would be disastrous if Samuel's sons, who had no sense of justice and fairness, were to continue as their judges. Samuel was placed in a dilemma. He was heartbroken at seeing the failures of his sons and at the same time displeased at the request to have a king. He truly believed that God was to be the only King of the people. He was convinced that the institution of kingship and monarchy would lead the chosen people away from being God's people and lead them toward being a worldly power. When Samuel prayed to God, He granted their request but with a warning of the difficulties associated with earthly kings: forced military drafting, taxation, possible tyranny, and exploitation. But the people were resolute in their request. God did not force them to change their minds but granted their request.

God was pleased with Saul, a member of the tribe of Benjamin. Saul exhibited great physical qualities and godly traits: "There was no other Israelite more handsome than Saul; he stood head and shoulders above other people" (1 Samuel 9:2). He was very devoted to his father, Kish, and his family. He believed in the power of God and acknowledged that God could speak through His spokespersons like Samuel. It came as no surprise when he anointed Saul as the first king of all the twelve tribes of Israel. God also provided many signs to Samuel that confirmed that Saul should be the king. At that moment, Saul was the best person for this important task.

Saul was anointed by Samuel, and God's Spirit rushed upon him. Saul gained the confidence and admiration of the people, and with the help of God, he achieved many victories in battle. Samuel stepped down as the leader of Israel and encouraged the people to be faithful to God at all times and to support their new king.

Saul's faithfulness to God did not last long. He thought he was in command and decided to overstep boundaries that included taking over religious duties, which displeased the Lord. When Saul was preparing to wage battle with the Philistines, Samuel had specifically instructed Saul to wait for his arrival to offer the sacrifice. Offering the sacrifice was the duty of a priest, and a holocaust at the onset of the battle was seen as asking God for victory in the battle. Samuel, who was the judge and high priest, was to offer this sacrifice. However, at Gilgal, Saul offered the holocaust, which was specifically the duty of the priest. Samuel viewed this act of Saul as foolish and presumptuous disobedience of God's specific commands. His anger was very clear in his words: "You have been foolish! Had you kept the command the Lord your God gave you, He would have established your kingship in Israel as lasting; but as things are, your kingdom shall not endure" (1 Samuel 13:13–14a). It was the first of many acts of foolishness and disobedience committed by Saul.

Saul began to exhibit a lack of discretion and degeneration of judgment in his warfare. He believed that through complete fasting, he could defeat the enemy. Though fasting was seen as a noble deed, it was an unwise instruction to be given to the soldiers. Had Saul sought God's guidance in prayer and if God had instructed Saul to command the soldiers to refrain from food, such an act could have been justifiable. If the instruction had come from God, it would have been a beautiful moment to reveal God's glory before the people. Such a moment would have deepened the conviction among the people that it was God's battle and the victory was gained by His power, not the military might of the king. But on his own, Saul commanded the people to refrain from food until they had defeated the enemy.

Not knowing of his father's command, Jonathan, the son of Saul who had secured many victories, ate honey from a honeycomb. Saul viewed this as an act of disobedience on the part of his son, and he wanted to put Jonathan to death. The soldiers, who had witnessed the valor of Jonathan and his victories, objected to Saul's intention. Saul was in danger of losing the support of his army. They said, "This must not be! As the Lord lives, not a single hair of his head shall fall to the ground, for God was with him in what he did today. Thus the soldiers were able to rescue Jonathan from death" (1 Samuel 14:45). Saul's bizarre behavior was being noted by all, especially by his son and the military forces.

Saul's disobedience to God also became visible when he ignored the explicit command received through Samuel, who wanted to have everything destroyed with the Amalekites. God had instructed Saul through Samuel, "I will punish what Amalek did to Israel when he barred his way as he was coming up from Egypt. Go now, attack Amalek, and deal with him and all that he has under his ban. Do not spare him but kill…camels and asses" (1 Samuel 15:2–3). The king of Amalek had attacked the children of Israel during their journey to the Promised Land (Exodus 17:8–15). The children of Israel had not military of adequate weaponry, and the whole situation had brought great fear among the people. God waged the battle for them through Moses, Joshua, Aaron, and Hur and obtained victory for them. The defeat and destruction of Amalek should have been viewed as a fitting punishment for the enemies, who had brought great suffering to the people of Israel wandering through the wilderness. Saul, on the other hand, spared the king of Amalek, Agag, and the best of his fat sheep, oxen, and lambs. He wanted to take the king as a military prisoner and declare his power before all. Looking at the fat sheep, oxen, and lambs, he must have thought he could make much greater use of them (including sacrifice) than complete destruction. Contrary to God's instruction, Saul wanted to store up the wealth and riches from the defeated nation.

Saul gradually slipped away from God, and he was losing God's Spirit due to his disobedience. In place of God's Spirit came an evil spirit, probably violent rage resulting from his jealousy, constantly tormenting him. When Saul took matters into his hands, contrary to specific instructions given to him, he was replacing God's purposes with his own goals. He forgot what his responsibilities were, and he sought after his own personal gratification. Saul's heart was tormented by a spirit of melancholy and depression. He found temporary comfort in the skillful music played by David, but no physical comforts and pleasures of life could give him lasting contentment. Human beings experience constant restlessness when they are separated from God and that was Saul's story. Centuries later, Saint Augustine would paraphrase this principle: "Our hearts are made for You, O Lord, they are restless until they rest in You."

The worst came when jealousy gripped the heart of Saul with the arrival of David. To make matters worse, the Philistines became stronger under their new hero, Goliath. Having lost the presence of the Spirit of God within him, Saul was gripped with fear. Until then, God's power had reassured Saul of victory in many battles. His own physical power did not match his giant opponent, Goliath. When David stepped forward to meet the challenge, Saul was concerned about the boy's safety and offered him his armor. However, David moved ahead with his God-given confidence and the slings in his hand. David trusted more in the Lord than in the armor of Saul, and he surrendered his heart to God's power. The power of God manifested through David as he was able to slay the mighty Philistines and rescue the children of Israel from their enemies.

The killing of Goliath by David should have been an occasion for great celebration, but soon it turned into a moment of great rage for the king. The women's song, "Saul has slain his thousands and David his ten thousands" (1 Samuel 18:7) annoyed Saul to such an extent that he wanted to kill David. Soon Saul the king became captive to his own evil feelings, totally forgetting the reason why he was chosen by God to be the king. Though David later on became his son-in-law and close friend of his son, Jonathan, nothing stopped Saul from his wicked desire to exterminate David. He had sold his soul to the devil and faced the tragic end. Having lost favor with God, Saul not only lost his final battle against the Philistines but also the lives of his three sons and his own life (1 Samuel 31:1–10).

Saul had a great start. He was courageous, charismatic, humble, and capable initially. Everything was going right for him as long as he remained faithful to the Lord. When he separated himself from the source of his life and nourishment, his life became miserable and a failure and eventually it withered away. As a result, Saul experienced in his life a loss of fervor and lack of purpose. What was sad in this case was that Saul did not even realize that he was losing God's Spirit.

Revelation 3:20 reads, "Behold, I stand at the door and knock. If anyone hears my voice and opens the door, I will enter his house and dine with him, and he with me." God stands at the door of every person's heart, waiting to be invited in. God does not force His way into a person's life. Even when He is invited, His Spirit remains in a person's life only as long as He feels wanted. Whenever God's Spirit experiences neglect and rejection in human life, He gracefully moves out.

*"I am the vine, you are the branches. Whoever remains in me and I in him will bear much fruit, because without me you can do nothing." —John 15:5*

139

## For Further Reflection and Discussion

1.  Saul had a great start but a poor ending. Discuss.

2.  At times we encounter people who come to the forefront with great promise. But tested with time, responsibilities, and challenges, they fail to live up to their potential. What are the implications of this?

3.  By taking on the duties of the priests, Saul demonstrated his belief that he was above the law. What are the dangers of not respecting the responsibilities of others?

4.  Saul did not know that he was losing the Spirit of God. In place of God's Spirit, there was an evil spirit tormenting Saul. What are the implications of this?

5.  Initial enthusiasm and determination should be matched with acts of commitment day after day. Discuss.

# JONATHAN:
## True Friendship Tested

*"Jonathan then spoke well of David to his father Saul, saying to him, let not your majesty sin against his servant David, for he has committed no offense against you, but has helped you very much by his deeds…Why, then, should you become guilty of shedding innocent blood by killing David without cause?"* (1 Samuel 19:4–6).

Sometimes parents can prevent their children from reaching their optimal development. Knowingly or unknowingly, some parents can thwart their children from reaching the heights they were destined to reach. Jonathan's story bears witness to that, as he should have been the automatic successor to his father, Saul, reigning over Israel as the second king. Had Saul continued as a faithful servant of God and ruled over the people with integrity, Jonathan would have inherited the throne. But Saul's continual disobedience and imprudent decisions proved that he was unfit to rule over the people.

The words of the prophet Samuel had sealed Saul's fate: "You have been foolish! Had you kept the command the Lord your God gave you, the Lord would now establish your kingship in Israel as lasing; but as things are, your kingdom shall not endure" (1 Samuel 13:13). These words of Samuel also meant that Jonathan, the prince, would not ascend to the throne but rather would have to watch someone else take his legitimate place. Upon hearing this news, any other prince should have been disappointed and grief-stricken. However, Jonathan did not exhibit any such sentiments. He was wise enough to realize that it was futile to go against the will of God. He believed that ultimately God's plan would come to its fulfillment. He knew his duty was to serve the people in the ways in which he was capable. He continued to be devoted to his father, and he eventually formed a unique friendship with the newly anointed king, David, based on trust, brotherly love, and loyalty.

Jonathan, the son of King Saul, was a young man of great courage, strength, and determination. He was elated at the knowledge that God had chosen his father, Saul, to be the first king of Israel. He admired his father and stood in awe of his commanding personality and courage. He showed his dedication and devotion when he vowed to serve his father. He knew that serving his father faithfully would ultimately lead to serving God and His people. Jonathan had proven his courage when he had fought against a battalion of Philistine soldiers with only his armor-bearer by his side. Jonathan had begun his battle against the Philistines with an invocation of the name of God and trusted that God would wage the war on his behalf. Jonathan's act of bravery inspired his father, Saul, as the king and six hundred men joined the battle against the Philistines. The Lord granted them a great victory over the Philistines, and Jonathan received many accolades and gained the admiration of the army.

Unlike Jonathan, who trusted God's hand in Israel's victory over their enemies, his father, Saul, relied on his military might. As Israel continued battling against the Philistines, Saul made a rash oath: "Cursed be the man who takes food before evening, before I am able to avenge myself on my enemies" (1 Samuel 14:24) and put his army under an irrational sanction. Jonathan, who had not heard of his father's oath and sanction, tasted honey and put himself in danger. As Saul was determined to punish anyone who had violated his commands, he was forced to order Jonathan to death due to his oath. However, those in Saul's army who had witnessed Jonathan's courage, stood with him as they said, "Is Jonathan to die, though it was he who brought Israel this great victory? This must not be! As the Lord lives, not a single hair of his head shall fall to the ground, for God was with him in what he did today" (1 Samuel 14:45). It was a moment that truly tested the integrity of Jonathan. If he had wanted, he could have overthrown the power of his father with the overwhelming support of the army and appointed himself as the king. Such a thought would never have crossed Jonathan's mind as he knew the importance of being faithful to his father.

Jonathan's heart grieved as the nation was threatened again by the mighty Philistines. When the fierce warrior Goliath singlehandedly challenged the Israelite army, Jonathan wanted to step up and fight the giant. However, his father convinced him that such a reckless act would only cause the loss of his life. Jonathan hesitantly agreed to his father's command and hoped and prayed for someone whom God would send to save Israel from shame and humiliation.

He was amazed at whom God sent in answer to his prayer. The young man, David, who stepped up in his shepherd's clothing, appeared to be no match for the giant Goliath. But as Jonathan watched the shepherd boy, David, with great interest, he felt that David surpassed Goliath in courage. Goliath was counting on his powerful weapons and his own enormous physical strength. David, on the other hand, seemed to rely on the power that came from within. The words of David to Goliath had a lasting effect on Jonathan: "You come against me with sword and spear and scimitar, but I come against you in the name of the Lord of hosts, the God of the armies of Israel that you have insulted. Today the Lord shall deliver you into my hands; I will strike you down and cut off your head…For the battle is the Lord's, and he shall deliver you into our hands" (1 Samuel 17:45–47). As Jonathan watched David, he realized that the source of David's strength was his trust in the almighty God. He lifted his heart and eyes to God, beseeching protection upon this young and courageous man who had stepped out to save the king and the people from great humiliation.

The slaying of Goliath brought great jubilation to the whole land of Israel. King Saul was elated at the victory David had won for him. For Jonathan, it was a moment of realization that God had chosen someone who could serve the people better than he could. The moment was not a bitter one as he experienced true admiration and love for David, whose courage had saved the people. David's courage and bravery deeply affected Jonathan. What touched Jonathan the most was David's exhibition of trust in God and his humility before the mighty God. Clearly David had not relied on his own physical strength, as he had been no match for the invincible Goliath. Jonathan was deeply moved with genuine brotherly affection for David. He realized that they shared much in common in the areas of courage, strength, bravery, and loyalty. He also realized that David surpassed him in his faith and trust in God.

Jonathan, who knew about Samuel's words that the kingdom would be taken away from Saul, believed that David was the one whom God would choose to succeed his father. He did not know that Samuel had already gone to the family of Jesse in Bethlehem and anointed David with oil. For any prince, such a moment should have caused great self-pity for himself and hostility toward the one who could be viewed as a "rival." His heart could have been tormented by jealousy and envy of David, similar to his father, Saul. However, for Jonathan, it was a moment of acceptance of God's mysterious ways. God blessed the goodness of Jonathan's heart and there began a true and genuine friendship that would find favor in the sight of God.

Jonathan's actions clearly indicated that he accepted David as the successor to his father's throne. He invited David to the palace and gave him his royal robe, his military dress, his sword, his bow, and his belt. Those were the prerogative of the prince and a clear sign before everyone as to who would succeed the throne after the death of the present king. Bowing in great respect, David accepted these gifts and vowed to be loyal to Saul and his son Jonathan. David and Jonathan promised to be true friends to each other and let nothing come between their friendship. Jonathan was greatly pleased to know his father had decided to make David the military commander of his army. He was elated to fight alongside David, and God granted them many victories.

While Jonathan rejoiced at the success of David over Goliath and David's victories in many military expeditions, Saul was consumed with jealousy of David. Saul constantly remembered the praises of the women—"Saul has slain his thousands, and David his ten thousands"—embittering him with the need to get rid of his new rival. He believed that nothing could give him satisfaction except taking the life of David. He had clearly forgotten what David had accomplished for the nation and how he had saved him from humiliation. Consumed with jealousy and envy, Saul sought to kill David. When Jonathan came to know his father's evil intentions, he begged his father to acknowledge what David had done for the nation and refrain from such a cruel act: "Let not your majesty sin against his servant David, for he has committed no offense against you but has helped you very much by his deeds...Why then, should you become guilty of shedding innocent blood by killing David without cause?" (1 Samuel 19:4–6). Saul, who loved his son, heeded Jonathan's request and promised that he would not raise his hand against David.

However, Saul had become very unpredictable, and his promise to his son did not last very long. He attempted time and again to kill David, but each time David escaped. There were times when Jonathan unveiled Saul's plans and warned David, thereby saving his life.

However, with each failed attempt Saul became increasingly furious. His anger flared up when he learned that Jonathan was behind some of David's escapes. He blamed Jonathan for not being courageous enough to stand up for his rightful claim to be the next king. He accused Jonathan of supporting David in his rise to power among the people. Jonathan put his own life in danger by standing up for David and by aiding David to escape multiple assassination attempts. While Saul exhibited bitterness and resentment against God's plan for David to succeed Saul, Jonathan, who had the rightful claim to be the next king, showed his acceptance of God's plans. If Jonathan had chosen to be a selfish and ambitious person, he would have sided with his father and helped him to kill David. But Jonathan showed greater character and readiness to accept God's decision than his father did. He had come to know and love David as the chosen instrument of God, and his friendship with David was one of great loyalty that surpassed his own ambitions.

As it had become increasingly difficult for David to survive in the open, he was forced to become a fugitive. Jonathan sought out David, and their last encounter clearly manifested the depth of their friendship. David bowed down before Jonathan and paid him homage, then they held each other, kissed, and wept aloud. Finally Jonathan said to David, "Go in peace, in keeping with what we two have sworn in the name of the Lord—the Lord shall be between you and me, and between your posterity and mine forever" (1 Samuel 20:42). They were real men, true friends, who were able to share the proper and right love of a brotherly friendship.

Saul's irrational behavior brought his premature end. Jonathan's faithfulness to his father would cost his own life. He could have easily avoided death by refusing to obey the commands of his father. However, as long as Saul lived and was viewed as the legitimate king of Israel, Jonathan followed the commands of his father. The final battle with the Philistines turned deadly, and on the same day, Jonathan and two of his brothers were slain by their enemies. King Saul, who was mortally wounded, refused to surrender to the enemies and killed himself. Saul had brought a cruel end upon himself and his family by his erratic behavior.

When David heard of this distressing news, he greatly grieved over the deaths of Saul and Jonathan. He expressed his sorrow in an elegy and praised the courage of Saul and Jonathan as well as Jonathan's devotion to his father. He spoke of Jonathan as "my brother, most dear have you been to me; more precious have I held love for you than love for women" (2 Samuel 1:26). David honored the promise of lasting friendship as he gave a fitting burial for Jonathan (2 Samuel 21:12–14), and showed kindness to the son of Jonathan, "Meribbaal, who was lame in both feet" (2 Samuel 9:1–13).

Jonathan and David were capable of loving one another—giving and receiving love. Probably Jonathan's love for David involved more self-sacrifice. Jonathan's love for David was totally selfless. It is sad and ironic that our modern society often casts a shadow of doubt and attributes ulterior motives behind genuine friendships, be it between man and man, woman and woman, or men and women. Many people have difficulty in believing the fact that there can be genuine friendship without physical intimacy. As a result, some look at the friendship between Jonathan and David through the lens of eroticism and miss out on the beauty of their genuine friendship that was built on trust, appreciation, and brotherly love.

> *"This was what love meant after all: sacrifice and selflessness. It did not mean hearts and flowers and a happy ending, but the knowledge that another's well-being is more important than one's own."* —Melissa de la Cruz

## For Further Reflection and Discussion

1.  What must have gone on in the mind of Jonathan when he came to know that God had rejected Saul?
2.  Jonathan had every reason to be jealous and angry at the thought that his claim to be the king was over. However, he showed dedication to God, to Saul, and to David. Discuss.
3.  Saul had power, but he was not free. Jonathan had no power as Saul did, but he was free. Discuss.
4.  What are the qualities that foster genuine friendships? Answer it from the perspective of the friendship between David and Jonathan.
5.  Sexual intimacy fulfills friendship in a proper context (e.g., marriage), or destroys the possibility of a genuine friendship in other contexts. Discuss.

# DAVID:

## "A Man After God's Own Heart"

*"David strengthened himself in the Lord his God"* (1 Samuel 30:6).

God often provides the best available person to serve His purposes. Saul was chosen as the king because he was the best available. When Saul turned his back on God through his foolish choices, He looked for the next best available in Israel. His eyes fell upon David, the shepherd boy, son of Jesse from Bethlehem. Samuel, who had anointed Saul to be the first king of Israel, was grieving over the failure of Saul. God commanded Samuel to go to Bethlehem to the house of Jesse and anoint one of Jesse's sons to be the new king. When he met Eliab, the first son of Jesse, he was convinced that Eliab would be the new king. But God clearly told Samuel, "Do not judge from his appearance or from his lofty stature, because I have rejected him. Not as man sees does God see, because man sees the appearance but the Lord looks into the heart" (1 Samuel 16:7). God was choosing a person of great devotion who would be known as a "man after God's own heart" (Acts 13:22). Nothing happens by chance with God. The election of David to be the king of Israel meant God was acting upon His promises, gradually unfolding His plan for the true, good shepherd king.

The shepherd boy, David, grew up to be one of the greatest personalities in the history of Israel. He is portrayed as the ideal king, a powerful warrior, a great musician, a psalmist, a sinner, and a "saint." It was from his family that the Savior of the world would come. Often when people would dream of the promised Messiah, they imagined someone like David, who would restore pride, peace, and prosperity in the kingdom. The best compliment came from God Himself, who said, "David is a man after my own heart" (Acts 13:22; cf. 1 Samuel 13:14).

Though David was a shepherd boy, he was destined for greatness. He was very handsome and talented. He was chosen by God as the king to succeed Saul. He was anointed by Samuel and would soon find himself in the court of Saul. Eventually, he became a national hero when he killed the Philistine giant, Goliath. The armies of the

Philistines and Israelites were camped opposite each other and were preparing for war (1 Samuel 17). The Philistine giant, Goliath, had continuously challenged the Israelites to choose someone from their army to fight against him. The mockery and insults lasted for over forty days, and neither Saul nor any soldier from the army or Israel stepped out to meet the challenge. Three of David's brothers were serving in Saul's army and they bowed out in shame, knowing well that facing Goliath would result in their death.

The courageous shepherd boy David volunteered to fight the mighty Philistine. Although many tried to persuade him from embarking on such a dangerous task, David announced with determination that he was armed with the strength of the Lord. When King Saul attempted to discourage David, citing his amateurish knowledge of war, David made clear his valor: "Your servant (David) has killed a lion and a bear, and this uncircumcised Philistine will be as one of them, because he has insulted the armies of the living God" (1 Samuel 17:36). David stepped out in faith, knowing that his armor was the presence and protection of the living God. He chose not to put on Saul's armor or use his weapons. David's weapons were a staff, five smooth stones, and a sling. The Philistines must have looked amused at the sight of this handsome young man in shepherd's clothes approaching the mighty warrior, Goliath, who wore a bronze helmet, bronze corselet of scale armor, bronze greaves, and carried a bronze scimitar and a javelin with an iron head. Many soldiers from the Israelites' army must have prayed for his protection, while a few must have sneered at him for what they thought to be a foolish action. Some must have cursed David as they believed that Goliath would kill David and then go on to slaughter everyone else.

Goliath was outraged at seeing David, who approached him in his shepherd's clothing. His contempt was clear in his words: "Am I a dog that you come against me with a staff? . . . I will leave your flesh for the birds of the air and the beasts of the field" (1 Samuel 17:43–44). David, who trusted in the power of God, remained unafraid at the words of the mighty Philistine. He used only one of the five smooth stones in his slingshot and expertly struck the forehead of the Philistine. Goliath, who was armed to the teeth, collapsed from the fatal blow of a simple stone. David not only saved the Israelites from shame and embarrassment but also demonstrated clearly his unwavering faith in the living God. As the Spirit of God was with David, he went on to achieve greater things in the sight of the Lord.

Despite all his successes, he faced some great troubles in life. David's troubles started when Saul became jealous of him and his fame. He escaped several assassination attempts, left his homeland, and hid in the wilderness and even among strangers. Seeds of jealousy and resentment were planted in Saul's heart when he heard the women of Israel lavishing praises upon David: "Saul has slain his thousands, and David his tens of thousands" (1 Samuel 18:7). Resentment had begun to grow in Saul's heart, and he viewed David as a rival and enemy.

When one does not have the power of God within oneself, insecurities, rage, and doubts can conquer one's heart. Saul, pierced with jealousy, sought to kill David, whose valor had saved the kingdom from the wrath of the Philistines. He plotted to have David killed by the Philistines (1 Samuel 18:20–27); Saul made his intention of killing David clear to his son Jonathan (David's dear friend) and the servants (1 Samuel 19:1). Even after David became a refugee, Saul searched for him with his army in order to kill him (1 Samuel 24:1–3).

On the other hand, David demonstrated great character and loyalty to God when he refused to kill Saul even though he had two opportunities to do so (1 Samuel 24:5–6; 26:8–12). David always acknowledged Saul as God's anointed (1 Samuel 26:9–10) and refused to harm Saul, who was constantly seeking to kill him. The situations and circumstances were just right to end his suffering and fugitive status. The words of the servants were compelling: "God has delivered your enemy into your hands" (1 Samuel 24:5). David could have seized the moment and could have killed Saul. There would have been no one to resent his action. The people who were miserable under Saul would have acclaimed David as their king immediately, but David did not take matters into his hands and commit the evil of inflicting harm upon God's anointed. David's integrity and character were clear in his words and actions: "The Lord forbid that I should do such a thing to my master, the Lord's anointed. With these words David restrained his men and would not permit them to attack Saul" (1 Samuel 24:7–8). David wept when he heard about the death of Saul and Jonathan, and he wrote an elegy for them. David was already living out the true dimension of love: "Love your enemies and pray for those who persecute you" (Matthew 5:44).

Even after David had unified all the tribes of Israel and established himself as the sovereign king, he always remained humble before God. He constantly remembered that his strength came from the Lord. When David brought the Ark of the Covenant to Jerusalem, he danced with joy like a common man in the sight of all. His psalms (73 of 150 psalms are attributed to David) clearly indicated that he relied upon God in every situation. He was not crestfallen when he was denied the request to build the temple and graciously accepted the fact that he had shed too much blood (1 Chronicles 22:7–9). He always trusted in the Lord his God and surrendered his life totally to Him.

Even David's great sins in his personal life have a moral lesson for all. He committed adultery with Bathsheba and plotted the murder of her husband, Uriah. Consumed by lustful passion, he committed the horrible sin of adultery. To hide his heinous sin, he plotted the murder of the innocent Uriah, the husband of Bathsheba. Confronted with the reality of his sin, he was stricken by guilt and shame. But these sins and subsequent feelings of guilt did not destroy David as he exhibited true remorse and repentance. Psalm 51 ("A clean heart create for me, God; renew within me a steadfast spirit") demonstrated his true contrition and desire to turn away from sin. Having experienced God's merciful love, David did not allow the troubles of life to destroy him. He faced the consequences of his sins courageously.

He had to face the death of his child, born from the adulterous relationship with Bathsheba. In his own home, his son Amnon raped his daughter Tamar; Amnon then was killed by his other son Absalom. Absalom later revolted against his father. Then to the great grief of David, Absalom himself was killed. The one closest to the Lord endured a great number of trials!

Unlike Saul, setbacks and problems never destroyed David. He never abandoned God. There may have been moments when his passion made him forget about God, but he never abandoned Him. Whenever this great person faced troubles, it became a moment to renew his strength and trust in the Lord. First Samuel 30:6 reads, "David strengthened himself in the Lord his God." The selection from 1 Samuel 30:1–6 has the context in which David arrived in Ziklag fleeing from Saul. He found that Ziklag had been raided by the Amalekites, leaving it in ruin and with all the people taken captive. Among the captives were his own wives, Ahinoam and Abigail. All were grief-stricken, but soon David became the target of the frustration and anger of the men around him who wanted to stone and kill him because he was not there when he was needed the most. Here is where the end of the sixth verse becomes a source of light for every person who has ever faced troubles: "David strengthened himself in the Lord his God."

As David renewed his strength in the Lord, he was able to face all the trials and tribulations of life. In every situation David always came back to the source of his strength, the strength of his life—God Himself. Different psalms that are attributed to David give us an indication of this aspect of his life. David did not try to solve the problems in his life by his own strength. Rather, he relied on the Lord and constantly turned to Him for guidance and direction.

Troubles in life can make one a better person or a bitter person. Troubles, inevitable in human life, can come unexpectedly or as a result of one's choices. They can be inflicted by others, inherited in life, be the result of great crisis or unwarranted calamities, or could even have no logical explanation. In David's case, troubles made him a better person as he constantly sought to renew his strength in the Lord.

*"Though I walk in the valley of darkness, I fear no evil, for you are with me; your rod and your staff give me courage."*
— A Psalm of David (Psalm 23:4)

## For Further Reflection and Discussion

1.  Human beings look at the outward appearance, but God looks into the heart. What are the implications of this statement?

2.  Why did David refuse to wear the armor of Saul?

3.  Goliath cursed David by his gods. David praised God when he said, "the Battle is the Lord's and He shall deliver you into our hands" (1 Samuel 17:47). Discuss.

4.  The one who is closer to the Lord faces many troubles in life. Have you faced trials in life as you have tried to walk closely with the Lord?

5.  "Every saint has a past. But every sinner has a future." Discuss this in the light of David's sin and redemption.

# NATHAN:

## Fearless Prophet of God

*"Then David said to Nathan, 'I have sinned against the Lord.'*
*Nathan answered, 'The Lord on His part has forgiven your sin. You*
*shall not die. But since you have utterly spurned the Lord by this deed,*
*the child born to you must surely die.' Then Nathan returned to his*
*house"* (2 Samuel 12:13–15).

David, the greatest king of Israel, succeeded in unifying the kingdom and establishing peace in the nation. God was with David in all of his endeavors and blessed him with many victories in battle. There was peace and prosperity in the land as David did everything that was pleasing to the Lord. David was humble enough to listen to the words that God spoke through his prophets: Samuel and Nathan. Samuel, the last judge and prophet, was advancing in years and so David received great counsel from Nathan, especially on three different occasions.

Nathan was called by God to be His prophet during the reigns of David and Solomon. The name Nathan means "God has given," or "a gift." Though not much was written about the life and activities of Nathan, he came to prominence when David was contemplating the idea of building a temple. David had brought the Ark of the Lord to the city of Jerusalem amidst great festivities, and it was placed in a tent. David was living in a palace, and he felt that having the Ark in a tent was dishonoring the dignity of the Lord. He called Nathan, the prophet, and said, "Here I am living in a house of cedar, while the Ark of God dwells in a tent" (2 Samuel 7:2). Nathan, who knew the goodness of David's heart, gave him the stamp of approval when he replied, "Go, do whatever you have in mind, for the Lord is with you" (2 Samuel 7:3). Nathan rejoiced at David's intentions as David was not forgetting the source of his blessings even in prosperous and peaceful times. As was his custom, Nathan turned to the Lord in prayer, and God revealed His plans. God instructed Nathan to go and tell David that He had chosen David's heir for this noble task.

Nathan knew that this revelation from God might be disappointing to David. He could have altered the revelation from God like other false prophets, who often gave prophecies that pleased their listeners. However, Nathan believed in being the true spokesperson of God and communicated to David exactly what God had revealed. David did not show any signs of disappointment but rather accepted the will of God wholeheartedly. David thanked God for all the blessings that He had bestowed upon him and the nation. The humility of David greatly pleased Nathan, and he assured David of God's continuous presence and protection in his life.

Even the best and faithful person has moments that can test his/her integrity. David, who had pleased the Lord in all things, let the weaknesses of his flesh overtake him in one decisive moment. Upon seeing the beautiful Bathsheba bathing, David was overcome with lust and he committed adultery with her. Bathsheba, who was the wife of Uriah the Hittite, was powerless to resist the demands of the king. Uriah, who was the armor-bearer of Joab, the nephew of David, was engaged in battle against the Ammonites. When David came to know that Bathsheba was with child, he decided to cover his sin of adultery. He asked Joab to release his armor-bearer. When Uriah came to David, he instructed Uriah to go home and be with Bathsheba. However, Uriah did not obey the order of the king, and he slept with the other soldiers instead of his wife. The faithfulness and dedication of Uriah were evident in his words: "The Ark and Israel and Judah are lodged in tents, and my lord Joab and your majesty's servants are encamped in the open field. Can I go home to eat and to drink and to sleep with my wife? As the Lord lives and as you live, I will do no such thing" (2 Samuel 11:11).

When David failed in his attempt to cover his sin, he instructed Joab to set up a trap through which Uriah would be killed. In his attempt to cover one horrible sin, he committed another—the murder of an innocent person. David exhibited no remorse at his evil actions, and he was happy to accept Bathsheba as his new wife. Apparently things seemed to have gone smoothly for David as he was content with his situation. David was able to hide his heinous sins from everyone else. However, nothing was hidden from God, and He could not be fooled like Joab. The cry of innocent blood reached heaven, and God sent His faithful servant Nathan to confront the powerful king.

Nathan, who remained firm in his convictions and did not compromise truths, did not hesitate when God asked him to go to David. Nathan knew that he had a difficult task at hand as he had to confront the king. Arriving at David's palace, he proposed a case to David and asked him to be the fair judge. Nathan knew that David was fair in his judgments when it came to matters of justice and injustice. Nathan proposed a parable, wherein a poor man's only possession, a little lamb, was stolen and killed by his rich neighbor for his visitor. Hearing the parable, David became very angry and pronounced death upon the evildoer. David stated that such an injustice could never be tolerated in his kingdom. David, exercising his royal judicial role, sentenced the guilty cruel man to death.

It was the right moment for Nathan to confront the real culprit. As he thought of David's sins and the injustice committed against Uriah, the prophet's anger escalated. He looked into the eyes of the powerful king and pronounced the words, "You are that man!" (2 Samuel 12:7). David realized then that the "case" was a parable and that he was that cruel person! The courageous prophet spoke to David the words from God: "I anointed you king of Israel. I rescued you from the hand of Saul...If this were not enough, I could count up for you still more...You have cut down Uriah the Hittite with the sword; you took his wife as your own, and him you killed with the sword of the Ammonites. Now, therefore, the sword shall never depart from your house, because you have despised me and have taken the wife of Uriah to be your wife" (2 Samuel 12:7–10). The words of Nathan resonated in the heart of David, and he realized the seriousness of his sins. Being the powerful ruler, David had placed himself above the law and had sought to use and abuse others for his own selfish gratification. David was the "man after God's own heart," and yet by his heinous sins he had greatly displeased the Lord. David's head hung in shame at the realization that he had seriously violated the statutes and commands of the Lord. The powerful king could not look into the eyes of the prophet.

Standing before Nathan, who was confronting him with the truth, David was forced to search his heart and shamefully acknowledge his crimes. The truth pierced David's heart and his repentance was clearly shown in his words, "I have sinned against the Lord" (2 Samuel 12:13). Out of his guilt, shame, and repentance emerged one of the most beautiful and profound psalms, in which David begged for God's mercy and forgiveness: "Have mercy on me, God, in your goodness; in your abundant compassion blot out my offense. Wash away all my guilt; from my sin cleanse me.... Against you alone have I sinned; I have done such evil in your sight.... A clean heart create for me, God; renew in me a steadfast spirit...My sacrifice, God, is a broken spirit; God, do not spurn a broken, humbled heart" (Psalm 51:1–19). Looking at the contrite David, Nathan's heart melted, and he begged God to forgive the repentant sinner. Nathan had truly loved David and when God revealed the sin of David to Nathan, his heart ached for David. He also realized how much the sin of David had grieved God, who considered David to be a man after His own heart. Though Nathan assured David of God's forgiveness, he made it clear that David would face the consequences of his actions in his life. Having completed the challenging task, Nathan returned to his home.

Nathan continued his faithful ministry among the people. There were moments when David turned to Nathan for counsel. When David experienced challenges and agonies in life, the prophet comforted him and encouraged him to remain faithful. God had revealed to Nathan that it was Solomon, the second son born to Bathsheba (the first child born from the adulterous relationship had died), who would succeed David as king. God had designated Solomon to build the temple in Jerusalem. David was advancing in years, and it was time for one of his sons to be enthroned as king. His ambitious sons were competing for the crown. Nathan's diplomacy and timely action ensured that Solomon would succeed his father, David.

Adonijah, the fourth son of David, assumed that he would inherit the throne as three of his older brothers were killed. He had succeeded in securing the support of his uncle Joab, the high priest Abiather, and many leading military commanders. He failed to procure the support of Nathan, the prophet, who had clearly told Adonijah that God had chosen Solomon to succeed David. Adonijah had looked down on Solomon and did not heed the counsel of Nathan. Adonijah proclaimed himself as king without the support of David, as he thought that David was frail and powerless.

Nathan approached Bathsheba and together they went to David. Although David's body was weak, he still possessed a clear mind. When he heard the news from his faithful servant Nathan, David acted quickly and proclaimed Solomon as his successor. He asked Nathan to accept the honor of anointing his son Solomon as the next king. When Adonijah's followers heard of David's decision, they deserted the prince. Nathan, the faithful and courageous prophet of God, anointed Solomon to be the king of Israel and advised Solomon to show mercy to Adonijah. Nathan's timely action helped to avoid civil war and secured the throne for Solomon. He acted with the best interest of the nation in mind. Beyond everything, his actions demonstrated faithfulness to God.

Nathan appeared on the scene at three decisive moments in history. Though his prophetic activities were brief, he presented himself as the courageous spokesperson of the Lord. Although he knew of David's desire to build the temple, he courageously communicated to David God's decision that denied David the privilege. He did not hesitate to confront the king when he had committed the horrible sin of adultery and the crime of premeditated murder. He acted swiftly to ensure that Solomon would succeed his father and the glorious temple would be built in Jerusalem. Indeed, Nathan stands before us as a powerful instrument of God.

> *"If your heart acquires strength, you will be able to remove blemishes from others without thinking evil of them."*
> —Mohandas K. Gandhi

## For Further Reflection and Discussion

1.   It is often easier to say what people want to hear, rather than what they need to hear. If you ignore challenges and focus only on pleasant tasks, you leave people with no lasting impressions. Discuss this in the light of Nathan's prophetic works.

2.   Sin begets sin: if you tell a lie, you might be required to say several to hide the first one. Discuss this in connection with David's sin.

3.   Nathan proved to be a courageous spokesperson of God. What was the true source of his strength?

4.   Did Nathan's view of David change after he confronted David with his sins?

5.   The biblical question, "Am I my brother's keeper?" can be applied to different situations. How adequate is its application when we find someone who persists in a life that is sinful?

# SOLOMON:

## Young and Wise . . . But?

*"When Solomon was old, his wives had turned his heart to strange gods, and his heart was not entirely with the Lord, as the heart of his father David had been"* (1 Kings 11:4).

From the perspective of worldly comfort, prestige, and prosperity, Solomon's period of kingship was greater than any other time for Israel, including the reign of his father, David. Solomon was born as if with a silver spoon in his mouth. He enjoyed all the comforts and convenience of life in the palace. Although David's sin of adultery and murder cast a gloom over the whole nation, his repentance and penance had made people forget about his failure and embrace the newborn with great joy. The parents called their newborn son Solomon, which means "peace." Perhaps what David and the whole nation needed at that time was the gift of peace. Solomon was truly loved by his parents, David and Bathsheba, and all the people. He admired his father, David, greatly, both for his courage and devotion to his people. But what left the greatest impression in his heart was the unchanging devotion his father had toward the living God. Although his father had experienced a fair amount of trouble in his life, he always seemed to renew his strength in the Lord.

Though his stepson Adonijah plotted to be crowned as the king, their father favored Solomon. David chose Solomon to succeed him as king, knowing that Solomon was humble before God and sought His guidance. More importantly, it was part of God's plan that Solomon would succeed his father (1 Chronicles 22:9), and nothing could change that plan. David blessed and instructed Solomon with these words: "Take courage and be a man. Keep the mandates of the Lord, your God, following His ways and observing His statutes, commands, ordinances and decrees as they are written in the law of Moses, that you may succeed in whatever you do and wherever you turn" (1 Kings 2:2–3). He became the third king of Israel, after Saul and David, and the last king of the united kingdom of Israel—all twelve tribes.

Solomon vowed to be faithful to God. He wanted to be a fair and just ruler for his people. He was blessed with a great dream in which God asked him to request any favor that He could grant Solomon. Solomon's faithfulness and intentions were fully portrayed in his request. He humbly prayed, "O Lord, my God, you have made me your servant, to succeed my father David, but I am a mere youth, I do not know at all how to act. I serve you in the midst of the people whom you have chosen, a people so vast that it cannot be numbered or counted. Give your servant, therefore, an understanding heart to judge your people and to distinguish right from wrong" (1 Kings 3:7–9).

What an awesome prayer! Solomon showed maturity and insight beyond his age to make such a request. God was highly pleased at this and granted his request and more. God's generosity knew no bounds, and His blessings for Solomon were abundant. God not only gave Solomon the gift of wisdom but also riches and glory. However, God commanded Solomon to be loyal and devoted to Him.

Solomon exhibited great wisdom in his life, as he had the ability to distinguish between right and wrong. Solomon's wisdom was clearly shown in the verdict he gave to the prostitutes who asked him to settle their dispute. Each of the women had given birth, and one of the babies died. The woman whose baby died claimed that the other had stolen her living baby. They approached Solomon for a verdict. As both of them claimed ownership of the baby, Solomon asked for a sword and commanded a soldier to cut the baby in two and give a portion to each woman. The woman who was lying agreed to the king's suggestion, as she said, "It shall be neither mine nor yours. Divide it." (1 Kings 3:26). The real mother was terrified at the thought of killing her baby. She was in great anguish and yet she begged that the baby be kept alive and be given to the other woman. Solomon commanded that the baby be given to the woman who was the real mother. He judged that no sensible mother would want to see her baby die right before her. Solomon's wise judgment was acclaimed by all the people.

He ruled the people fairly, and his name and fame spread to the whole world. Peace and prosperity were the earmarks of this period, and the time of his reign was known as the golden age of Israel. Rulers of surrounding nations were in awe of this young king. The visit of the Queen of Sheba, who came from southern Arabia (current Yemen) to

Solomon's court, and the words of appreciation and praises she showered on Solomon clearly set Solomon apart as a wise, powerful, and fair king of his subjects. She was greatly impressed with Solomon and everything she witnessed. In awe she said, "Your wisdom and prosperity surpass the report I heard. Happy are your men, happy these servants of yours, who stand before you always and listen to your wisdom. Blessed be the Lord, your God, whom it pleased to place you on the throne of Israel" (1 Kings 10:7–9).

He was given the greatest privilege of all: to build the temple of the Lord. Though David desired to build the temple, it was Solomon whom God chose to carry out this task. David had fought many wars and solidified the nation. He had brought the Ark of the Lord to Jerusalem. Solomon lavishly used his wealth to build the temple of the Lord. It took seven years to construct the magnificent temple. The construction of the first temple gave the people a sense of identity and great pride. The temple became the new sign of God's covenant with His people. Solomon dedicated the magnificent temple to God and made a peace offering: twenty thousand oxen and one hundred and twenty thousand sheep. He felt grateful in making these huge offerings and vowed once again to remain faithful to God forever. He also built a large palace for himself, constructed the wall of Jerusalem, and many cities.

Occasionally we hear people say, "I was young and stupid." In Solomon's case, one could easily say, "He was young and wise but became old and stupid." Normally, experiences in life and age help people to correct mistakes and to make better choices. In the case of Solomon, the opposite was true. Solomon's downfall came with his age. Twice the Lord appeared to him and promised His blessings upon Solomon. He also had given ample warning, not to stray from His protection and stoop down to worship foreign gods. Eventually, Solomon forgot God's blessings and warnings.

The demise of Solomon is a classic example of how one can fall from the state of greatness to total ruin. Ignorance could not be seen as an excuse for his situation, as he was the wisest living person. Solomon, with his gift of wisdom, could discern right and wrong, but somehow he did not possess the prudence or character to practice it consistently in his own life. Somehow Solomon replaced his love and dedication for God with other realities of life.

Solomon's marriages to the foreign women took his heart away from God. The Bible states that Solomon had seven hundred wives and three hundred concubines (1 Kings 11:3). As part of military and trade alliances, Solomon had taken many foreign princesses as his wives. His downfall began when he allowed his foreign wives to continue the worship of their pagan gods. Having had the great experiences of the divine in his life and having enjoyed abundant favors from God, Solomon should have been the instrument to bring his pagan wives to a true faith in the living God. Rather, he allowed them to build shrines for their deities and offer sacrifices at their shrines. He even built temples for pagan gods and, along with his wives, he burned incense and offered sacrifices. Solomon failed miserably, first by tolerating their pagan practices; eventually compromising with them in his life; and finally embracing them for himself. Solomon committed the abominable sin—idolatry.

Within his kingdom he began to levy heavy taxation, which displeased the people, and they became bitter. He granted special privileges to the tribes of Judah and alienated the northern tribes. All the evils Solomon committed would eventually catch up with him as his glorious kingdom would be divided into two. Toward the end of his life, troubles began to appear through powerful factions, and enemies rose up both within and outside the nation, threatening the unity and stability of the glorious kingdom. After the death of Solomon, his son Rehoboam would become the king of one tribe, Judah in the south, while the enemy of Solomon, Jeroboam, would become the king of the rest of the eleven tribes.

God still did not give up His plan for the salvation of the human race. The natural consequence of Solomon's sin was the downfall of his kingdom, which eventually became divided. The divided kingdom was a true portrayal of Solomon's divided heart in his old age. Yet God preserved Judah and Jerusalem for the sake of fulfilling His promise— the promised Messiah would be born through the family of David.

Three realities of life that can make or break a person are power, money, and love (specifically, lust of a man for a woman or vice versa). They are true blessings if they are used wisely according to one's situation. They can become evil and take control over a person and make him a slave if one fails to have control over them. Solomon had all

163

three and was given the special gift of wisdom to distinguish between what was right and wrong, or good and evil. However, all of Solomon's wisdom did not help him when he became a slave to his passions. Wisdom, though a wonderful gift in itself alone, will not help a person to uphold what is right and good. One also requires true character and deep convictions, and above all courage to stand up for what is good and right. Solomon gave up his convictions and gave in to the conniving and manipulative ways of his foreign wives. His devotion became divided as he began to focus more on himself than on God or the people God entrusted to his care.

Money, power, and love are realities that can be used for one's selfish purposes or for the good of oneself and others and ultimately for the glory of God. When the focus is shifted from God and others to oneself, these realities can enslave a human person and deprive him/her from realizing the true meaning of human life.

*"No one can serve two masters. He will either hate one and love the other, or be devoted to one and despise the other. You cannot serve God and mammon."* —Matthew 6:24

## For Further Reflection and Discussion

1. Solomon had a challenging task ahead of him as he had to succeed his father, David, as king. In simple terms, we can say "he had big shoes to fill," as David was well accepted by all and was viewed as the "man after God's own heart." Naturally there were huge expectations from people. If you are called to succeed someone who was extremely successful, how would you prepare to face the challenge?

2. Solomon started out right. His prayer for wisdom is marveled by all. God not only gave him wisdom but also riches and glory. What are the implications of Solomon's humble beginning before God?

3. Wisdom alone is not enough to live an upright life. You need character and convictions to live out your knowledge of what is good and right. Discuss this based on Solomon's choices.

4. Did Solomon break God's commands by marrying so many foreign princesses?

5. Money, power, and love are beautiful realities. They are not evil in themselves. They can make you or break you. Discuss this based on Solomon's life.

# ELIJAH:
## Prophet Par Excellence

*"This is enough, O Lord! Take my life, for I am no better than my fathers. He lay down to sleep...an angel touched him and ordered him to get up and eat"* (1 Kings 19:4–5).

Ahab was one of the worst kings of Israel: "Ahab, son of Omri, did evil in the sight of the Lord more than any of his predecessors" (1 Kings 16:30). His sin surpassed all others as he went on to marry the Sidonian princess Jezebel, and erected an altar to Baal in the very temple that he had built in honor of Baal in Samaria. He also erected a sacred pole, symbolizing the life-giving power of Baal. He had completely forsaken the true God and went on to commit the abominable sin of idolatry as he worshiped Baal with his wife. He also urged the people to leave behind their faithfulness to Yahweh and forced them to worship Baal. When one moves away from worshipping the living God, one's moral life degenerates; as a result, one clings to the ways of the world. Ahab's moral deterioration and the gravity of his sin are clearly shown in these words, "He did more to anger the Lord, the God of Israel, than any of the kings of Israel before him" (1 Kings 16:33).

God sent the best to counter the worst. From the beginning, Elijah's heart was with God. He avoided everything that was evil and devoted his life solely to God. He truly lived out the meaning of his name "Jehovah is God," when he upheld faith in the living God and opposed the worship of false gods. When he saw how people were forsaking God and following the path of Ahab and Jezebel, he grieved over their unfaithfulness. Yes, he was not a person who let evil grow by his silence. He was so zealous for God that he courageously proclaimed His word to Ahab the king: "As the Lord, the God of Israel lives, whom I serve, during these years there shall be no dew or rain except at my word" (1 Kings 17:1).

Ahab, whose heart was totally closed to God, might have laughed along with Jezebel and her prophets at Elijah and ordered him to leave his kingdom. God's powerful word, spoken through Elijah, was ful-

166

filled as the whole kingdom was stricken with famine. At God's command, Elijah lived in the Wadi Cherith, east of Jordan, wherein he was miraculously provided for during the famine: "Ravens brought him bread and meat in the morning, and bread and meat in the evening, and he drank from the stream" (1 Kings 17:6). The whole experience deepened Elijah's trust in God.

When famine advanced, God touched the heart of the widow of Zarephath, who provided for Elijah. Elijah found her collecting sticks to cook her last meal for her son as severe famine had resulted in total scarcity of food. He asked her to bring him some water and bread, and she sadly conveyed that all that she had was a bit of flour and some oil. She was going to use her last supplies to prepare the last meal for her son and herself before they died of hunger. But Elijah repeated his request and assured her that she would not die of hunger. The woman could have seen the whole episode as a scam and completely ignored the request of this stranger. However, she yielded to his request and decided to put the need of this stranger above her own. God honored her obedience and rewarded her goodness and generosity as her little provision of flour and oil never exhausted! God protected His chosen one and at the same time blessed the widow of Zarephath and her son, who showed generosity in sharing the little provisions they had with Elijah. When her son became sick and died, Elijah called upon the power of God, and God showed His compassion by raising her son from the dead. The widow of Zarephath, a foreigner, had come to believe in God and His spokesperson, in contrast to the king and God's chosen people who had forsaken Him.

In the third year of the famine, God asked Elijah to go back to Ahab. Famine had severely affected Samaria. It had become a national disaster. People were greatly suffering on account of the abominable acts of the king, the queen, and her prophets. Queen Jezebel, the wife of Ahab, had accused the prophets and all who feared Yahweh as being the reason for the famine. She was enraged and killed the prophets of the Lord who refused to worship Baal.

When Ahab saw Elijah, he was outraged and called him a disturber of Israel. Elijah stood his ground boldly and proclaimed that it was the king and his family who were disturbing Israel by forsaking the living God and His commands, and by worshiping Baal. He challenged the prophets of Baal, who were four hundred and fifty in number, at Mount Carmel, to offer an acceptable sacrifice to Baal. It was a contest between Elijah, the true prophet of the living God, and the hundreds of false prophets of Baal. It was going to be a moment of truth for all to see. Ahab, Jezebel, and the prophets of Baal were convinced that they could discredit Elijah because they believed in the power of Baal. Jezebel had made the decision to kill Elijah after the contest under the pretext that Elijah was a traitor and a disturber of the peace. The prophets of Baal prepared the sacrifice and called upon their deity to accept the offering. When there was total silence even after mutilating themselves, Elijah mocked them and suggested, "Call louder, for he is a god and may be meditating, or may have retired or may be on a journey. Perhaps he is asleep and must be awakened" (1 Kings 18:27).

Hours passed and Baal's prophets seemed exhausted and exasperated. Elijah began to set up his altar before all the people. After drenching the altar and its offering with water three times, Elijah called upon the name of the living God. The fire of the Lord consumed the sacrifice and manifested His greatness before all the people. "Seeing this, all the people fell prostrate and said, 'the Lord is God'" (1 Kings 18:39). Elijah was consumed with zeal for the Lord and ordered the people to capture all the false prophets of Baal. The people who witnessed the greatness of God and the victory of Elijah captured them all, and Elijah slit the throats of the wicked prophets. Elijah also announced to Ahab that the famine would end soon with imminent rain.

The victory seemed to be short-lived, as the whole affair had outraged Jezebel. The humiliated woman sought the life of Elijah. Her fierce anger intimidated Elijah, and he escaped from her grasp. In the desert he asked the Lord to take his life because he was so discouraged by the turn of events and the uncertainty of his life. He felt that his mission had been an utter failure. How could the great prophet of God, who had seen God's awesome power, succumb to fear and desperation? He could possibly have been affected by his constant struggle for truth, the continuous rejection of the people, the threat of the evil enemy, and his own feelings of failure. Through him, God had provided every possible sign required for the conversion of the king, the queen, and the people. Elijah was heartbroken at seeing the uncertainty of Ahab and the vengeance of Jezebel. For a moment he allowed doubts to seep through his being and he wanted to give up. His desperation was so great that he wished to die.

Probably this was exactly what Jezebel wanted. By his fleeing, Jezebel had every reason to boast that she was more powerful than Elijah and his God. God was not going to permit His chosen one to be discredited at the hands of a wicked woman. God once again provided Elijah with food and ordered him to get up and eat for the long journey ahead. Elijah, who always obeyed the words of his Master, did as he was told: "He got up, ate and drank; then strengthened by that food, he walked forty days and forty nights to the mountain of God, Horeb" (1 Kings 19:8). The journey of forty days and forty nights must have given him new realizations about himself and God. By his running away from Jezebel, he demonstrated his failure to trust in the providential care of the Lord. He was only looking at himself. In some ways he was like the Israelites during their wilderness journey, who often failed to trust in God's providential care. Their repeated failures to trust in God had resulted in forty years of wandering. By his running away, he acted in ways that were similar to the Israelites. He also must have thought about the forty days Moses spent in the presence of God on Mount Sinai (Horeb).

At the very mountain where Moses spent forty days with God and the people of Israel received the Ten Commandments, Elijah was assured of God's protection. He witnessed the powerful experiences of violent forms of nature in the form of a mighty wind, earthquakes, and fire. But, alas, God was not present in any of them. Then there was a tiny whispering sound, and when Elijah heard it, he had to cover his face in his cloak and went and stood at the entrance of the cave. Through these events, God was telling Elijah that while He manifests His awesome power in stupendous acts of nature, He is not in nature. He accomplishes His purpose through His gentle voice, the voice of truth. The marvelous acts of nature might get people's attention, but what truly leads them to repentance and a change of heart is the message of truth, which is like a small voice always present but often neglected. The message of truth has always been there. And all the prophets of God are to proclaim it through their lives as Elijah did. He was instructed to anoint new kings for the people and to anoint Elisha as the prophet to succeed him.

The best—Elijah—then visited the worst—Ahab—for the last time. Ahab had coveted the vineyard of Naboth, who had refused to part with his ancestral property. The wicked queen Jezebel took the matter into her own hands and through treachery had Naboth killed and took possession of the vineyard. Elijah uttered the words of doom to Ahab that all of his household would be killed, and Ahab's blood would be licked by the dogs and Jezebel would be eaten by dogs at the wall of Jezreel. They had brought this punishment upon themselves by their evil deeds. Having completed his work and after having anointed the young Elisha to succeed him, Elijah was taken up to heaven in a flaming chariot. In the Jewish worldview, he was expected to return before the arrival of the Messiah.

The zealous Elijah always carried on the work of the Lord. There were moments when natural human fear and doubt took control over him. However, he remained faithful to the end. This greatest prophet is mentioned several times in the New Testament. In the gospels, he is likened to John the Baptist, the herald of the Messiah: "He (John) will go before him in the spirit and power of Elijah to turn the hearts of fathers towards their children and the disobedient to the understanding of the righteous, to prepare a people fit for the Lord" (Luke 1:17). Elijah, the greatest prophet, would be seen with Moses, the greatest lawgiver, conversing with Jesus at the moment of His transfiguration, where Jesus revealed His glory and when the Father confirmed His Son's mission (Mark 9:4).

*"Expecting the world to treat you fairly because you are a good person is a little like expecting the bull not to attack you because you are a vegetarian."* —Denn Wholey

## For Further Reflection and Discussion

1. Elijah prophesied about the lack of rain to the Baal worshippers, who considered Baal as the god of rain. What are the implications of this?

2. God provided for Elijah in the most unusual circumstances. Have you ever experienced God's extraordinary providential care?

3. Was Elijah's act of slaying the prophets of Baal justified?

4. Consider those moments when fear prevented you from seeing God's presence and care. Discuss.

5. There is a tendency to look for God in stupendous things. However, God often makes His presence known through the simple things of life. Discuss.

# JEZEBEL:

## Manipulation Exemplified

*"When Jezebel learned that Naboth had been stoned to death, she said to Ahab, 'Go on, take possession of the vineyard of Naboth the Jezerite which he refused to sell you, because he is not alive, but dead'"* (1 Kings 21:15).

If Ruth is admired for her filial piety and devotion, Jezebel is frowned upon for her wickedness and evil ways. Both were Gentile women. One is remembered for embracing the truth, and the other for constantly trying to destroy it. One has gone down in the history of the Bible as a heroine of faith, while the other has been portrayed as the epitome of evil, division, and confusion. Jezebel cannot even be compared with other "bad girls of the Bible" (Potiphar's wife, Delilah, Herodias, or Salome). These other women were bad, but Jezebel is by far the worst, and her life was an epitome of wickedness.

Ahab, the worst king of Israel, married Jezebel, the daughter of Ethbaal, the king of the Sidonians. Ahab was already wicked; however, Jezebel contributed her share in making him the most infamous king who ever ruled over Israel. As her father was both king and priest of Baal, she was initiated into the cult practices at an early age. She embraced them enthusiastically as such practices appealed to her sensuality and gave her a sense of power.

Like many surrounding cultures, the worship of Baal involved activities of sensual natures and sexual pleasures. Temple prostitution was commonly practiced as part of their religious ceremonies. Activities of a sexual nature played a significant role in their fertility cults. Jezebel had the power of being a princess, and her greatest asset was her beauty. Her charm gave her an advantage in winning over the hearts of many powerful men. She was not only beautiful, but she also possessed a cunning personality. She had realized early on that physical beauty had a depreciating value, but power always gave constant control. She set out to gain control of everything, as she was in possession of a dangerous mix of traits: beauty, cunning, power, and ambition.

172

The marriage between the Israelite king Ahab and the Sidonian princess Jezebel created a new alliance between the two nations. For Jezebel, this was the best opportunity to introduce her culture and religion to her newly found home. She had always regarded Yahweh, the God of Israel, as her enemy. She believed Baal to be the true god and wanted to destroy every other alleged supernatural power in existence. She knew that Ahab was not a strong person of principles and convictions and she could easily manipulate him and bring him under her control. Subtly she brought Ahab under her control through the use of her charm, and when she suggested building a temple for Baal, he did not object. She wanted the temple to be indicative of great power, beauty, and majesty. She urged Ahab to increase the taxation to obtain her goal of building a splendid monument for her deity.

After constructing the temple, she urged Ahab to erect an altar for Baal, and eventually led him to denounce Yahweh by worshiping Baal. She convinced him of Baal's mighty power and ridiculed the God of the Israelites. The religious practices she introduced immensely appealed to the heart of the people as these practices were of great sensual nature. She was surrounded by a multitude of Baal's prophets who were able to perform many wonders before the people. People were spellbound at the work of her magicians, whom she gainfully used to impress people with the power of Baal. She demonstrated her power through the use of witchcraft (2 Kings 9:22). She won over the trust of the vast majority of people in Israel through her charm and sensual cult practices. She was able to intimidate and sow seeds of fear in others through her practices of witchcraft. Through her cunning, she was able to lead people away from God. She also unleashed persecution and death upon those who remained faithful to Yahweh. She was set to destroy people's faith in Yahweh either by her seduction or through persecution.

She met her rival, Elijah, who presented himself to be the prophet of the God of Israel. The moment she saw him, she flinched and wanted to destroy him by any means. She laughed at the words Elijah spoke to Ahab, "During these years there shall be no dew or rain except at my word" (1 Kings 17:2). She told Ahab and the people that their god, Baal, could discredit the words of Elijah and make everyone believe that he was the true god. She boasted that Baal had supreme power over rain and storm. She consulted Baal's prophets, and they assured her of imminent rain and prosperity in place of drought and famine. But as months rolled into years with no sign of rain and with increased famine, they convinced her that Baal was angry because of those who worshipped Yahweh. She believed that unless and until she killed Elijah and all the prophets of Yahweh, Baal would not be appeased. She did not view the widespread famine and drought as a sign of her false beliefs. She went on a rampage and began killing all the prophets of the Lord. As she could not find Elijah, she concluded that he must be dead. There is no way he could have survived this severe famine, she thought.

Unknown to her, God had safeguarded His chosen prophet and miraculously made provisions for him. He sent Elijah back to Jezebel and Ahab with the hope that they would repent and turn from their wickedness. However, the obstinate and evil Jezebel refused even to consider any wrongdoing on her part. She was livid with anger to know that Elijah was alive and looking healthy even after three years of famine. He presented himself to challenge her to see whose god was the true god—Yahweh or Baal. Jezebel had no doubt Baal would strike down Elijah and establish his superior power. As the events unfolded, Elijah won the contest, as God revealed His overwhelming power. Jezebel was horrified to hear that Baal did not answer the petitions of his prophets. She was outraged to hear of the slaughter of all the prophets of Baal with whom she had committed many abominable sins. The moment of truth should have challenged her to realize her mistakes and turn from her wicked ways. But Jezebel, whose heart was firmly shut against truth and the living God, refused to change her ways and vowed revenge on Elijah.

She was annoyed at seeing Ahab exhibiting traits of remorse and a desire to return to Yahweh. Ahab had witnessed the power of God and the defeat of Baal and his prophets. Right before his eyes, he saw how desperately the prophets of Baal repeatedly called on their deity to accept the sacrifice and saw the futility of their endeavor. Ahab had witnessed the devotion of Elijah and the power of God when God accepted the sacrifice. He knew it was the might of God that had brought rain upon the earth after three years of famine. But Jezebel had such a firm control over Ahab that she did not allow him to dwell on his new realizations. Ahab once again lost the opportunity to correct his ways. She vowed to take revenge on Elijah and had him on the run. She diligently searched for him to have him punished. She convinced Ahab that killing Elijah would demonstrate the power of Baal and usher in a new age of peace and prosperity.

Her control over Ahab and her manipulative powers were best portrayed in the episode of Naboth (1 Kings 21). Ahab had coveted the vineyard of Naboth, which was next to his palace. Although Ahab promised to exchange it with another vineyard or pay him money for it, Naboth refused to part with his ancestral property. Naboth was a God-fearing man who valued the long-standing tradition that inherited property should not be sold to anyone outside the family. When Ahab heard of Naboth's decision, he was both angry and depressed. For Jezebel, this was the best opportunity to both demonstrate her loyalty to her husband and to prove her power. She had enjoyed unlimited power at her palace and she could not stand anyone objecting to the desire of the king.

Though she did not believe in or observe any of the religious laws of Israel, she knew them well. She knew that the testimony of two witnesses would be sufficient to condemn someone to death (Deuteronomy 17:6). She forged a letter with Ahab's name and sealed and sent it to the elders and nobles, whom she had brought under her manipulative control. The letter stated: "Proclaim a fast and set Naboth at the head of the people. Next, get two scoundrels to face him and accuse him of having cursed God and the king. Then take him out and stone him to death" (1 Kings 21:9–10). With a cold-blooded nature, she executed her plan and had the innocent Naboth killed. She felt triumphant at her achievement and informed Ahab of his newly acquired possession. Naboth's innocence and his commitment to ancestral law meant nothing to her.

The cry of the innocent reached to the heavens. God instructed Elijah to confront Ahab and Jezebel for the last time. All of God's signs and warnings had been completely rejected by this cruel and vicious couple. Ultimately their evil deeds would catch up with them. At God's prompting, Elijah proclaimed their impending deaths: "Because you have given yourself to doing evil in the Lord's sight, I am bringing evil upon you…The dogs shall devour Jezebel in the district of Jezreel" (1 Kings 21:20–23).

Eventually, Ahab and Jezebel would lose control over the kingdom. Elijah's prophecy came to pass as both Ahab and Jezebel faced cruel deaths. Ahab was wounded in a battle and died due to loss of blood: "The (wounded) king, who was propped up in his chariot, facing the Armeans, died in the evening...When the chariot was washed at the pool of Samaria, the dogs licked up his blood and harlots bathed there" (1 Kings 22:35–38). The evil Jezebel too faced a cruel death as she was flung from the window to the ground. Jehu, the newly anointed king of Israel, destroyed the family of Ahab and fulfilled the prophecy of Elijah on Jezebel: "Jehu ordered to throw Jezebel down. They (her attendants) threw her down, and some of her blood spurted against the walls and against the horses...and the dogs devoured her flesh" (2 Kings 9:32–37).

The "spirit of Jezebel" would continue to hound true believers. In the New Testament she is portrayed as the false prophetess who seeks to mislead the people and draw them away from true faith: "You tolerate the woman Jezebel, who calls herself a prophetess, who teaches and misleads my servants to play the harlot and to eat food sacrificed to idols" (Revelation 2:20). God's people are constantly challenged to embrace and live by the truth.

When one lives the life of a lie, there is no sense of fairness or justice. In place of honesty, manipulation and deception reign over one's heart, and determine one's actions. Such a person often views those who live honest and godly lives as his/her enemies. The sooner a person realizes the fact that the true enemy is within oneself, the sooner will be the possibility of escape from the pitiful state of lies and deception.

*"Deception is a cruel act. It often has many players on different stages that corrode the soul."* —Donna A. Favors

## For Further Reflection and Discussion

1.   Beauty, money, and power can be wonderful things. They can also be dangerous things. Discuss.

2.   When you face truth, you can either embrace it or seek to destroy it. What are the implications of this statement?

3.   King Ahab acted like a puppet in the hands of his wife, Jezebel. What are the dangers in the family when the wife becomes a domineering figure over her husband?

4.   Can Elijah's fleeing from Jezebel be viewed as Jezebel's victory and a failure on the part of the prophet?

5.   The "spirit of Jezebel" is a dangerous thing. It can bring about confusion and division. Discuss.

# ELISHA:

## Empowered by a Double Portion of the Spirit

*"Elijah set out, and came upon Elisha, son of Shaphat, as he was plowing with twelve yoke of oxen; he was following the twelfth. Elijah went over to him and threw his cloak over him...Elisha left him and, taking the yoke of oxen, slaughtered them; he used the plowing equipment for fuel to boil their flesh, and gave it to his people to eat. Then he left and followed Elijah as his attendant"* (1 Kings 19:19–21).

When the mighty prophet of God, Elijah, called the humble farmer, Elisha, he immediately followed Elijah with great devotion. He not only left his profession, but he was also determined that he would never return to it. He left forever his former way of life, and he embraced the new way with vigor and enthusiasm.

Elisha was the faithful son of Shaphat, who lived in the northern kingdom of Israel. His parents gave him the name "Elisha," which means "God is Savior." From the beginning Elisha believed that salvation came from God. He devoutly worshipped God and was never lured into idolatry. Idolatry was rampant during his day, and his heart grieved as people turned away from the worship of the true God. He lamented when King Ahab and Queen Jezebel forced the people to worship the pagan god Baal. He was determined that he would bow down only before the true God, and he refused to worship idols. He had heard of the mighty deeds of Elijah and prayed earnestly that he would have the opportunity to meet the mighty prophet. The encounter took place in a most unusual fashion, and it was to change the life of Elisha forever. The call of God did not come to Elisha in the temple or when he was deeply engrossed in prayer. Rather, the call came when he going about his daily tasks along with other hired men on his father's farm.

He was startled when Elijah, the mighty prophet, cast his mantle upon him. He knew by implication it meant that Elijah was inviting him to follow him. He had heard that Elijah had a number of disciples whom he had instructed in God's ways to be His prophets. He was overwhelmed by the powerful experience and remained spellbound for minutes. As he realized that Elijah was walking away, he ran after him and made one humble request: "Please let me kiss my father and mother goodbye and I will follow you" (1 Kings 19:20). Elisha was a loyal and affectionate son of his parents. Elijah understood the importance of his family loyalty when Elisha wanted to say farewell to his parents. Elisha must have felt the pain in his heart to leave behind his loving parents. However, when he returned from saying farewell to his parents, his actions surprised even Elijah. Elisha slaughtered his oxen, used the plow as firewood, boiled the flesh, and gave it to the people. His radical actions were clear indications of giving up totally and completely his current way of life and embracing the call of God with enthusiasm and total commitment. Elijah must have smiled contentedly in his heart at the dedication of Elisha. He was convinced that he finally had a committed successor to carry on the work of God among the people.

Elisha witnessed the many mighty deeds of his master and greatly admired the holy man of God. Elijah taught Elisha the ways of the Lord and commanded him to remain faithful to the Lord always and fulfill the duties of the prophet with great diligence. Although Elijah had guilds of prophets who were instructed by him, none matched the spirit and diligence of Elisha. Elijah had reminded them that there would come a day when he would be taken up by God, and they would have to continue the work of God. He urged them to remain unafraid as they would be guided by the power of God's Spirit.

However, Elisha was not prepared to let his beloved master go. He faithfully followed him from Bethel to Jericho. Though Elijah asked him to go back to begin the prophetic work on his own, he insisted upon staying with his master. It was not an act of disobedience. His action resonated with the spirit of Ruth, who decided to remain with Naomi despite Naomi's insistence that Ruth go back to her people (Ruth 1:16). When they arrived at the banks of the river Jordan, Elijah took his mantle and struck the water; it divided and they crossed over to the other side. Having reached the other side of the river, Elijah looked lovingly at his beloved disciple and asked him what he wanted from him. Elisha, who had followed faithfully his master, looked at him with tears and said, "May I receive a double portion of your spirit" (2 Kings 2:9). He was not asking for a favor that would make him greater than his master, but he was acting on the biblical understanding that the firstborn son inherited a double portion of his father's inheritance (Deuteronomy 21:17). The greatest and best inheritance Elisha could possess was the spirit of Elijah, which in fact was the Spirit of God. Elisha was granted his request, which made him the principal prophet to continue the work of his master.

As he saw his master being taken away from him in a fiery chariot, he cried like an orphaned child. His anguish was so great that he ran after the chariot that was ascending to heaven, with a loud cry, "My father, my father." As soon as the last trace of the fiery chariot that carried Elijah vanished from his sight, he caught hold of Elijah's mantle and returned to the banks of the river Jordan. His distress was so great that he used the mantle to strike the water with these words: "Where is the Lord, the God of Elijah?" (2 Kings 2:14). He had not realized that he was no longer an "orphan," that God's Spirit was with him. Right before him the water parted, and he crossed over to the other side to begin his prophetic ministry. The sons of the prophets who were watching the whole incident from the other side of the river bowed down before him and acknowledged him as their new leader.

Empowered by the Spirit of God, Elisha was able to perform many miracles that saved people from calamities. In Jericho, where Elisha resided, the inhabitants came to him and complained about the poisonous water. The water had caused many deaths and miscarriages, and the land became unyielding due to the contaminated water. Elisha dropped some salt into it and pronounced that he had purified the water. The power of God was revealed though him, and the water became clean and pure, causing no more deaths or harm.

Elisha demonstrated his love for a poor widow who was harassed by a creditor, when he multiplied the little oil she possessed to such a great quantity. She was able to sell the oil, pay her creditor, and live comfortably with what remained of this miraculous deed. He never forgot anyone who bestowed on him any kindness. He often received hospitality at the home of an influential woman at Shunem. When he came to know that she was barren, he interceded to God who heard Elisha's prayer and granted her a son. On another occasion, he blessed the humble offering of a man who had brought twenty barley loaves made from the first fruit. The loaves would have been enough to feed only a handful of people. However, Elisha asked him to set the loaves before one hundred men, who ate and were satisfied.

Elisha's actions were not limited to his own people. He showed the universal love and compassion of God to anyone who turned to God in faith. Naaman, the commander for King Aram in Syria, had contracted leprosy. He came before Elisha at the request of his wife's maidservant. The maid was taken from Israel and knew about the power of God working through His mighty prophet Elisha. The humble girl, who was truly devoted to God, revealed to her mistress things she had heard about Elisha. She was convinced that Elisha would be able to heal the commander of his leprosy. She knew that she was putting herself in a very precarious situation. She could lose her life if Naaman returned unhealed. The general heeded this courageous young girl and arrived in Israel with all his military entourage. Elisha, who loathed vainglory and extravagance, did not go out to meet him. Rather he sent a message, asking Naaman to go and dip himself seven times in the river Jordan. Upon hearing this, Naaman was very perturbed and decided in anger to return to Syria. He felt that the prophet was disrespecting him by not coming forth and paying him homage. He was a man of great wealth and power and thought that he deserved the respect of everyone. He must have chided himself for listening to the foolish words of the slave girl. However his servants urged him to change his mind and do what the prophet said.

When finally Naaman changed his mind and acted on the message of Elisha, he would not only receive physical healing, but he would also receive the gift of salvation. As he came up from the water on the seventh time, his flesh was clean and smooth, and he was completely healed of leprosy. Naaman was healed not only physically but also emotionally and spiritually. He realized that true power came from God and not from material things and possessions. He acknowledged his faith in the living God, when he said, "Now I know that there is no God in all the earth, except in Israel" (2 Kings 5:15). He was singing praises to God, whose kindness knows no bounds. Elisha refused the rich gifts that were offered by Naaman but allowed him to take some soil from Israel, that he might build an altar for Yahweh in Syria.

Elisha's prophetic ministry lasted for about sixty years through the reigns of Ahab, Jehoram, Jehu, Jehoahas, and Joash. He was instrumental in bringing to completion the great conflict that had existed between his master, Elijah, and Ahab, the notorious king. The prophet

Elijah had prophesied horrible deaths for Ahab and Jezebel for the sin they committed against the innocent Naboth.

Elisha fulfilled his master's prophecy when he asked one of the guild prophets to proceed to Ramothgilead (2 Kings 9:1) and anoint Jehu, the military commander of King Joram. King Joram was the son of the notorious King Ahab and his evil wife, Jezebel. Empowered by the Spirit of God, Jehu brought about the punishment that was uttered by Elijah for the crimes committed by Ahab and his wife. Jehu massacred King Joram and the entire household of Ahab. He had Jezebel hurled down through the window, and the dogs came and tore up her flesh. Jehu, who was anointed at the instruction of Elisha, murdered all the prophets of Baal and destroyed the temple of Baal.

The "double portion of the Spirit" that Elisha had received enabled him to perform many great miracles, destroy those who led the people to the evil of idolatry, and restore once again peace and prosperity in the land. Through the activities of Elisha, God demonstrated His love for everyone who acknowledged His sovereignty.

> *"Above all else, know this: Be prepared at all times for the gifts of God and be ready always for new ones. For God is a thousand times more ready to give than we are to receive."*
> —Meister Eckhart

## For Further Reflection and Discussion

1. When Elisha decided to follow Elijah, he left his former life. His new life gave him purpose and meaning. God constantly calls us to new life, challenging us to leave behind our old way of life. Discuss.
2. Why did Elisha ask for a "double portion of his master's spirit"?
3. Elisha performed many miracles that convinced people of the power of God. What are the benefits of witnessing miracles? What are the miracles that we are able to witness today?
4. What are the dangers when miracles become the source of one's faith?
5. Elisha's encounter with Naaman reveals many things about Elisha, Naaman, and God. Discuss.

# HOSEA:

## The Undying Love of a Passionate Lover

*"When Israel was a child I loved him, out of Egypt I called my son. The more I called them, the farther they went from me, sacrificing to the Baals and burning incense to idols. Yet it was I who taught Ephraim to walk, who took them in my arms...I fostered them like one who raises an infant to his cheeks; yet, though I stooped to feed my child, they did not know that I was their healer"* (Hosea 11:1–4).

Hosea is part of the "Twelve Minor Prophets," which includes the works of other prophets: Joel, Amos, Obadiah, Jonah, Micah, Nahum, Habakkuk, Zephaniah, Haggai, Zechariah, and Malachi. These are called Minor Prophets not because their ministries were less important but because their books are much shorter than the books of Isaiah, Jeremiah, Ezekiel, and Daniel, who are called the Major Prophets. Fitting to their call to the office of the prophet, each one of them challenged the people to remain faithful to the covenantal relationship with the Lord and give up the worship of idols and their wicked ways.

Hosea's prophetic career began in the last days of King Jeroboam II in the northern kingdom of Israel. Under Jeroboam II, the northern kingdom of Israel had reached its height in terms of prosperity. Jeroboam came to power when the Assyrians were becoming powerful. The Assyrians defeated the Syrians and as a result they had become weak and defenseless against Israel. Jeroboam expanded his borders, and the country became as large as it had been under Solomon. Because of this expansion, Israel could control the trade routes. Israel constantly came in contact with surrounding cultures, their traditions, practices, and cult worships. Eventually, many began to forsake their ancestral practices and embrace elements of other cultures that included cult practices and worship of idols.

King Jeroboam led the way when he began Baal worship and introduced worship of the golden calf. He set up altars and sanctuaries for idols in Bethel, the religious center of the northern kingdom. The kings, their aristocratic supporters, and priests became increasingly corrupt and led people away from the worship of God. The moral degradation and gravity of Israel's sins were best captured in these words: "There is no fidelity, no mercy, no knowledge of God in the land. False swearing, lying, murder, stealing, and adultery! In their lawlessness, bloodshed follows bloodshed" (Hosea 4:1–2).

This dismal condition of rebellion, immorality, moral degradation, and corruption led to the right moment for the wrath of God to flare up and destroy the wicked people. However, what is revealed so powerfully through Hosea the prophet was the relentless love of God for His people. When the people showed their faithlessness, God demonstrated His faithfulness by sending Hosea among them. Very little is known about the personal background of this great prophet of God. His name, Hosea, means "salvation," and he lived out the message that salvation can be found only in God. God asked Hosea to do some unusual things, as His message and life were to be a powerful testimony to God's ways and His dealing with the people of Israel. In the book of Hosea, the nation of Israel is compared to a harlot woman, and her children were identified as the fruit of harlotry. God's undying love was clearly manifested through His continued faithfulness even when what He received in return was unfaithfulness. God, the supreme Lover, never gave up even though His heart ached at the rejection and unfaithfulness He experienced. The personal life and message of Hosea were so intertwined that one would lose the significance of the book if one overlooked either part.

God directed Hosea to marry Gomer, who was a woman of ill repute. We do not know whether she was already a prostitute or simply possessed traits of unfaithfulness in her heart. Regardless, God asked Hosea to marry Gomer, who would prove to be unfaithful. Hosea did as God directed, but he began to fall in love with his wife and became totally devoted to her. Initially, she returned his love and remained faithful. However, her faithfulness did not last long as she began to demonstrate her unfaithfulness through her association with her former lovers. The marriage between Hosea and Gomer symbolically represented the covenant between God and the people of Israel. God loved them, protected them, and set them apart for a special purpose. However, the nation often rebelled against God and went away from the covenantal relationship. The lovers of Gomer symbolically represented the foreign gods the children of Israel worshiped in different times, demonstrating the nation's spiritual adultery.

The children who were born to Hosea and Gomer were given names that befit the attitude and actions of Israel and their leaders. The firstborn son was named Jezreel, referring to the valley in which much blood had been shed by Jehu, who killed everyone in the household of Ahab and Jezebel (2 Kings 9:21–37). By naming his son Jezreel, Hosea was reminding the people of their impending punishment, death, and destruction in the hands of the Assyrians. The name Jezreel means "God sows," and it has a great significance in an agricultural context. A farmer scatters the seed, and the seed literally has to die to produce new life. The name of Hosea's child Jezreel could also imply the fate of the nation under Assyria—they would be scattered, many would die, but God would restore their future and there would be a harvest.

When Gomer became pregnant a second time and gave birth to a girl, God commanded Hosea to name her Lo-ruhamma, which meant "no more mercy or pity." As the kings, leaders, priests, and people persisted in their sinful ways, the name of the second child would powerfully remind the people of God's patience, which was running out. Hosea warned the people that God did not have any more pity and compassion because they refused to repent and return to Him. The name of the third child was Lo-ammi, which literally meant "not Mine," or "you are not My people, and I will not be your God" (Hosea 1:8). For Hosea, the name indicated that he doubted if the third child born to Gomer was his own or the result of Gomer's adulterous relationships. From God's point of view, it described Israel's alienation from Him and their desire to give allegiance to other gods. These names pointed out the loss of protection the people enjoyed and the special privileges they had as the chosen people when they remained faithful. As they deliberately chose other gods above the true God and lusted after wealth and prosperity by ignoring His precepts and commands, God was about to reject them.

Despite all these warnings and God's acts of love, the Israelites refused to turn back to their God. They were content to lead a sinful life. Evidently this saying did pertain to them: "Doing good is not easy; if it were, everybody would be good." They had been lured into a sinful life and wickedness, and the sinful ways gave them pleasure, thrills, and fleeting joy. The attitude of the people was accurately portrayed in Gomer, when she refused to do good and remain faithful. Forsaking the faithful love of Hosea, she went after her former lovers, who gave her pleasure, thrills, and fleeting joy. God had warned the people through His prophets that such a way of life would lead to their destruction. The consequences of their sins were symbolically depicted in the consequences that Gomer faced in life. While Hosea was challenging the nation to come to the Lord, his own wife at home was leaving him. Gomer was not interested in the prophetic activities of her husband. She was not interested in upholding her duties as a wife and mother. In her desperation to obtain pleasures, Gomer left Hosea and went to live with one of her lovers. However, as time went on, she was ignored by her lovers, and she sold herself to slavery. She had hit rock bottom!

Yet at the heart of true love is forgiveness, and that is best manifested in God and in His relationship with His chosen people. God, the supreme Lover, was about to forgive and give the people yet another chance. His love is relentless, and He remained steadfast in His faithfulness despite the rejection He endured. So He told Hosea to bring Gomer back and continue to love her. When he went to get Gomer, who had a become slave to survive, she was in a wretched condition. Hosea paid money for her release and brought her home as God directed him. He deeply loved his wife and hoped that she had learned lessons from her erratic behavior and attitudes. He told her, "Many days you shall wait for me; you shall not play the harlot or belong to any man; and I in return will wait for you" (Hosea 3:3). Hosea denied her conjugal privileges to make her realize her mistake and understand the depth of his love. He wanted her to come back to him with true and lasting love.

Symbolically God was telling Hosea that when He would take Israel back, they would be deprived of privileges and things they had enjoyed before: "The people of Israel shall remain many days without king or prince, without sacrifice or sacred pillar, without ephod or household idols" (Hosea 3:4). God wanted the people to realize that, though He would forgive them and restore them back to the covenantal relationship, they would have to pay the consequences of their sins. God makes it clear that He hates sin, yet He loves sinners. The nature of God is such that He loves sinners, diligently seeks them out, and offers them His loving forgiveness.

God's love is expressed with great tenderness in Hosea 11:1–4. It speaks about God remembering Israel when she was a "child." God liberated the people from Egypt and gave this newly formed nation the Promised Land. Israel is compared to a child learning to walk, and God is like a Father, who is helping the child to take little steps in life. He takes them in His arms to care for them and heal them. He dealt with them with "cords of human kindness and bands of love," not with chains of authority. The vivid description of a father raising his son to his cheek powerfully depicts the tender love God has for His people. Despite all these, what the father receives in return is rejection and denial of love.

Through Hosea, God called the people back to Him. He assured them forgiveness when they repented and returned to Him, just as Hosea demonstrated in his life when he dealt with Gomer upon her return. The significance of God's covenantal relationship was illustrated powerfully through the husband-wife relationship of Hosea and amplified further through a father-child relationship. Hosea was pleading with the people to change their ways and be converted. He warned them of their impending suffering under the Assyrians. However, his pleading fell on deaf ears as his contemporaries totally ignored him. Then Hosea would speak about captivity, exile, and eventual restoration as a proof of God's relentless and undying love. Though captivity and exile were inevitable realities of the future, Hosea assured them that the faithful remnant would know God's forgiveness, restoration, blessings, and relentless love.

*"I believe that unarmed truth and unconditional love will have the final word in reality. This is why right, temporarily defeated, is stronger than evil triumphant."*
—Dr. Martin Luther King Jr.

## For Further Reflection and Discussion

1.  Your life is your message. Discuss this in the light of Hosea's life.
2.  The book of Hosea depicts God's relentless love for His people and the continuous rebellion of the people. God is dishonored and angered by the unfaithfulness of His children. What are the ways people react when they are dishonored and angered by ungrateful people?
3.  Love propels one to do the difficult and impossible things. Discuss this in the light of Hosea taking Gomer back from slavery.
4.  Hosea and Gomer seemed to have possessed different interests in life. What are the dangers when spouses go after their own interests and totally ignore the interests of the other?
5.  God can always forgive a sinner who repents. But He cannot often keep the sinner from experiencing the consequences of their choices. Discuss.

# AMOS:

## God's Angry Prophet

*"I was no prophet, nor have I belonged to a company of prophets; I was a shepherd and a dresser of sycamores. The Lord took me from following the flock, and said to me, go, prophesy to my people Israel"* (Amos 7:14–15)

Many readers of the book of Amos might wonder about the relevance of his message in today's context. They might wonder as to why they should read the prophetic oracles that were directly linked to a nation and its destruction. The words of Amos were fulfilled and Israel was completely destroyed by the Assyrian superpower in 722 BC. They might also wonder about the relevance of the "fire and brimstone"–type message of Amos in today's context. They would argue that it would be better to showcase the mercy and compassion of God rather than punishment and destruction. In simple terms, for many the Christian message of "God is love" is more appealing than the "just world theory" of the Old Testament (where good is rewarded and evil is punished). However, we act at our own peril if we only live by the understanding of "God is love" and forget that "God is just." The message of Amos today challenges us to understand the true nature of God, which is both just and loving. Justice and mercy are at the heart of God, and we cannot ignore either of these characteristics of God.

Amos was from the southern kingdom of Judah, and yet God had called him to prophesy in Israel, the northern kingdom (the division had come about at the end of Solomon's reign). Amos was a shepherd from Tekoa, a town in Judah. He was called to be a prophet during the reign of Uzziah, who was the king of Judah, and Jeroboam II, who reigned in Israel. Under Jeroboam II the northern kingdom of Israel had reached its height in terms of prosperity. Jeroboam came to power when the Assyrians were becoming powerful. The Assyrians defeated the Syrians, and as a result they had become weak and defenseless against Israel. Jeroboam expanded his borders, and the country became as large as it had been under Solomon. Because of this expansion,

Israel could control the trade routes.

However, as the nation increased in its prosperity, it deteriorated in its morality. When people became comfortable in their lives, they often forgot the source of their blessings—God. They began to replace God's statutes and decrees with their own precepts and standards. The saying, "The more wealth you have, the more wealth you want," became part of their thinking and actions. In order to obtain more wealth, they began to exploit the weak and vulnerable. When gaining wealth becomes the ultimate goal, often the morality of the means to obtain it is overlooked. They employed deceitful ways in their trading, oppressed the workers by inadequate compensation, and exploited the poor and ignorant. Greed had completely consumed their way of thinking and living among the powerful of the north.

God's statutes and precepts were forgotten and as a result there existed total erosion of all moral and spiritual values. Those who were rich and powerful had embraced for themselves a hedonistic way of life. They were living as if the comfort and convenience of this world were more important than the world to come. They had completely cast aside any thoughts about heaven and eternal life. It grieved God to realize that people did not see their prosperity as a gift from Him to ennoble the earth and to help those who were less privileged.

God sent Amos to warn them to repent before it was too late. Amos was not from a priestly family or a guild of prophets. He described himself as a shepherd and a dresser of sycamore trees: "I was no prophet, nor have I belonged to a company of prophets; I was a shepherd and a dresser of sycamores. The Lord took me from the flock, and said to me, go, prophesy to my people Israel" (Amos 7:14–15). Amos, being a shepherd, belonged to the lower strata of society. Shepherds were viewed as unclean people as they were unable to keep the Sabbath regulations and purification laws. Shepherds were often exploited by corrupt and greedy traders. As both Judah and Israel were increasingly becoming strong centers of commerce and trade, they attracted traders from surrounding cultures. Very often middlemen and shrewd merchants gained the bulk of their profit from trading, as they exploited the illiterate farmers and shepherds. God viewed Amos as His powerful instrument to give the message of justice and repentance as Amos himself had faced injustice and exploitation in his own life.

Amos was well aware of the political and social situation of his time. God gave him the vision to understand the dangers both Israel and Judah were bringing upon themselves by becoming worldly powers. He began his prophetic activity by giving a series of warnings, first against the surrounding nations and finally against his own people who were living in Israel and Judah. Centuries later, St. Paul would paraphrase the same warnings: All have sinned, both Jews and Gentiles (Romans 3:23). Amos pronounced punishment upon those nations that oppressed God's people and coerced them to go away from the true God and give themselves to idolatry. Though they had not received the law of God, they should still have lived under the natural law that exists in every society.

Finally Amos turned his attention to the people of Judah and Israel and held them accountable for their sins. Unlike other nations, the Hebrews had received the special law of God. They were God's chosen people, and He had manifested His glory many times in their lives. He had taught them through His prophets, judges, and kings the importance of living a righteous life in accordance with His precepts and statutes. He had instructed them to care for the poor, the widows, and the orphans, and had warned them against exploiting the poor and defenseless. Their crimes were more serious as they had been given the knowledge to live righteously.

It must have been gratifying for the people of Israel to hear about God's punishment on the pagan nations. They may even have rejoiced at the impending doom that Amos had prophesied against Judah. However, they were shocked at the greater form of punishment that God had in store for Israel. Amos criticized Israel for a variety of their sinful actions. Shamefully they had carried out slavery on poor people: "They sell the just man for silver, and the poor man for a pair of sandals" (Amos 2:6). They had reduced poor people to the level of goods, and bought and sold them as cheap commodities. Though a higher price could not justify such a practice, the act of selling and buying people for a piece of silver or for a pair of sandals demonstrated how they viewed powerless people. Their abominable sins included the rampant practice of prostitution, where father and son committed acts of impurity with the same woman. The kings were supposed to protect the innocent people, but they failed miserably in their duties. The rich and powerful people took away the grains from the peasant farmers, but the kings did not intervene on behalf of the poor. Their courts sided with the rich and the elite as many poor people were thrown into prison. Innocent people were accused of crimes, and many notorious criminals walked away from the courts exonerated. They practiced many forms of pawning and charged excessive interest from people who were trying to survive and provide for their families.

Amos warned the people that their wickedness had brought the fearsome wrath of God upon themselves. He challenged them to repent from their evil ways and turn to God, who is abounding in mercy and kindness. He categorically stated that if they refused, their cities would be destroyed and they would be taken away as captives. In order to get their attention, Amos used a familiar theme: "the Day of the Lord." From the worldview of the Israelites, "the Day of the Lord" entailed specific acts of God in history in which God would destroy all their enemies. However, Amos said "the Day of the Lord" would not only bring upon punishment on their enemies but also on the people of Israel, who had become enemies of God because of their wickedness.

To emphasize the seriousness of Israel's sins, Amos spoke about several symbolic visions God had given him. These visions clearly showed God's wrath and the impending punishment He had in store for the rebellious people. One of the visions involved locusts destroying the harvest of the people. Amos was talking about the scarcity of food that would cause tremendous suffering for the people. At a time of prosperity, his message once again fell on deaf ears.

Amaziah, the priest of Bethel, who served himself rather than God, was greatly annoyed by the message of Amos. Bethel had become the center of religious worship in the northern kingdom of Israel, and Amaziah was the priest who supervised the activities of its temple. He had moved away from the true worship of Yahweh and had incorporated many cult practices that greatly offended God. Amaziah sided with the rich and the powerful, and he viewed the many prophecies of Amos as a threat to his powerful position in Bethel. He acted shrewdly when he sent false testimony to King Jeroboam against Amos. Amaziah accused Amos of giving pronouncements against the king and the kingdom: "Amos has conspired against you here within Israel; the country shall not endure all his words...Jeroboam shall die by the sword, and Israel shall surely be exiled from its land" (Amos 7:10–11). It was a clever way to set the king against Amos. To Amos, Amaziah said, "Off with you visionary, flee to the land of Judah! There earn your bread by prophesying but never again prophesy in Bethel; for it is the king's sanctuary and a royal temple" (Amos 7:12–13). Amos stood his ground and boldly proclaimed to Amaziah that it was God who had commissioned him to warn the people of their impending punishment. He was not going to let the threat of Amaziah deter him from the message that he was sent to proclaim. He made it clear to Amaziah that he, the priest, was equally responsible for leading the people astray, and God would hold him responsible for his actions.

Amos made it clear to the Israelites that they could not count on their past glory to escape from their future destruction. Israel had been chosen by God for a special purpose. They had been chosen not because of their merits but to bring to completion God's plan for the whole world. God had no favorites, as He had shown through His actions when he delivered the Ethiopians, Philistines, and Arameans: "Are you not like the Ethiopians to me, O men of Israel, says the Lord? Did I not bring the Israelites from the land of Egypt as I brought the Philistines from Caphtor and the Arameans from Kir?" (Amos 9:7–8). Amos made it clear that everyone was equal before God, irrespective of their color, creed, culture, or nationality. Amos seemed to indicate what St. Paul would say centuries later: "There is no distinction between Jew and Greek; the same Lord is the Lord of all, enriching all who call upon him. For everyone who calls on the name of the Lord will be saved" (Romans 10:12).

Amos realized that the sins of the Israelites were numerous and that they would experience severe punishment in the hands of the Assyrians. Yet he recalled the promise of God and gave a sense of hope to them by repeating it: "I will not destroy the house of Jacob completely…On that day I will raise up the fallen hut of David; I will wall up its breaches, raise up its ruins and rebuild it as in the days of old" (Amos 9:8b–11). The proclamations of Amos and other prophets were constant reminders to Israel that its sins had brought about the destruction of Jerusalem and had flung Israel into exile, but Israel also realized that God had not definitively abandoned or utterly destroyed it. God's mercy is always greater than the greatest of human transgressions.

Human sin might impede the plan of God, but it cannot totally frustrate the loving designs of God. Ultimately, Amos gave glory to God while he acknowledged human failures. He invited the people to look beyond their sins to the great mercy and compassion of God. Centuries later, when people would acknowledge their sins, they would vindicate the words of Amos: To us belong shame and confusion, but to you, O Lord, glory and grace! (cf. Daniel 9:7–10).

> *"God grant me the serenity to accept the things I cannot change; courage to change the things I can; and the wisdom to know the difference."* —The Serenity Prayer

## For Further Reflection and Discussion

1.   Justice and mercy are at the heart of God. What are the dangers of ignoring one and holding firm to the other?
2.   Amos was called from the southern kingdom to prophesy in the northern kingdom. What were the challenges he faced? What are the challenges that are faced by ministers today "who are not from the people"? What are the challenges people face when they are ministered to by "foreigners"?
3.   Materialism often leads to moral corruption. Is this premise true in our modern society, the community we belong to, our family, and our individual life?
4.   Religious institutions can act as a moral voice of the people. What are the dangers when a religious institution itself becomes corrupt? Discuss this in the context of the encounter between Amos and Amaziah.
5.   Human sins can impede God's plans, but they cannot totally frustrate the loving designs of God. Discuss.

# ISAIAH:

## Ever Ready for Service

*"He touched my mouth with it. 'See,' he said, 'now that this has touched your lips, your wickedness is removed, your sin purged.' Then I heard the voice of the Lord saying, 'Whom shall I send? Who will go for us?' I said, 'here I am, send me'"* (Isaiah 6:7–8).

Of all the prophets who were called to serve the people of Israel, Isaiah ranks as one of the most prominent. He is one of the "Major Prophets" in the Bible, along with Jeremiah, Ezekiel, and Daniel. In his long prophetic career of about sixty years, he witnessed many important events in the history of the people of Israel—the rise and fall of many kings in Israel, the rise and fall of surrounding kingdoms, Israel's defeat, their misery in exile, and God's act of deliverance. In his own life he experienced God's power, the effectiveness of his prophetic ministry, acceptance among the people initially followed by their rejection, and the challenge of giving an unpopular message. His long book of sixty-six chapters provides a wide variety of themes that includes judgment, holiness, captivity, the fall of the nation, comfort, hope, and most importantly salvation through the coming of the Messiah. The overarching theme of the book, however, is God's free gift of salvation. Many of Isaiah's prophecies are fulfilled in the person of Jesus Christ, the Savior of the world.

The name Isaiah means "the Lord is salvation." He lived out the meaning of his name, proclaiming loud and clear that salvation can be found only in the Lord. He challenged the people to turn back from their wickedness to God, the source of salvation. He reminded the people of their covenantal relationship and spoke about how God acted on His promises. Isaiah's prophetic activities also include an emphasis on hope in the midst of doom and desolation. He urged the people to remain hopeful as God would deliver them from their current state of despair, which they themselves caused due to their lawless life. He foretold the events of the distant future, which included the coming of the Messiah and His gift of salvation, as well as events to come in the last days, such as the Second Coming of the Savior. Of all his prophecies, the most prominent are those connected with the Suffering Servant, who by His death would bring about the gift of salvation once and for all: "Yet it was our infirmities that He bore, our sufferings that He endured…upon Him was the chastisement that makes us whole, by His stripes we were healed" (Isaiah 53:4–5).

Isaiah was called to prophetic activity in the same year King Uzziah died (742 BC). The vision of Isaiah, where he saw God seated on a high and lofty throne, and the call he personally received are key to understanding the life and message of Isaiah. Chapter 6 provides the vision: "I saw the Lord seated on a high and lofty throne, with the train of his garment filling the temple. Seraphim were seated above…Holy, holy, holy is the Lord of hosts!…all the earth is filled with his glory! At the sound of that cry, the frame of the door shook and the house was filled with smoke" (Isaiah 6:1–3).

Standing before God, who is absolutely holy, Isaiah instantly realized his unworthiness and sinfulness. Although Isaiah had attempted to live a righteous life and avoid all that was evil, he still felt unholy and worthless as he stood before the all-powerful and holy God. He was aware of his personal inclination to sin and the collective sinful nature of the people when he said, "I am a man of unclean lips, living among a people of unclean lips" (Isaiah 6:5). One of the seraphim flew to the altar, took a burning coal, touched Isaiah's mouth, and proclaimed to him that his guilt was now taken away and all his sins were atoned for. Isaiah was cleansed for a special purpose to announce the message of salvation to the people. Once Isaiah had met the Lord, been pardoned of his sins, and cleansed from his guilt, then he was ready to serve the Lord.

Isaiah was one of the few persons in the Bible who did not hesitate to answer God's call. He did not present any excuses like Moses or Jeremiah. When God asked, "Whom shall I send?" Isaiah responded, "Here I am, send me" (Isaiah 6:8). Isaiah was sent to minister to the people of Judah and Jerusalem, who had turned their backs on God. His message resonated the familiar theme of the time as he urged them to repent, turn away from their wicked ways, and look to God for mercy and forgiveness.

Isaiah's prophetic activities are inextricably tied to the political events of his time. Historically speaking, the events described in the book occurred from the eighth century BC to the sixth century BC. Some Bible scholars divide the book into three different sections: Proto-Isaiah (chapters 1–39), Deutero-Isaiah (chapters 40–55), which is also called the book of consolations, and the Third-Isaiah (chapters 56–66), which speaks about the return of the captives from exile. As a result of the extended historical events that are mentioned in the book, many scholars are of the opinion that the authorship of the book cannot be credited to one single person. There is general consensus that the first thirty-nine chapters of the book are connected directly to the activities of the prophet Isaiah, the son of Amoz.

Isaiah hailed from an aristocratic family, and he became an influential figure in the lives of several kings. They often consulted with him for the course of action they needed to take in the changing political scenarios. Sometimes they listened to his advice, but other times they discarded his counsel and faced the consequences of their actions.

Isaiah 1:1 begins, "The vision which Isaiah, the son of Amoz, had concerning Judah and Jerusalem, in the days of Uzziah, Jotham, Ahaz and Hezekiah, kings of Judah." It was a time when the militant Assyrian empire was on the rise to becoming a great power in the east. Isaiah challenged the people to trust in God and not in military might for their safety and security, and ultimately for their salvation. When Assyria was rising in power, the northern kingdom of Israel formed a pact with Syria and invited the southern kingdom of Judah to join them to form a coalition. Isaiah advised King Ahaz to refrain from such an action and urged him to trust in God's saving plan. Though Ahaz refused to join the treaty, he sought help from Assyria to withstand the pressures of Judah and Syria. Isaiah viewed it as Ahaz's inability to trust in God's providential care. Isaiah went on to press Ahaz to ask the Lord for a sign that could convince the king and change his evil alliance with Assyria. However, Ahaz refused under the false pretense of piety: "I will not ask! I will not tempt the Lord" (Isaiah 7:12). Ahaz was being hypocritical. He was hiding the fact that he preferred the might of Assyria more than the protection of the Lord. It became a powerful moment for Isaiah to give one of the greatest promises of God for the salvation of the world: "The Lord Himself will give you this sign, the virgin shall be with child, and bear a son, and shall name him Immanuel" (Isaiah 7:14). However, nothing changed the mind of Ahaz, as he had been captivated by the power and might of Assyria.

Tiglath-pileser, the king of Assyria, offered help with an ulterior motive of making Judah one of Assyria's subsidiary kingdoms. Ahaz greatly displeased the Lord when the king took the silver and gold that were in the temple and sent them as gifts to the Assyrian king, encouraging apostasy (2 Kings 16:1–18). Against Isaiah's warnings, Ahaz even visited the Assyrian king and paid him homage and pledged his loyalty. When he was in Assyria, he saw fascinating altars and shrines of Baal and decided to construct similar altars in Judah and Jerusalem for Baal and Asshur. He offered sacrifices at those pagan altars and burned offerings to idols. He even offered one of his sons as a child sacrifice. With the king leading the way, the people embraced idolatry and pagan practices. Isaiah not only witnessed the failures of the king but also the moral degradation of the people. Increasingly they were lured by material wealth and a hedonistic way of living. Practices of idolatry were rampant in different quarters. Isaiah witnessed severe social injustices committed against those who were vulnerable, particularly the widows, the orphans, and the poor. He constantly warned the king and the people about their impending doom.

As Isaiah had prophesied, Assyria defeated Syria and completely destroyed the northern kingdom of Israel, dismantling its capital, Samaria. Assyria did not destroy Judah, as it was one of her subsidiaries. King Ahaz thought that his timely pact with Assyria had rescued his nation from destruction. However, Isaiah warned the king that God was giving them another opportunity to repent and turn away from their apostasy. Judah was saved and Isaiah reminded the people that God spared Judah to fulfill the promise that the kingdom of David would last forever, as the promised Messiah would come from the family of David.

Hezekiah succeeded his father, Ahaz, and he initiated a serious of religious reforms, which Isaiah wholeheartedly supported. Hezekiah believed in God and wanted to purge the pagan religious practices and idolatry. He began destroying the Assyrian shrines in Judah that were the result of his father's alliance with Assyria. Removing Assyrian shrines and altars signaled Hezekiah's decision to get out of the alliance his father, Ahaz, had made with Assyria. It was a time to show his faith in God, but he failed at this important moment. Unlike Ahaz, who sought the Assyrian help to withstand pressures of Syria and Israel, Hezekiah sought the help of Egypt to withstand any future Assyrian invasion. Isaiah vehemently opposed such an alliance and said, "Woe to those who go down to Egypt for help, who depend upon horses; who put their trust in chariots because of their number...but look not to the Holy One of Israel nor seek the Lord" (Isaiah 31:1).

Hezekiah had refused to pay tribute to Assyria, counting on Egypt's help to withstand any military invasion from Assyria. Sennacherib, the king of Assyria, decided to retaliate against Judah, and he marched to the south, destroyed many cities of Judah, and besieged Jerusalem. Egypt did not come to the rescue of Judah. Hezekiah realized his grave mistake and turned to the Lord for help. The God of compassion heard the cry of the king, who was faithful in many matters, and delivered them from the Assyrians. The angel of the Lord brought severe punishment upon those in the camp of Assyria, and King Sennacherib retreated to Nineveh (2 Kings 19:35). The deliverance of the Lord should have radically changed the minds of the people. However, their faithfulness only lasted as long as Hezekiah was alive.

Isaiah's activities ended with the prediction that eventually Jerusalem would be destroyed and its inhabitants would be carried off to Babylon. The threat from Assyria dissipated with the emergence of the Babylonians. As the Babylonians were becoming powerful, the king of Babylon sent his messengers to visit Hezekiah, who was recovering from an illness (Isaiah 38–39). Hezekiah was impressed with this kind gesture and showed his visitors all of his wealth in the treasury. Isaiah was greatly displeased at this imprudent act of the king and prophesied: "Behold, the days shall come when all that is in your house, and everything that your fathers have stored up until this day, shall be carried off to Babylon; nothing shall be left, says the Lord" (Isaiah 39:6). The warnings of this great prophet would come true as people persisted in their sinful ways.

The destruction came almost two centuries later, during the time of the notorious King Zedekiah, who refused to listen to the words of prophet Jeremiah. Against Jeremiah's warning, Zedekiah formed an alliance with their old nemesis, Egypt. Nebuchadnezzar, the king of

Babylon, marched into Judah, destroyed Jerusalem, and carried the captives to Babylon. The repeated warnings of many prophets had not drastically changed the people.

However, God was not going to let human failure frustrate His plan completely. In a time of captivity, when the people were without a king, the temple, sacrifice, worship, or even freedom, they remembered their true Deliverer. In the second part of the book of Isaiah (chapters 40–56), the writer gave comforting words of hope and promised them that in the near future they would return to their homeland. Isaiah's prophecies not only entailed a better future for the captives but also pointed to the time when the Promised Savior would come and save the world.

Each year the hearts of the believers leap for joy and expectation (especially during the season of Advent) at all the promises Isaiah spoke centuries ago: "The people who walked in darkness have seen a great light" (Isaiah 9:1); "In the desert prepare the way of the Lord! Make straight in the wasteland a highway for our God. Every valley shall be filled in, every mountain and hill made low" (Isaiah 40:3); "O that you would tear open the heavens and come down" (Isaiah 63:19). They hear again the words of Isaiah at the beginning of Jesus' public ministry: "The Spirit of the Lord is upon me, because the Lord has anointed me. He has sent me to bring glad tidings to the poor...Today this scripture passage is fulfilled in your hearing" (cf. Luke 4:18–22; Isaiah 61:1–2). During the season of Lent they are reminded of the great sacrifice of Jesus, which was foretold by Isaiah, referring to the Suffering Servant (Isaiah 53), who would redeem the world by His sacrifice: "Upon him was the chastisement that makes us whole, by his stripes we were healed" (Isaiah 53:5).

*"To trust Him means, of course, trying to do all that He says. There would be no sense in saying you trusted a person if you would not take his advice. Thus if you really handed yourself over to Him, it must follow that you are trying to obey Him. But trying in a new way, a less worried way."*
—C. S. Lewis

## For Further Reflection and Discussion

1.   Isaiah readily accepted the invitation to be a prophet, while many persons in the Bible gave a myriad of excuses. Isaiah felt that he was "saved and set free to serve." How does his response, "Here I am, send me," challenge us today?

2.   Why did Ahaz refuse to ask the Lord for a sign?

3.   Isaiah spoke against different alliances with other nations that were to detrimentally affect the well-being of Israel. What are those "alliances" in our own lives that can stifle our spiritual growth?

4.   Great crises in life can turn out to be moments of realization of God's promises and power. Discuss this in the light of God's different promises in Isaiah.

5.   Identify and discuss five passages in Isaiah that are directly linked to the person of Jesus.

# EZEKIEL:

## "You Shall Never Lose Hope"

*"Thus says the Lord God to these bones: See! I will bring spirit into you, that you come to life...I will put my spirit in you that you may live, and I will settle you upon your land; thus you shall know that I am the Lord. I have promised, and I will do it, says the Lord"* (Ezekiel 37:5–14).

Ezekiel was the only prophet in the Old Testament who was called in a foreign land to give a message of comfort and hope to the people of God. The name Ezekiel means "God will strengthen," and his message of hope and new life was aimed at alleviating hopelessness among the people living in exile. The Babylonians had conquered Judah in 597 BC and had taken King Jehoiachin and ten thousand men as captives to Babylon (2 Kings 24:14–16). Ezekiel was one of the captives taken to the foreign land. He was twenty-five years old when he was deported to Babylon. Being born the son of a priest, Ezekiel had longed for the day when he would minister to the people as a priest in the temple of the Lord. His hopes were shattered when the Babylonians plundered and desecrated the temple and took away the sacred objects to Babylon. In Babylon he languished for more than five years without knowing what his destiny would be.

Yet God had great plans for Ezekiel as he was a chosen instrument of God to bring comfort to the people who were in exile. God provided Ezekiel with a vision that changed his understanding of the nature and power of God. Ezekiel and the people in exile were to realize that God was not confined to the land of Israel, but rather He is the Lord of all the nations. Ezekiel began to understand that God was the God of the universe, and He was in command of everything in the world. God called Ezekiel and said, "Son of man, I am sending you to the Israelites, rebels who have rebelled against me; they and their fathers have revolted against me to this very day. Hard of face and obstinate of heart are they to whom I am sending you...they shall know that a prophet has been among them" (Ezekiel 2:3–5). The children of Israel had constantly rebelled against God and ignored all the warnings God's prophets had given them. Even though they found themselves to be in exile, they had not totally repented and turned back to God. But God remembered the covenant that He had made and decided to send His prophet to assure the people that He had not left them. The call of Ezekiel once again demonstrated the nature of God, whose love and care could not be completely overshadowed by the rebelliousness of human beings.

God knew that the messenger He was about to send to the people had to understand the message completely before conveying it. God asked Ezekiel to do something very strange. He directed Ezekiel to eat the scrolls and then go and speak to the people. When Ezekiel looked at the scroll, his stomach churned, as what was written on the scroll entailed lamentation, wailing, and woe. It was indeed a difficult task as he had to preach a message of lamentation to a group of people who were already experiencing extreme hardship and pain as captives in Babylon. But Ezekiel understood that what the people were facing were the consequences of their actions. At the same time he felt empowered, realizing that God was with them even in the midst of their suffering and pain. God commissioned Ezekiel to be the watchman for the house of Israel to warn them from impending dangers. The duty of the watchman, who was stationed at the city gate, entailed watching for any form of threat that might come from the enemies. It was the duty of the watchman to alert the people to the dangers at hand.

In the first part of his ministry, Ezekiel acted as a true watchman as he gave warnings about what was to happen to God's chosen people. King Nebuchadnezzar had brought only ten thousand people to Babylon as captives, leaving behind a great number of people in Judah and Jerusalem. Ezekiel shared the suffering of the people as captives in a foreign land. However, he was surprised at their attitudes. Although the people had experienced defeat, deportation, and alienation from their land, they still had not repented. Those who were brought to Babylon and those who remained in Judah did not completely give up their belief in false gods.

Ezekiel was heartbroken to find that many among the captives in Babylon were deserting the precepts of the Lord and embracing the pagan form of worship and idolatry. Some of them must have felt the

203

need to play it safe as they were in a foreign land. Some of them must have seen it as a way of appeasing their current leaders, whose mercy was necessary for their well-being. As a result, many would leave their ancestral traditions, as well as the statutes and commands of God, and embrace foreign traditions and forms of worship that included idolatry. Those who were left behind in Jerusalem persisted in their sinful ways. His message about Jerusalem would be hard to speak and still harder to hear. Given this context, Ezekiel would prophesy that Jerusalem would be destroyed totally if the people did not repent, and there would be a second deportation of captives to Babylon. The fact that Israel was God's chosen people and that Jerusalem was the city of His temple would not bring an early release of those who were in captivity in Babylon or prevent Jerusalem from being destroyed.

While Ezekiel was in Babylon urging the people to return to God, the prophet Jeremiah was giving the same message to those who were left behind in Judah and Jerusalem. Jeremiah and Ezekiel received the same form of rejection from leaders and the people. They refused to listen to the warnings and mend their ways. God had spoken through His prophets about the dangers of forming alliances with the Egyptians. Against all such warnings, King Zedekiah initiated a treaty with Egypt and attempted to revolt against the Babylonian rule. King Nebuchadnezzar viewed it as a rebellion and the Babylonian army conquered Judah a second time. The Babylonians laid siege to Jerusalem in 588 BC, completely destroyed the temple of Jerusalem, plundered and brought to ruin the majestic temple, and took all able-bodied men and women to Babylon. While Jeremiah remained in Jerusalem among the ruins, Ezekiel shared the plight of the vast number of people who were deported to Babylon. Yet the two great prophets of God remained faithful to their calling.

The destruction of the temple, the defeat of the nation, their alienation from their land, slavery under the might of the Babylonians, and loss of identity as a chosen people were the ultimate results of the continuous sins and rebellion of the people. Suffering and grief became the hallmark of the people, who were living as slaves in Babylon. Yet the greatest promise of God shone forth amidst gloom and desolation: a faithful remnant would return to Jerusalem and God would reestablish His covenant. However, Ezekiel made it clear that God desired that people acknowledge His sovereignty and power over the whole universe. Ezekiel used the words, "They will know that I am the Lord" (Ezekiel 12:15), to testify to this divine desire and intention of God. The people of Israel, who rebelled against God, would know that He was the One who was in control of their destiny. The nations, who perpetuated idolatry and lured the chosen people away from God, would know that God's judgment was upon them. The chosen people in exile would know that God's presence was not confined to Israel and the temple in Jerusalem alone—He would be there with His children exiled in Babylon.

The words of the prophet Ezekiel not only contained messages of doom and destruction but also the great tenderness and mercy of God. God's faithfulness to His covenant and His desire to save the people were so great that He would reach out to them once more. God, who had seen the failures of His chosen leaders, would give one of His greatest promises through Ezekiel: "I myself will look after and tend my sheep. As a shepherd tends his flock when he finds himself among his scattered sheep, so will I tend my sheep. I will rescue them from every place where scattered...And gather them from the foreign lands and bring them back to their own country...I myself will pasture my sheep; I myself will give them rest, says the Lord God. The lost I will seek out, the strayed I will bring back, the injured I will bind up and the sick I will heal, shepherding them rightly" (Ezekiel 34:11–16). God was going to be their King, their Leader, and their Shepherd. These words of God that were spoken through Ezekiel would be fulfilled in the person of Jesus Christ. Centuries later, the children of the remnant who were brought back from exile would hear these words: "I am the good shepherd. A good shepherd lays down his life for the sheep" (John 10:11). Even in the midst of utter turmoil and hopelessness, the mercy and compassion of God shone forth, and through Ezekiel, provided words of comfort and consolation.

Of all the great visions God gave to Ezekiel, the vision of the dry bones clearly showed God's initiative to restore the people and bring them back to Himself. The people who were in exile were compared to those who had lost vitality, energy, and life itself. God asked Ezekiel if these bones could come to life, and Ezekiel humbly acknowledged that only God would have the answer. Ezekiel knew that no human being would be able to provide life to these dead bones. He knew God's initiative, grace, and His gift of the Spirit were imperative to bring about new life. God made it clear to Ezekiel that the dry bones represented the physical, moral, and spiritual status of the people of Israel: "These bones are the whole house of Israel. They have been saying, 'our bones are dried up, our hope is lost, and we are cut off'" (Ezekiel 37:11). Evidently, hopelessness was pervasive among the people in such dire circumstances. Although the rebellious people had brought this condition upon themselves, God was about to provide them with yet another opportunity.

God asked Ezekiel to speak to the dry bones the word God was giving. When Ezekiel obeyed and spoke God's word, he heard the tremendous noise of the rattling of bones, as the bones that were scattered in the valley began to come together, bone joining bone. Although flesh soon covered the bones, there was no life in the newly formed bodies. This lack of life symbolically represented the condition of spiritual death the children of Israel experienced as they went away from the living God to the worship of idols. The rattling of the bones and the covering of the flesh represented changes Israelites attempted in different moments in history. However, those cosmetic changes were inadequate for them to truly experience the new life that God was willing to offer. God made it clear that the people had to make a complete turn to God and open their hearts to receive the grace that He was willing to give to them. When the "breath," or the Spirit, of God came upon the lifeless bodies, Ezekiel saw them rising as if from a slumber and standing up as a large army. God was picturing for Ezekiel what He intended to do for a "dead" nation. There would be new life, new hope, and a new beginning. Restoration would begin when people exhibited true repentance. The temple would be rebuilt, and God would establish a new covenant with His people. God assured the people through Ezekiel that the exile would come to an end and God's plan for the world would begin to unfold.

*"I want to encourage you by letting you know that there's hope for you and your situation, whatever you are dealing with. God is intimately involved with every detail of your future and His desire is for you to be an overcomer."*
—Sue Augustine

## For Further Reflection and Discussion

1.   Ezekiel was the only prophet who received God's call in a foreign land. What are the implications of this statement?

2.   The call of the Lord came to Ezekiel five years after his exile to Babylon. What must have been going on in the mind of Ezekiel during those five years?

3.   Ezekiel had a hard message to preach, and the message he preached was still harder to hear. Discuss.

4.   God made it clear through Ezekiel that He would shepherd His people. How is God shepherding His people today?

5.   The vision of the dry bones can be compared to those moments in which we may have felt "dried up and lost hope." What were the factors that sustained you under such circumstances?

# DANIEL:

## The Greatest Test, the Greatest Testimony

*"Even after Daniel heard that this law had been signed, he continued his custom of going home to kneel in prayer and give thanks to God in the upper chamber three times a day, with the windows open towards Jerusalem"* (Daniel 6:11).

Despite all the warnings given to the people about the urgency to abandon their evil ways and return to the Lord, they persisted in their sinful ways. When the Assyrians destroyed the northern kingdom of Israel, God's powerful prophets such as Isaiah, Jeremiah, and Hosea challenged the southern kingdom of Judah to return to God. However, as people persisted in sin, the prophecies of doom and destruction came to pass. Nebuchadnezzar, the king of Babylon, conquered Judah, destroyed the city of Jerusalem, and took all able-bodied men and women as captives to Babylon. The majestic temple of Jerusalem that was built by King Solomon was destroyed, and the Babylonians carried off many of the sacred vessels of the temple to their homeland. Nebuchadnezzar, being a visionary, knew that prisoners of war could certainly contribute to the growth of riches in his country in more ways than the conventional slave labor.

In order to extract the best service from his captives, King Nebuchadnezzar devised a plan and commanded his chief chamberlain to identify and select "the Israelites of royal blood and of the nobility, young men without any defect, handsome, intelligent and wise, quick to learn, and prudent in judgment, such as they could take their place in the king's palace; they were to be taught the language and literature of the Chaldeans; after three year's of training they were to enter the king's service" (Daniel 1:3–5). Among those chosen were Daniel, Hananiah, Mishael, and Azariah. These four young friends possessed many virtues and good qualities. However, their greatest virtue was their faith in the living God, which the Babylonians did not fully understand. From their early years, they had come to know and love God. They were diligent in practicing the precepts and commands of the

Lord. Though their hearts grieved at the defeat of Judah in the hands of the Babylonians, they never dared to question God as to why His chosen people had to suffer. As they had witnessed the failures of their kings, priests, and leaders, they realized that the nation had brought this chastisement on themselves due to their continuous disobedience.

King Nebuchadnezzar wanted to train the young Hebrews in the Chaldean (Babylonian) culture, literature, and traditions. The Chaldean culture was greatly influenced by the popular Hellenistic (Greek) language and culture. The king knew how to identify people of great intelligence, virtue, and nobility from other cultures and train them in a new culture to serve his purpose. He lavishly provided all the young chosen ones with food and wine from the royal table during their period of training.

All the young Hebrews were given Babylonian names. Daniel's name was changed Belteshazzar, Hananiah to Shadrach, Mishael to Meshach, and Azariah to Abednego. These young men, who had deep convictions and faith in God, had decided to remain pure in the sight of God. Daniel knew the importance of remaining undefiled before God, even in a culture that was greatly affected by pagan practices and idolatry. Having known the rules and regulations about food (those that were viewed as clean and those seen as unclean), he intended to refrain from the royal food that was provided. When Daniel expressed his decision, his three companions gladly accepted it.

God touched the heart of the chief chamberlain of the king, and he provided these four young men with vegetables and water as they requested. Daniel and his companions did not taste any of the rich food and wine that were lavishly made available to everyone else. God's favor was upon these young men as He gave them the gifts of wisdom, understanding, and knowledge and enabled them to surpass the knowledge of everyone else during the time of their training. Daniel and his companions, who did not defile their bodies with the king's food and wines but instead consumed vegetables and water, appeared much healthier than all the others. God's hand was upon them as He kept them strong and healthy, despite consuming food that was not as nourishing as the food of the palace. God especially blessed Daniel with the unique gift of understanding dreams and visions, and interpreting them correctly. This divine gift served Daniel well many times during his service to the king. God's Spirit was with them as they presented them-selves before the king, who was extremely delighted at their knowl-edge, wisdom, and understanding: "In any question of wisdom or prudence which the king put to them, he found them ten times better than all the magicians and enchanters in his kingdom" (Daniel 1:20).

Daniel's special knowledge and wisdom aided him in gaining greater favor with the king. The king was tormented with a strange dream, and he consulted all his wise men in the courts to relate to him his own dream and then provide satisfactory interpretations of the dream. The king was demanding an impossible task from his inter-preters as he did not reveal to them the content of his dream. The wise men in the king's court were helpless, and they did not know what the dream of the king was. As they all failed in this task, the king became enraged and commanded all of them to be executed. Next, the king de-cided to seek the interpretation from the newly trained Hebrew men. He asked specifically for Daniel and his companions, as they had im-pressed him with their wisdom and knowledge. When the news reached the young Daniel, he retreated to be alone with God in prayer. He knew that human knowledge alone was not enough to face the challenge at hand. If his interpretations displeased the king, Daniel could be endan-gering his own life and the lives of his companions. Daniel humbly asked the Lord to reveal to him the correct interpretation of the dream. God answered Daniel's prayer and provided him a vision through which the mystery was revealed. He was granted access to the king, and Daniel first related the dream and then its interpretation.

Daniel had struggled with the interpretation of the dream. The cor-rect interpretation of the dream indicated that the Babylonian kingdom was about to be destroyed. Daniel could have altered its correct inter-pretation and given one that would be favorable to the king. However, Daniel trusted in the Lord and gave the king the true interpretation of the dream. The dream of the king was about a great statue made up of various kinds of material, and about a rock that was hewn from a mountain. The rock struck the feet of the statue, which was made of tiles. The whole statue crumbled and the different materials were scat-tered by the powerful wind. The rock that struck the statue became a great mountain and filled the whole earth. Daniel interpreted that the different materials represented different monarchies and kingdoms that would rise in the future, and the rock prefigured a universal and ever-lasting kingdom, which would be the work of God. King Nebuchadnezzar was not perturbed at this revelation but rather felt relieved as he knew what was ahead of him in the future. He thanked Daniel and praised the God of Daniel for the wisdom given to Daniel. He elevated Daniel as the ruler of a province in Babylon and chief prefect over all the wise men of Babylon, whose lives Daniel had saved. Daniel did not forget his friends, and he requested that the king grant them notable positions in the kingdom. The grateful king heeded the request of Daniel and made Daniel's friends the administrators in the kingdom.

The companions of Daniel—Hananiah (Shadrach), Mishael (Meshach), and Azariah (Abednego)—were grateful to the king for the favors he bestowed upon them. But their power and position in the kingdom did not corrupt their faith and trust in God. King Nebuchadnezzar had erected a golden statue of his image and commanded that at the sound of the trumpet everyone should fall down and worship it. Anyone who refused to obey the command of the king was cast into the fiery furnace. He made this command at a time when he had sent Daniel away on a special mission. The command of the king was obeyed by all, except Shadrach, Meshach, and Abednego. They knew that bowing down before a golden statue and worshipping it entailed idolatry and disobedience of the first commandment. As the news reached the king, he ordered that the furnace be heated seven times more and that the strong men bind and cast these rebels into the fire. The courageous friends of Daniel preferred to die than to disobey God. As they were cast into the fiery furnace, they were singing praises to God and asking Him for protection. The God of mercy and compassion heard the prayer of His faithful servants and sent His angels to be with them. Though they were in the midst of the burning furnace, no flame touched them. This became a powerful moment of transformation for the king as he granted Hebrews freedom to worship their God.

When Nebuchadnezzar died, Belshazzar succeeded him. He was not as prudent as his father and disrespected the Jewish people and their traditions. In one of his feasts, he ordered that the sacred vessels that were taken from the Jerusalem temple be brought out. The king, his nobles, and his entertainers began drinking wine using the sacred vessels. It was indeed an act of great sacrilege. To the bewilderment of everyone, suddenly a human hand appeared and began writing on the wall. Daniel was called in to interpret the cryptic handwriting. Daniel courageously announced that the "writing on the wall" indicated an end of the kingdom and the death of the king, who had profaned the sacred vessels. As Daniel interpreted the words, Persians invaded Babylon, killed Belshazzar, and Darius succeeded the throne.

Darius, the king of the Persians, found Daniel to be the most trustworthy and capable among all his administrators. There were many administrators and nobles who were jealous and annoyed at the honesty and integrity of Daniel. They were powerful men in Babylon who were dishonest. They all formed an alliance and approached the king to issue a decree: "No one is to address any petition to god or man for thirty days, except to you, O king; otherwise he shall cast into a den of lions" (Daniel 6:8). The king issued such a strange decree without realizing their wicked intentions. These wicked men knew that Daniel often prayed to God and asked for His guidance and direction in life. Although Daniel knew of the decree, he did not deviate from his normal custom of kneeling down and praying three times a day. He could have played it safe by not praying for a month, or he could have closed his window when he prayed. His courageous faith enabled him to trust in the Lord and not fear the human wickedness. His conspirators joined together in petitioning that Daniel violated the decree and therefore he should be cast into a den of lions.

Darius, who had come to love Daniel, was greatly distressed by this. Yet, unwilling to violate his own decree, he cast Daniel into the den of lions. Daniel, whose faith in the Lord gave him courage to face any challenging situation, raised his heart and mind to God and prayed for deliverance. The Lord shut the mouth of the lions, and he was preserved unharmed. The king, who had refused to eat and had refrained from any form of entertainment on account of Daniel, hurried early the next morning to see what happened. When he found Daniel alive and well, the king was ecstatic and gave praise to the God of Daniel. Darius issued a decree enjoining reverence for the God of Daniel. The courage and faithfulness of Daniel became the catalyst for gaining religious freedom for the Hebrews in this foreign land.

God gave Daniel several visions about the events that were to be unveiled in the future. Many of those visions were aimed at creating greater faithfulness on the part of the people in the face of adversity. Daniel was challenging the people to remain loyal to God in the midst of the struggles and difficulties of life. His message to the people was clear and concise: "You can resist temptation and conquer adversity if you have faith." Daniel's life clearly demonstrated that a person of faith can survive the trials and tribulations of life. God is able, and the One with whom all things are possible will not abandon His faithful children. Daniel's vision ultimately pointed toward God's actions in the future, which would be fulfilled in the person of Jesus Christ.

*"When you have come to the edge of all light that you know and are about to drop off into the darkness of the unknown, faith is knowing one of two things will happen: there will be something solid to stand on or your will be taught to fly."*
—Patrick Overton

## For Further Reflection and Discussion

1. "Without a test, there is no testimony." Discuss this in light of Daniel's experiences.

2. Daniel was away from his homeland. Even though he was required to learn a new culture and tradition, he did not give up his basic convictions. Identify situations in which you could be challenged to give up your convictions.

3. Daniel's friends walked among the burning flames and yet they were unharmed. What are the implications for our lives today?

4. There were many situations in which Daniel could have played it safe (given a false interpretation of the dream or avoided praying for a month). Instead, he believed that his ultimate safety was with God. Discuss.

5. Persons of faith can resist temptation and courageously face adversities in life. Discuss.

# JOB:

## Even the Righteous Suffer Greatly

*"Where were you when I founded the earth? Tell me if you have understanding. Who determined its size? Who stretched out the measuring line for it?"* (Job 38:4–5).

One of the most difficult questions ever posed is "Why should good and innocent people suffer?" No satisfactory answer is readily forthcoming. The closest answer could be found in the life of Job, but still the answer remains vague at best. Often there are no rational explanations that can give a satisfying answer to such an important question. Ultimately one is challenged to realize how small one is in comparison to the mysteries of God.

Job constantly said yes to God and no to evil. His piety and devotion were well known to all. Every aspect of his life was determined by his relationship with God. He loved God above all things and never questioned Him even when things did not go according to his plans. Like everyone, there were ups and downs, and twists and turns in his life. But he never allowed any of those to affect his relationship with God, his family, or his neighbors. He always said, "My blessings are too numerous for me to fret over the little struggles of life." Indeed, God had blessed Job abundantly: "Seven sons and three daughters were born to him; and he had seven thousand sheep, three thousand camels, five hundred she-asses, and a great number of wild animals, so that he was greater than any of the men of the East" (Job 1:2–3). All the members of his family loved and cared for each other, and the foundation of love and unity was built on their love for God. Job often reminded his children to remain holy before God and often offered sacrifices for any sins they might have committed. He was truly an upright and righteous man.

While Job was busy with his routine activities, there was an interesting development in the heavens that included Job without his knowledge. God was speaking so proudly of His servant Job. But the adversary, Satan, very interestingly countered, "True, when things go well, it is easy to lead a good and upright life." He challenged God to change the fortunes of Job and see how he would fare in moments of crisis. "Is it for nothing that Job is God-fearing? Have you not surrounded him with family and all that he has with your protection? You have blessed the work of his hands, and his livestock are spread all over the land. But now put forth your hand and touch anything that he has, and surely he will blaspheme you to your face" (Job 1:9–11). God allowed Satan to have control over Job by inflicting adversities but never causing any harm to his life.

In one day, there was a complete reversal of Job's fortunes. Four messengers brought Job news of the complete ruin of his servants, all his animals, all his possessions, and—the most painful of all—the death of all his ten children. One day he was blessed with ten children, and enjoyed many possessions, servants, immense wealth, and a happy life. And the next day he found himself childless, poor, and destitute. He was absolutely stunned at hearing of all the unfortunate events. He tore off his cloak, cut his hair, and fell prostrate on the ground. He could have had every reason to be angry and question God for these unexpected calamities in his life. Rather, he uttered these incredible words to express his absolute dependence on God: "Naked I came forth from my mother's womb, and naked I shall go back again. The Lord gave and the Lord has taken away; blessed be the name of the Lord" (Job 1:21). Even difficult events had failed to shake Job's unconditional trust in the Lord.

As Job remained innocent and uncomplaining after losing all his possessions and posterity, Satan suggested that Job had not yet been fully tried and tested. Job still had his good health and faced no physical pain. God granted Satan a second permission to inflict sufferings on Job's body but to spare his life. Job's body was covered with severe boils from the soles of his feet to the crown of his head. His physical pain was severe, and he sat on ashes and scraped his skin with a piece of broken pottery. Overwhelmed by agony and frustration, Job's wife went on to suggest, "Curse God and die" (Job 2:9). Job held on to his conviction that all things came from God as gifts, at times in the form of good, and at times in the form of evil. In truth, God had not caused any evil upon Job; rather it was the work of Satan. Job, who thought everything came from God, seemed to believe that even the sufferings in his life were somehow part of God's plan.

The three friends of Job—Eliphaz, Bildad, and Zophar—came to be with Job to offer him their sympathy and support. For seven days and seven nights they silently sat with Job. None of them were ready to talk. They were trying to make sense of the unexpected tragedies that had happened to Job. Job's pain was great and his troubles numerous. As hours turned to days, his pain became too intolerable. Job, finally overwhelmed by his suffering, opened his mouth and cursed the day he was born. This initiated a conversation that probed into the reasons for Job's suffering. In trying to make sense of the situation, Job's friends suggested that he was either impatient, or may have committed evil and probably deserved greater punishment than he was experiencing. They were unable to pinpoint what sin Job might have committed, but they held on to their belief that God rewarded those who did good and punished those who were evil in His sight. As Job faced suffering and punishment, they felt he must have committed evil at some point.

Eliphaz stated that Job had attempted to comfort many. According to Eliphaz, misfortunes had affected Job's patience, and it seemed clear that Job never understood the pain of others when Job offered them his advice. Eliphaz also believed that Job might have committed some serious sin to offend God. Bildad thought the reason for all Job's calamities might have been Job's children. Zophar implied that whatever be the wickedness that Job had committed, the punishment seemed insufficient. Job increasingly began losing patience with his friends and grew irritated. They were fine when they were quiet. He asked them to be silent rather than giving him false remedies and lies. His heart grieved at their accusations.

Job was confident of his innocence and maintained that his suffering was unjustified. As he had not committed any sin, there was no reason for God to punish him. Through it all, Job did not curse God, as his wife had suggested, or accuse Him of any injustice; but rather he looked for vindication from God. He searched for God to reason with him, but he could not see God physically. Job also admitted that he did not know how to plead his case effectively with God. Hearing this, his friends then categorically said that Job lacked appropriate fear of God.

A fourth friend, Elihu, who was introduced in chapter 32, stated that Job seemed to spend too much time defending himself instead of

God: "He was angry with Job for considering himself rather than God to be right. He was angry also with the three friends because they had not found a good answer and had not condemned Job" (Job 32:2–3). In his speech, Elihu argued for God's power, gift of salvation, and absolute rightness in all His conduct. Elihu stated that while Job might be righteous, he certainly was not perfect.

When God finally interrupted, He did not give logical answers to the questions concerning Job's suffering. Rather, He patiently tried to teach Job by inviting him to broaden his understanding rather than foolishly believe that he could find all the answers. He asked Job questions about the details of creation. Job only humbly acknowledged God's unlimited power and the limitations of human knowledge. God's speech emphasized His dominion and sovereignty in the creation and care of the world. God made it clear that He was supremely free and did not need the approval of His creatures.

He made it clear to Job that his friends (the first three—Eliphaz, Bildad, and Zophar) were seeking to find justification for Job's suffering, but it was beyond their comprehension. Job, on the other hand, admitted his limitations and renewed his trust in the Lord. His acceptance of God's sovereignty and the realization of his foolish attempt to have God vindicate him were clear from his words: "I know You can do all things, and that no purpose of Yours can be hindered. I have dealt with great things that I do not understand; things too wonderful for me, which I cannot know. I have heard of you by word of mouth, but now my eyes have seen you. Therefore I disown what I have said, and repent in dust and ashes" (Job 42:1–6).

God instructed Job's three friends to offer a sacrifice for their offenses and beseech Job to pray for his gullible friends. God's acceptance of Job's prayer clearly indicated that Job always remained blameless and righteous before God. Job's family and possessions were restored and his later days were more blessed than the earlier ones: "For he had fourteen thousand sheep, six thousand camels…. And he had seven sons and three daughters…and he saw his children, his grandchildren, and he even his great-grandchildren" (Job 42:12–16).

There are no satisfactory answers to the questions, "Why should good and innocent people suffer?" or "If God is so loving and good, why is there so much suffering and pain in this world?" The story of

Job does make it clear that God does not cause suffering. It is, rather, the work of the devil to turn people against God. One might not be able to find justifiable answers for the causes of one's pain. One may never understand. Job had to humbly realize his human limitations and accept the mysteries of God's ways. Ultimately, Job surrendered himself totally to God.

Unexpected sufferings and moments of crisis may cause a person to ask this question: "Where is God?" A parent who is faced with the untimely death of his/her only child may cry out to God with this same question. Could God answer, "I AM with you as I, too, lost My only Son—on the cross"?

From the cross on Calvary a cry was heard, "My God, My God, why have You abandoned Me?" Sometime later, from the same cross these determined words were heard: "Father, into Your hands I commend My spirit."

> *"He tells us to trust Him enough to believe He knows what He is doing. When His actions don't make sense, trust Him...When the bottom falls out and life turns hard, trust Him. Good times and bad, happy and sad, trust Him. When I try to explain Him away or reduce Him to neat little formulas, I show a lack of faith, not a wealth of it."*
> —Mark Tabb

## For Further Reflection and Discussion

1. "It is easy to remain faithful to God when things go your way." Discuss the implications of this statement.

2. There are some who forget God in good times and remember him only in moments of crisis. Job was different. Discuss.

3. What are the implications of Job's statement, "Naked I came forth from my mother's womb, and naked shall I go back again? The Lord gave and the Lord has taken away; blessed be the name of the Lord"?

4. In frustration Job's wife said, "Curse God and die." Job replied, "We accept good things from God; and should we not accept evil?" Did Job think that God caused evil?

5. What are your thoughts on the following questions: "Why should good and innocent people suffer?" and "If God is all loving and good, why is there so much suffering in this world?"

# ESTHER:

## An Orphan Who Saved the People

*"Go and assemble all the Jews who are in Susa; fast on my behalf, all of you, not eating or drinking, night or day, for three days. I and my maids will also fast in the same way. Thus prepared, I will go to the king, contrary to the law. If I perish, I perish"* (Esther 4:16).

Esther is hailed as a courageous woman whose valor saved the Jewish people from annihilation in the foreign land of Persia. Events in the book of Esther occurred after the Medes and Persians had conquered Babylon. The story of Esther reveals God's mighty power as He saved His people from destruction by using a young woman in a strange land. Although the book of Esther seldom uses the name God (except in its prologue and epilogue), the whole story beautifully portrays God's work of using ordinary people to accomplish extraordinary things for His people.

Esther was an orphan, as she had lost both of her parents during the Babylonian captivity. Mordecai, a devout Jew of the tribe of Benjamin, took care of this young girl and adopted her as his daughter. The name her parents had given her was Hadassah, meaning myrtle. Mordecai, who wanted to hide her Jewish identity, gave her the name Esther after the Babylonian goddess Ishtar. As they were deported to Persia, Mordecai knew that a Babylonian name was safer than a Jewish name. Esther was an extremely beautiful girl, and Mordecai took great pride in his adopted daughter.

The rise of Esther into prominence came about as a result of an unusual set of circumstances. King Ahasuerus, the mighty king of Persia, decided to display his abundant wealth for one hundred and eighty days. His kingdom extended from India to Ethiopia and included the whole of the Middle East, so he was in possession of great wealth. He exhibited his vast collection of weaponry, precious stones, gold, ivory, expensive royal clothing, vessels made of every conceivable material, and various kinds of artifacts. People from all over the land were invited to view this extraordinary display of expensive items. At the end of the one hundred and eighty days of exhibition, the king organized a great feast for all in his kingdom. His wife, Queen Vashti, provided a great feast for all the women in the royal palace. Queen Vashti was a woman of exceptional beauty. She was at the same time a modest woman, who did not believe in displaying her beauty before others.

As with many extravagant feasts, unusual things occurred at King Ahasuerus's feast as well. On the seventh day of the feast, when the king was merrily drunk with wine, he dispatched attendants to his wife with an unusual command. She was ordered to present herself before everyone else wearing only her royal crown to display her exceptional beauty. Queen Vashti, who loved and honored her husband, refused to obey this royal command. Her refusal angered the king, as he felt totally humiliated before everyone else by the disobedience of his wife. He was in no normal state to realize that his royal command to display his wife's nakedness before everyone was a greater act of humiliation than her refusal to submit to such a command. The king sought advice from his top-ranked advisors. As they shared the same fury of the king, they advised him to banish Queen Vashti from the royal palace and seek a new queen who would be obedient to the king. The king issued a decree banishing Queen Vashti from the royal palace and sent letters in different languages to different parts of his kingdom to the effect that every man should be lord of his own home (Esther 1:22).

King Ahasuerus and his advisors made elaborate preparations to choose the next queen. All young virgins were ordered to come to the capital city of Susa and undergo an elaborate beauty treatment for a period of twelve months: "Of this period of beautifying treatment, six months were spent with oil or myrrh, and the other six months with perfumes and cosmetics" (Esther 2:12) Esther, who was living with Mordecai in Susa, was taken to the royal palace and placed under Hegai, the custodian of the women. As Esther was extremely beautiful and gifted, she was quickly noticed by Hegai. He provided her with cosmetics and provisions and transferred her to the best place in the harem. As she was strictly forbidden by Mordecai from revealing her identity, she did not provide any information about her Jewish heritage.

Mordecai was keenly watching the developments. He earnestly prayed to God that Esther would be chosen as the next queen. He knew that Esther possessed great virtues and if she were to be chosen queen, she would be placed in a position to help his people. Although Esther was naturally beautiful, she went through the elaborate beautifying period to prepare herself to meet the king. She earnestly hoped and prayed that the king would take note of her. God heard the prayer of Mordecai and Esther as the king was greatly pleased with her and loved her more than any of the other virgins. So he placed the royal diadem on her head and made her queen in place of Vashti (Esther 2:17). The king arranged a great feast in honor of Esther and declared a holiday in her honor in all of his one hundred and twenty-six provinces. Esther earnestly prayed to God that the king would refrain from making the same demand he made to Vashti to appear at the feast wearing only the crown. The feast should have been the perfect opportunity for the king to force the new queen to obey his order and show before all that he was the lord of his own house. However, the Lord touched his heart, and the king demonstrated great love and honor for his new wife. Esther's heart was filled with gratitude to God, and she devoted herself to love and honor God for the rest of her life.

Mordecai continued to keep close watch at every development in the palace. He was an honorable man and often had access to the king's palace. God provided him a great opportunity to win great favor with the king. As Mordecai was passing through the gate of the palace, he discovered a secret plot of the guards to murder the king. Mordecai reported it to Queen Esther, who in turn revealed it to the king. Both Mordecai and Esther hoped and prayed that the king would be able to verify such a plot and take action against the wicked guards. The matter was investigated and the plot was verified. The king hung the evil guards. The incident increased the king's love for Esther and the matter was written in the annals of the king.

Haman the Agagite was a high-ranking officer of King Ahasuerus. Although Haman was greatly successful in taking care of many of the king's affairs, he was also extremely cunning. As the king was greatly pleased with Haman's ability, he elevated him to the highest position any of the king's officers could aspire to. The privilege made Haman blind with pride, and he demanded that everyone should kneel and bow at his sight. Mordecai, a devout Jew who only knelt down before his God, refused Haman's order. Haman was livid with fury at the disobedience of Mordecai. Upon learning that Mordecai was a Jew, he hatched a plan to destroy all the Jews in the kingdom. He falsely accused them of rebellion and informed the king that the Jews in the kingdom were disobeying the laws of the king. Believing the false report of his close confidant, the king gave Haman permission to destroy the Jews. For Haman, such an order provided the best opportunity to destroy the Jews and plunder their wealth for himself. In the name of the king, he issued a decree that ordered the murder of all the Jewish people in the kingdom on the thirteenth day of the twelfth month.

The decree cast great fear among the Jewish people. There were loud cries and lamenting among the Jews. The Jewish people turned to God with prayers, penance, and fasting. Mordecai immediately knew who the culprit was behind such a treacherous act. He knew the right time had come to approach Esther to seek her aid in helping her people. However, it greatly alarmed him at the thought that they had concealed Esther's identity from the king. Mordecai fasted and ardently prayed for God to show them a way to protect the people.

As he approached Esther with the news, her heart was greatly troubled at the whole development. However, she felt powerless at the moment as she knew well the practice in the palace. No one was allowed in the inner court of the king without being summoned, and the same rule applied even to the queen. Her next opportunity to be with the king was after thirty days. Mordecai knew that he was racing against time, and so he sternly reminded the hesitant Esther about the predicament that the people were in: "Do not imagine that because you are in the king's palace, you alone of all the Jews will escape…you and your father's house will perish. Who knows but it was for a time like this that you obtained the royal dignity?" (Esther 4:13-14). Esther felt extremely vulnerable as she was caught between the dangerous plight of her people and the rule of the king. She turned to the source of her strength, God, for guidance and direction. She knew that the desperate prayer and supplication of His people would always be answered and she believed in the power of prayer. She asked Mordecai to request all the Jewish people to fast and pray for her. She was well aware that she needed God's favor to succeed in her mission.

Esther took off her royal garments and put on her mourning clothes. She fasted and prayed unceasingly for the next three days. At the end of the third day, she gathered all her courage and made her appearance before the king. The royal clothes and demeanor of the king greatly intimidated her and she felt about to faint. However, God had touched the heart of the king as he came off his royal throne and took her gently in his arms. He assured her that there was no reason for her to be afraid. She invited the king to attend her first banquet as queen and requested the presence of Haman as well. In the meantime, Haman was plotting with his family to execute Mordecai. They erected a gibbet to execute Mordecai.

That night the king was unable to sleep as he was troubled by the events of the day. He asked the attendant to read the chronicles of notable events from the annals. As the plot against the king and Mordecai's role in saving the king was read, he inquired if Mordecai had been rewarded in any way for his good deed. When he realized that no reward had been given to Mordecai, he called in Haman and asked him what a fitting gesture should be to honor a person. Haman gullibly thought the king was going to reward him for his good work, and he proposed a series of lavish honorable favors to be bestowed to that person in public. To the horror of Haman, the king ordered him to perform all those honorable favors for Mordecai in public. Mordecai returned to the royal palace with great honor, while Haman returned to his home in shame.

The day for the banquet arrived, and the king was in a joyful spirit. He drank his favorite wine to his heart's content and promised Esther any favor that she might choose to ask. Knowing that the appointed time had come, she revealed her identity and asked the king to spare her life and the lives of her people. When the king came to know the cruel plot of Haman, he was enraged. He ordered that Haman be hung immediately. The king's order was carried out, and Haman was hung on the same gibbet he had prepared for Mordecai's execution. The courageous act of a young woman saved the lives of the Jewish people.

Esther's life teaches us a valuable lesson today. She was an orphan and yet God exalted her and used her in such a mighty way. God does not look for individuals with flawless track records to do His work. He looks for an individual's willingness and ability to wait on Him. Esther did not act impetuously to save her people. She waited for the right moment to approach and make her requests known. She also believed in the power of prayer, as she had asked Mordecai to request the intercession of the people on her behalf. While she believed in the power of intercession, she herself fell on her knees and prayed unceasingly to God for mercy and protection. The prayer of the faithful Esther was heard and her courage was rewarded.

*"Trust in what you love, continue to do, and it will take you where you need to go."* —Natalie Goldberg

## For Further Reflection and Discussion

1. Queen Vashti was dethroned because of her disobedience, but she continues to be seen as an honorable woman. Discuss.
2. Esther went through elaborate preparations to become a queen. How important is preparation to be an effective instrument in the hands of God?
3. Mordecai refused to kneel and bow down before Haman. He was greatly punished for his determination to be faithful to God. Devotion to God may bring about struggles and sufferings in life. Discuss.
4. Haman attempted to murder Mordecai. God turned his plot around. What are the ways God has turned around something bad in your life for good?
5. Esther could have chosen to forget about her people as she was comfortable in the palace. However, she chose to remember her humble beginning. Success in life can cause people to forget about the roles others played toward it. Discuss.

# JONAH:

## A Jealous Prophet?

*"This is why I fled at first to Tarshish. I knew that you are a gracious and merciful God, slow to anger, rich in clemency, loathe to punish. And now, Lord, please take my life from me; for it is better for me to die than to live"* (Jonah 4:2–3).

Jonah was pretty happy to be God's spokesperson. He loved giving God's messages, especially those that were in line with fire and brimstone. Constantly he demanded conversion and repentance from the people. He wanted his people to walk in God's ways. However, he was very careful to avoid those people outside of his Hebrew tradition. To him, those others were worthless and destined to be destroyed. He could not wait to see the day when only God's chosen, holy people would survive and thrive in the world.

It came as a great shock to Jonah when he was commanded by the Lord to go to Nineveh, the traditional enemy city of Israel. Jonah loathed the inhabitants of Nineveh and had heard of their sinful lives and practices. They worshipped idols, and their fertility cults often lured many children of Israel away from their faith in the true God. Jonah must have secretly prayed many times that they be destroyed with all their wickedness because he did not want his people to be influenced by their lawlessness and impurity. It would have been wonderful if God had called him to witness the destruction of the city, but God's message here looked like a mere warning. Many times Jonah could not fathom God's ways, especially when it came to His boundless mercy that He seemed to offer to all who called upon Him. If it were left up to Jonah, Nineveh and its inhabitants, and all sinful nations and peoples, would have been destroyed a long time ago. *Well,* Jonah thought, *the best thing to do is to go away from the Lord in the opposite direction.* So he set out and boarded a ship for Tarshish, which was in the opposite direction of Nineveh.

Jonah was peacefully sleeping when a violent storm began to rock the boat. There was absolute chaos, and all were calling upon their gods to rescue them from the impending calamity. The captain might have been enraged to see one of the boarders fast asleep instead of calling for help. The boarders on the ship concluded that someone must have brought the misfortune upon them due to their wickedness. They decided to cast lots to determine the culprit, and Jonah's name was drawn out. When Jonah told them about the whole situation and how he ended up on the ship and from whom he was running, the whole crew was frightened. They seemed to exhibit more awe and fear for the living God than Jonah himself. The only option he was able to come up with was to tell them to toss him off the boat into the sea. The goodwill of the crewmembers who were Gentiles was visible as they tried hard to steady the ship and thereby save Jonah. However, nothing seemed to work, and they reluctantly agreed to cast Jonah into the sea. They begged for God's mercy on their action as they threw Jonah into the sea.

*It is better to be in the sea than to be in Nineveh*, Jonah might have thought. He would have preferred to die than to see those wretched people escape God's punishment. As he was thinking this he saw a huge whale approaching him with its wide-open mouth. Jonah did not realize that God was giving him another opportunity to change his narrow-minded attitude. As minutes turned into hours, and hours to days, Jonah began to pray for deliverance. For three days and three nights he languished in the belly of the whale. Finally, in desperation he cried out, "Out of my distress I called to the Lord, and He answered me. From the midst of the nether world I cried for help, and you heard my voice...But I, with resounding praise, will sacrifice to you. What I have vowed I will pay: deliverance is from God" (Jonah 2:3–10). The compassionate God heard the helpless cry of Jonah and delivered him from death.

Having been spewed up onto the shore by the whale, Jonah knew that it was useless to run away from God. The popular words of king and psalmist David, "Where can I hide from your Spirit...If I ascend to the heavens, you are there; if I lie down in Sheol, you are there too" (Psalm 139:7–12), might have resonated in his heart. Realizing that it was futile to ignore God's commands, he reluctantly succumbed to God's will. When God commanded a second time, he decided to obey Him. The city of Nineveh was enormous, and it should have taken him over three days to proclaim the message of God in all the important locations. Jonah made several shortcuts in one day and announced to the people in a condescending and judgmental fashion, "Forty days more and Nineveh shall be destroyed" (Jonah 3:4). He did not care whether his message reached everyone. His message was one of judgment and condemnation, not one that included conversion or repentance. He did not announce to them that if they turned from their wickedness, God would show them mercy and deliver them from the impending destruction. Strangely, Jonah did not want the people to believe his words and amend their ways. He wanted his mission to be a failure!

He was dismayed to see the change in their attitude, beginning with the king and spreading to the people. They believed in Jonah's words and wanted to repent and convert! The king of Nineveh led the people in repentance as he took off his royal robes and put on sackcloth and sat in the ashes. He wanted his kingdom to be spared from destruction. Hence he made a decree, "Neither man nor beast, neither cattle nor sheep, shall taste anything; they shall not eat, nor shall they drink water. Man and beast shall be covered with sackcloth and call loudly to God; every man shall turn from his evil way and the violence he has in hand. Who knows, God may relent and forgive, and withhold His blazing wrath, so that we shall not perish" (Jonah 3:7–9). They accepted Jonah as the prophet of God and believed in his message. Their conversion was genuine, and God accepted their repentance and decided to withhold the punishment He had planned to inflict.

That was not what Jonah had hoped. Still Jonah thought, *They are so wicked, God will surely destroy them in forty days. My words will come to pass.* He waited in anticipation to see the destruction of these wicked people. He could not understand why God should show mercy to the Gentiles. He complained to God, "This is why I fled at first to Tarshish. I knew that you are a gracious and merciful God, slow to anger, rich in clemency, loathe to punish" (Jonah 4:2). His frustration at the mercy of God is clear in his wish for death: "Lord, please take my life from me; for it is better for me to die than to live" (Jonah 4:3). He felt that God should have left him in the belly of the whale to perish than to rescue him to go through this disastrous moment of shame and embarrassment. He was too angry and disgusted to respond when God asked him, "Have you any reason to be angry?" (Jonah 4:4)

Jonah did not want to understand God's graciousness and mercy. He felt that the only people who deserved God's favor were the chosen ones, who acknowledged the living God and obeyed His commands. Those who worshiped foreign gods and led lives contrary to God's commandments were to be destroyed. He could not understand how God could grant forgiveness to those who had done abominable things. He truly felt that his anger was justifiable and God's mercy extremely unrealistic.

Hoping against hope, Jonah waited in the hot sun at the outskirts of the city to see its destruction. When a tree grew fast and provided him shade, Jonah was very happy. God sent a worm on the next day and it attacked the tree and it withered. When the sun rose, God sent a burning east wind, and Jonah became extremely furious. He did not understand that God was teaching him a valid lesson. In spite of Jonah's arrogance and narrow-mindedness, God still loved him and wanted Jonah to look beyond himself and his pettiness. The conversation that took place between Jonah and God was quite hilarious. Jonah was like a child, pouting when things did not turn out according to his whims. God patiently told him, "You seemed to be concerned over a plant that cost you no labor, so how much more should I be concerned over whole hosts of peoples and other living beings in Nineveh?" (Jonah 4:10–11). Jonah must have gasped in disbelief when God said, "They, too, are My children."

The same love of God, incarnate in the person of Jesus, would challenge the narrow-mindedness of some of His listeners. Jesus would invite them to go beyond their pettiness and self-centeredness. Simon the Pharisee represented all who thought of God's favor as being limited only to the chosen perfect ones (Luke 7:36–49). Jesus would constantly remind His listeners that God is the God of second chances, who constantly invites all people to enter into a loving relationship with Him. Jesus was critical of those who exhibited self-righteousness and smugness. God's patient love is revealed in the words of Jesus: "I have not come to call the righteous, but sinners to repentance" (Luke 5:31). Yes, God's love manifests itself to all, regardless of the divisions and distinctions people create that are often based on nationality, culture, language, race, ethnicity, sexual orientation, gender, age, economic status, and social standings. God's love cannot be compartmentalized and showcased. His mercy knows no boundaries. He is accessible to anyone who calls upon Him in faith.

It is so easy to pronounce judgments on others and blame them for their misgivings. At times, human hearts might even rejoice at the calamities that others face, especially if they belong to a rival family, tribe, nation, or even religion. The God of love does not want us to rejoice in the misfortunes of others but requires us to pray and help to alleviate the pain and suffering of others.

> *"Unforgiveness is like drinking poison, hoping that your enemy will die."*

## For Further Reflection and Discussion

1.   Jonah wanted to run away from God and His plans. However, God brought him back. St. Paul says in Ephesians 2:10 that God has plans for each one of us and that He will see to it that we conform to those plans. Discuss.

2.   Jonah possessed narrow-mindedness and excluded people who were different from his life. What are the dangers of these attitudes?

3.   Jonah wanted the people of Nineveh to be destroyed. He did not want God to show them His mercy and compassion. What does this reveal about Jonah and God?

4.   God tried to teach Jonah the value of human life with the example of the tree. Did Jonah finally understand the lesson?

5.   What is the purpose of this amazing book, Jonah? How was God challenging the Israelite view of exclusivism?

# JEREMIAH:
## The Struggle of a True Prophet

*"The days are coming, says the Lord, when I will make a new covenant with the house of Israel and the house of Judah.... I will place my law within them, and write it upon their hearts; I will be their God and they shall be my people" (Jeremiah 31:31–33).*

No true prophet had a smooth ride when he took his call seriously. Jeremiah, whose prophetic activities lasted for over a period of four decades, took his mission to heart and had to endure severe heartaches and pain. There were times in his life when he struggled with God and the difficult vocation he received. But he persisted, always being faithful to the living God. Continuing the legacy of his predecessors, he preached on important themes of true piety, social justice, absolute loyalty to the one true God, individual responsibility, repentance, and conversion. Like a true prophet, he upheld truth and criticized all who sided with falsehood. He was constantly targeted for his unpopular messages, which often challenged the way the kings, priests, false prophets, and many of the people lived.

Jeremiah, the son of Hilikiah, was born near Jerusalem in the priestly family of the tribe of Benjamin. The call of Jeremiah revealed God's plan for the young man. He was surprised to hear the powerful words of God: "Before I formed you in the womb, I knew you. Before you were born I dedicated you, a prophet to the nations I appointed you" (Jeremiah 1:5). In contrast to Isaiah, who readily accepted the call to be a prophet, Jeremiah willingly declined it. He was similar to Moses in his response to God. Though Jeremiah protested, citing personal inadequacies and his young age for such a gigantic task, God assured him that he was the right person. Jeremiah seemed to have no choice but to accept the challenge. It was as if God were telling Jeremiah, "I do not call the qualified, but rather qualify those whom I call." God had set Jeremiah apart for a mission that only he could fulfill. He was commissioned to "uproot and tear down; to destroy and to demolish; to build and to plant" (Jeremiah 1:10). It was a mission that involved constant challenge, radical change, and new beginnings.

The changing world events of the time demanded the presence of a person who would not run away when he faced great challenges. The Assyrians, Egyptians, and Babylonians were all constantly trying to overpower the chosen people of Israel. During Jeremiah's time the Assyrian empire had collapsed, only to be replaced with the powerful Babylonians. The leaders of the chosen people were corrupt, causing people to forget the living God and embrace the worship of foreign gods. In the midst of this chaos, there existed a pressing need to bring people back to God. Jeremiah had a difficult task at hand! God assured him of His constant presence and protection. Jeremiah's call in some ways was symbolic of what God has in store for every person. How comforting and strengthening it would be if every person acknowledged that God knew and called each one even before a person is formed in the womb!

Jeremiah had wholeheartedly supported the religious reforms initiated by King Josiah, who had tried to implement many steps to bring people back to God. King Josiah was a godly man who wanted to serve God and His people. Both Josiah and Jeremiah believed that the dismal plight of the people was caused by their own infidelity to God's covenant. Josiah had come to power at a time of extreme religious corruption, which had led to many forms of idolatry. He also had initiated a restoration of the temple and believed that if the people turned away from their wicked ways, God would not carry out His threat of destruction. King Josiah truly enjoyed the support of Jeremiah, whose message always entailed repentance and conversion. Unfortunately, Josiah was unable to complete the reforms as he was killed in a battle with the Egyptians.

It was a great setback for Jeremiah. After the death of King Josiah, the nation of Judah (the southern kingdom, with Jerusalem as its capital) completely abandoned God and ignored His statutes and precepts. Jeremiah began to witness corrupt leaders emerging everywhere and leading people astray. Kings, priests, and leaders of the people were wicked in their lives and affairs. He felt that the evil forces were corrupting the leaders, and as a result, the whole nation was drifting further and further from God's ways and embracing idol worship. He compared Judah to a prostitute: "Lift your eyes to heights, and see, where have men not lain with you? But the wayside you waited for them like an Arab in the desert. You have defiled the land by your wicked harlotry" (Jeremiah 3:2). Time after time he warned the people against taking for granted the mercy and patience of God. They were constantly testing God with their abominable acts of idolatry and cruel deeds of social injustice on the weak and powerless.

Jeremiah wondered how painful it must have been for God to see His people constantly turning their backs on Him. He also knew that God loved them too much to leave them in their state of ruin. He neither feared for his safety, nor looked for popular acceptance. He knew that his message of truth would make many turn against him. Jeremiah did not mince his words when he addressed the powerful. He criticized the greed of the priests and the false prophets, who continually gave a message that people wanted to hear. He challenged the false prophets, who avoided the actual situation and preached popular messages of prosperity and success: "Lies these prophets utter in my name, the Lord said to me. I did not send them; I gave them no command nor did I speak to them. Lying visions, foolish divination, dreams of their divination, they prophesy to you…I did not send them who say, 'sword and famine shall not befall this land.' By sword and famine shall these (false) prophets meet their end" (Jeremiah 14:14–15). He chastised them for giving false messages of peace and prosperity when in reality they were faced with danger from every side.

Jeremiah boldly criticized King Zedekiah for his wicked ways. Zedekiah was put in place as a puppet king under the Babylonians. However, he was planning to rebel against Babylon with the help of the Egyptians. God had revealed to Jeremiah what His plans were for the chosen people: "Submit your necks to the yoke of the king of Babylon; serve him and his people, so that you may live" (Jeremiah 27:12). He made it clear to them that forming an alliance with the Egyptians would anger Nebuchadnezzar, the king of Babylon. He warned them that such an act would lead to the total destruction of Judah and Jerusalem. However, the false prophets accused Jeremiah of treason and had him imprisoned. Jeremiah had to pay a heavy price for his prophetic activities: He was forbidden to enter the temple precinct; he received death threats; he was imprisoned; he was thrown down a well; he was called a traitor; he experienced rejection and loneliness.

In the midst of such agonizing moments, Jeremiah struggled with his own awareness of failures and inadequacies. There were times when he struggled with God and felt that God had duped him and he was paying too great a price for his obedience. We can imagine Jeremiah on his knees in front of God, crying out in great pain and despair for the anguish he was experiencing in his heart. He was convinced that his message was a failure. Worse still, Jeremiah even felt that God had tricked him into His service and had now abandoned him. His words show frustration, disappointment, pain, agony, rejection, and loneliness: "You duped me, O Lord, and I let myself be duped...Yes, I hear the whispering of many, 'denounce, let us denounce him.' All those who were my friends are on the watch for any missteps of mine...cursed be the day on which I was born!...why did I come forth from the womb, to see sorrow and pain, to end my days in shame?" (Jeremiah 20:7–18).

He prophesied the destruction of Jerusalem and the temple, but his words fell on deaf ears. King Zedekiah refused to listen to the words of Jeremiah and attempted to form an alliance with the Egyptians. Nebuchadnezzar, the king of Babylon, viewed it as a rebellion, and the Babylonian army surrounded Judah and the famine began that Jeremiah had predicted. It lasted for eleven months, and the people suffered severely due to lack of food. Nebuchadnezzar then totally destroyed Jerusalem, plundered and brought to ruin the majestic temple, and took all able-bodied men and women to Babylon. When his prophecy came to pass, Jeremiah was left in Jerusalem among the ruins. His heart was aching as he stood by the ruins where the majestic temple had once stood. People had witnessed the splendor of God many a time, and yet they were lured away to the worship of false gods. Even though God's chosen people were scattered by the Assyrians and Babylonians, Jeremiah knew that God would bring them back and fulfill His promises. He knew that there would be an end to the exile, the people would return, and the temple would once again be restored. He would remind the people of a loving and forgiving God who in time would unveil better days for them.

He believed that God's act of restoration would lead to the establishment of a new covenant, written in the hearts of the people. The new covenant would not be written on stone tablets but rather on the hearts of human beings. It would be an act of God and therefore everlasting. It would be made with the house of Israel and the house of Judah, indicating all the people. This would lead to a conversion of heart and a change of mind for all and result in the forgiveness of sin and inheritance of eternal life.

God would initiate the new covenant with the people through His Son, Jesus. The new covenant would be established by Jesus and ratified by His blood. At the Last Supper, Jesus would take the cup, fill it with wine, and say, "This cup is the new covenant in my blood, which will be shed for you" (Luke 22:20). The new covenant involved entering into a life-giving relationship with Christ and accepting Jesus as the Savior of the world, and more importantly committing oneself to Jesus Christ.

*"No sustainable change is possible unless it begins from within as a response to God's invitation and grace."*

## For Further Reflection and Discussion

1. Jeremiah was called by God from his mother's womb. In faith each of us can apply this to our own lives. What are the implications of God knowing us and calling us from our mother's womb?
2. Jeremiah had to convey a very difficult message that was not popular. As a result, he underwent extreme persecution and trials. What are the implications of Jeremiah's commitment in today's world?
3. Jeremiah criticized priests, kings, and false prophets. When should we criticize authority and when should we refrain from it?
4. Jeremiah underwent extreme personal trials and internal struggles. He even felt that God had duped him. He felt frustrated, discouraged, and disappointed. Discuss.
5. Jeremiah stood at the ruins of the temple with an aching heart. Centuries later, Jesus would weep over Jerusalem (Luke 19:41). Discuss these passages based on what you understand by "lost opportunities."

# JESUS:

## Fulfillment of All Promises

*Have among yourself the same attitude*
*That is also yours in Christ Jesus,*
*Who though he was in the form of God,*
*Did not regard equality with God*
*Something to be grasped.*

*Rather he emptied himself,*
*Taking the form of a slave,*
*Coming in human likeness,*
*And found human in appearance,*
*He humbled himself,*
*Becoming obedient to death,*
*Even death on a cross.*

*Because of this, God greatly exalted him*
*And bestowed on him the name*
*That at the name of Jesus*
*Every knee should bend,*
*Of those in heaven and on earth*
*And under the earth,*
*And every tongue confess that*
*Jesus Christ is Lord,*
*To the glory of God the Father.*
(Philippians 2:5–11)

This early Christian hymn, or Christological hymn, that we find in St. Paul's letter to the Philippians is rich with many levels of meaning. It can speak to us about the need to imitate Christ in humility and to aspire to the same attitudes that He exhibited in His life. It can remind us of the great self-emptying of Christ, the second Person of the Trinity, who took on flesh at a decisive moment in history, becoming one like us. It can tell us much more than the historical Jesus of Nazareth, who walked on this earth and died on the cross. It can remind us that the Son was with the Father at all times and by His obedience to the Father's will, He obtained redemption and salvation.

Jesus stands before us as the final fulfillment of every promise of God. By self-emptying, or "kenosis," Paul does not mean that Jesus was stripped of His divinity, but rather He took upon Himself human nature as well. It is as if to say His self-emptying is not any kind of depletion but rather by an addition of the human nature into His one person. Only this God-man (true God and true man) could restore human beings' lost friendship with God.

So far we have reflected upon forty persons in the Old Testament of the Bible. We came across their many experiences, strengths, weakness, struggles, and triumphs. Each one of them, in one way or another, can teach us something about Christ. But none can take the place of His mission for humanity.

**Jesus and Adam**: The first Adam yielded to the temptation of evil, allowing the power of evil to intimidate and trick him. Through this act of disobedience, sin and death entered the world. Jesus, the New Adam, resisted temptation and defeated evil by His act of obedience to the will of the Father. Through Him, redemption and salvation were reclaimed.

**Jesus and Eve**: The first Eve's act of disobedience brought about the continuous struggle between human beings and the power of evil. Jesus, born of the new Eve, Mary, would crush the head of the serpent, the symbol of evil, and claim the decisive victory for human beings.

**Jesus and Cain**: Cain, consumed by jealousy and anger, murdered his innocent brother, Abel. Jesus, filled with compassion and love, would give up His life for sinful human beings.

**Jesus and Abel**: Abel's death would remind us that even an innocent person can be a victim of unexpected tragedies and raging violence. Jesus would remind His followers, "Do not be afraid of those who kill the body but after that can do no more...but be afraid of the one, who, after killing, has the power to cast into Gehenna" (Luke 12:4–5).

**Jesus and Noah**: Noah's righteous living spared humanity from total extinction. Jesus' act of sacrifice would redeem human beings from eternal death.

**Jesus and Abraham**: Abraham believed, hoping against all hope, and surrendered himself totally to God against all odds. "By faith Abraham, when put to the test, offered up Isaac...He reasoned that God was able to raise even from the dead, and he received Isaac back as a symbol" (Hebrews 11:17–19). Jesus became the priest and sacrificial victim on the altar of the cross. There was no other creature to replace Him, and He surrendered totally when He said, "Father, into Your hands I commend My spirit" (Luke 23:46).

**Jesus and Sarah**: Sarah's impatience caused enormous problems in her family. When she decided to solve the crisis in her own way, she was inviting troubles into her life. Time after time, Jesus would remind His listeners to be patient and have faith. St. Paul says, "Have no anxiety about anything, but in everything by prayer and supplication with thanksgiving let your requests be made known to God. And the peace of God, which passes all understanding, will keep your hearts and your minds in Christ Jesus" (Philippians 4:6–7).

**Jesus and Hagar**: Hagar was a foreigner. Initially she did not know God. Eventually she would come to know the goodness of God, and He blessed her abundantly. Jesus would demonstrate the universal love of God when He responded to the request of the Canaanite (Syrophoenician) woman. She had come before Jesus, believing that He was able to heal her daughter. Commending her faith, Jesus would say, "O woman, great is your faith! Let it be done for you as you wish" (Matthew 15:28).

**Jesus and Ishmael**: Ishmael was sent away from his father's house at the insistence of Sarah. It was indeed a painful moment for Ishmael and his mother, Hagar. At the age of twelve, Jesus was found sitting among the teachers and asking them questions. To His anxious parents, Jesus would ask, "Why were you looking for me? Did you not know that I must be in my Father's house?" (Luke 2:49).

**Jesus and Isaac**: Isaac lay on the altar, expecting to die at any moment. As Abraham raised his knife, they heard the voice of the messenger: "Do not lay your hand on the boy" (Genesis 22:12). Centuries later, there was a loud cry from the cross: "Father, into Your hands I commend My spirit" (Luke 23:46).

**Jesus and Rebekah**: Rebekah offered hospitality to Abraham's servant. He was greatly impressed by her virtues. She would be chosen as Isaac's bride. When Jesus was in the house of Simon the Pharisee, a sinful woman would approach Jesus, sit at His feet, shed tears of repentance, and wipe His feet with her hair. Commenting on her actions, Jesus would say: "When I entered your house, you did not give water for my feet, but she has bathed them with her tears and wiped them with her hair...So I tell you, her many sins have been forgiven; hence she has shown great love" (Luke 7:44–47).

**Jesus and Esau**: Esau sold his birthright for a bowl of soup. He seemed more interested in satisfying his physical needs than being part of a covenant relationship with God. Jesus would say to the devil, "One does not live by bread alone, but by every word that comes forth from the mouth of God" (Matthew 4:4).

**Jesus and Jacob**: Jacob exemplified perseverance and oriented his life to achieve greatness. Once he knew that it was through him God's promises would pass down to the next generation, he was determined to achieve it. Jesus would instill in His disciples that true greatness is achieved only through a life of service (Mark 9:35).

**Jesus and Joseph**: Joseph was sold by his own brothers to the Ishmaelites for twenty pieces of silver. Jesus would be betrayed by His disciple Judas for thirty pieces of silver.

**Jesus and Miriam**: Miriam was one of the five women who played a role in saving the life of Moses. When Joseph knew that Herod had decided to kill the baby Jesus, Joseph would take Jesus and His mother, Mary, and depart for Egypt (Matthew 2:13–15).

**Jesus and Aaron**: Aaron, who was chosen by God as the priest among His people, was a forerunner of Jesus Christ, the true High Priest. Jesus would offer Himself on the altar of the cross: "When

Christ came as high priest of the good things that have come to be, passing through the greater and more perfect tabernacle not made by hands, that is, not belonging to this creation, he entered once for all into the sanctuary, not with the blood of goats and calves but with his own blood, thus obtaining eternal redemption" (Hebrews 9:11–12).

**Jesus and Moses**: Moses would give the Ten Commandments to the people of Israel at Mount Sinai. Jesus, the New Moses, would teach the true implications of the Commandments at His Sermon on the Mount and give the great New Commandment of Love: Love God, and love your neighbor.

**Jesus and Joshua**: Joshua was instrumental in the conquest of the Promised Land. Jesus, through His message of love, His death, and His resurrection, would show a new way to conquer the world, change lives, and enter the eternal heavenly kingdom.

**Jesus and Deborah**: Deborah was called by the Lord to be a judge, a prophetess, and a military commander of His people. Jesus would call twelve ordinary men (fisherman, tax collector, and zealot) and would appoint them to be His apostles to carry on his work in the world.

**Jesus and Gideon**: Gideon would look at his downsized army of three hundred men and wonder how he would fight against the vast army of the Medianites. Commenting on the importance of faith, Jesus would say, "If you have faith the size of a mustard seed, you will say to this mountain, move from here to there, and it will move. Nothing will be impossible for you" (Matthew 17:21).

**Jesus and Samson**: Samson won the admiration of everyone due to his amazing physical strength. The deeds and words of Jesus amazed everyone and they asked, "Where did this man get all this? What kind of wisdom has been given him? What mighty deeds are wrought by his hands?" (Mark 6:2).

**Jesus and Ruth**: The humble filial piety of Ruth was blessed beyond her imagination, as she became an ancestress of the Savior. Jesus would make it clear that every single good act is seen and rewarded by God as He lovingly praised the sacrificial offering of the poor widow at the temple (Mark 12:41–44).

**Jesus and Saul**: Initially Saul had everything in him to be remembered as one of the greatest kings of Israel, but as he moved away from God's ways, his life became a failure. Jesus continuously taught the disciples to abide in Him to produce abundant fruit.

**Jesus and Jonathan**: Although Jonathan knew that David would succeed Saul as the next king, he did not allow his ambition to affect the friendship he had with David. Jesus would say, "No one has greater love than this, to lay down one's life for one's friends" (John 15:13).

**Jesus and David**: Under David, the twelve tribes of Israel would come together as a united kingdom. The new kingdom, initiated by Jesus, would embrace people of every nation, language, and culture. The church, built upon the foundation of the twelve apostles (symbolic of the twelve tribes), would become the new home for all peoples.

**Jesus and Nathan**: Nathan would courageously stand before King David, who had committed adultery and murder, and say, "You are the man" (2 Samuel 12:7). Pilate would utter these words, "Behold, the man!" (John 19:5). Though Pilate knew that Jesus was innocent, He was handed over to be crucified.

**Jesus and Solomon**: Solomon was given the great gift of wisdom that enabled him to distinguish right from wrong. God blessed him abundantly with riches, possessions, reputation, and fame. Yet Solomon, in his old age, turned his back on God. "Jesus advanced in wisdom and age and favor before God and human beings" (Luke 2:52). Jesus' wisdom enabled Him to complete His mission as He surrendered Himself totally to the will of His Father.

**Jesus and Elijah**: The great prophet who was running away from the wrath of Jezebel would lie down in the desert, wishing to die. The angel ministered to him, asking him to get up and eat for the long journey ahead. Jesus would experience tremendous agony and pain in the Garden of Gethsemane. The angel ministered to him, strengthening Him to face the cross and death ahead.

**Jesus and Jezebel**: Jezebel's belief in her false god became her ultimate downfall. Even after she was confronted with the truth, she did not want to change her evil ways. Jesus would warn the church to be very careful about the spirit of Jezebel that could lead believers away from the truth (cf. Revelation 2:20–22).

**Jesus and Elisha**: Empowered by the Spirit of God, Elisha was able to perform many mighty deeds among the people. Jesus would say that those who believe in Him and receive the gift of the Spirit would do greater works: "Amen, amen, I say to you, whoever believes in me will do the works that I do, and will do greater ones than these, because I am going to the Father" (John 14:12).

**Jesus and Hosea**: Hosea demonstrated the greatness of God's love through his marriage to the unfaithful Gomer. Jesus would show His compassion to the disciples who deserted Him. He continues to show His love and mercy to us, who often desert Him.

**Jesus and Amos**: Amos would criticize Amaziah, the corrupt priest of Bethel. He was very critical of the leaders for their failures in taking care of those who were poor and vulnerable. Jesus would be very critical of the religious leaders of His time for their hypocrisy and false piety (Luke 11:39–52).

**Jesus and Isaiah**: Isaiah foretold the Suffering Servant, who would voluntarily take upon Himself the sins of the people: "He was pierced for our offenses, crushed for our sin, upon him was the chastisement that makes us whole, by his stripes we were healed" (Isaiah 53:5). The centurion who witnessed the death of Jesus on the cross would say, "This man was innocent beyond doubt" (Luke 23:47).

**Jesus and Ezekiel**: When the "breath," or the Spirit, of God came upon the lifeless bodies, Ezekiel saw them rising as if from a slumber and standing up as a large army. The disciples of Jesus would be huddled together in fear after their Master's death. However, when the promised Spirit descended upon them, they would come out as courageous men to begin the mission Jesus entrusted to them.

**Jesus and Daniel**: Daniel was protected by God in the lions' den. Jesus would assure His disciples, "These signs will accompany those who believe: in my name they will drive out demons, they will speak new languages. They will pick up serpents, and if they drink any deadly thing, it will not harm them. They will lay hands on the sick, and they will recover" (Mark 16:17–18).

**Jesus and Job**: Job, who sought answers from the Lord for his suffering, ultimately agreed that many things in life would be unintelligible to a mere human mind: "I have dealt with great things that I do not understand; things too wonderful for me, which I cannot know" (Job 42:2). Every form of suffering and pain has a redeeming value when seen from the perspective of Calvary, where Jesus suffered and died for our sins.

**Jesus and Esther**: Esther was an orphan and yet God exalted her and used her in a mighty way. God does not look for individuals with flawless track records to do His work. Jesus would call and appoint a hated person, Matthew, the tax collector, to be one of His apostles. Matthew not only preached the message of Christ through his life, but he also became an instrument of the Holy Spirit when Matthew wrote the gospel that has come down to us.

**Jesus and Jonah**: Jonah did not want God to show mercy and forgiveness to the people of Nineveh. He wanted God to destroy them. Jesus said, "For God so loved the world that he gave his only Son...God did not send his Son into the world to condemn the world that the world might be saved through him" (John 3:16–17).

**Jesus and Jeremiah**: Jeremiah announced the coming of days when God would establish a new covenant with all the people. At the Last Supper, the night before He died, Jesus would take the cup and give it to His disciples, saying, "This cup is the new covenant in my blood, which will be shed for you" (Luke 22:20).

# About the Author

Sebastian Myladiyil, SVD, a native of India and a naturalized citizen, is a Divine Word Missionary priest. He has been working in the Southern Province of the Society of the Divine Word in the United States since 1999. He began his ministry as associate pastor at St. Edward/St. Jude Church in New Iberia, Louisiana. From 2001-2010 he served as pastor at St. Rose de Lima Church in Bay St. Louis, MS.

Under his leadership, St. Rose became an important place in the relief and recovery efforts after Hurricane Katrina. He was a member of the Mississippi Governor's commission for rebuilding Hancock County. Through St. Rose Outreach and Recovery (SOAR), an organization established by Fr. Sebastian, more than 5000 volunteers helped more than 500 families. He captured the efforts of St. Rose and his experience in his second book *Blown Together: The Trials and Miracles of Katrina*. He was recognized as one of the Outstanding Citizens of Hancock County in 2007 by the Hancock County Chamber of Commerce. He was the 2010 recipient of the Gold Medal National Award for Service, conferred by the Knights & Ladies of Peter Clever. In 2010 he earned a Master's degree in Moral Theology from Notre Dame Seminary.

Since July 2010, Fr. Sebastian has been serving as the pastor at Immaculate Conception Church in Liberty, TX. He published a first and shorter version of this book, *His Instruments: If God Could Use Them He Can Use Us* in December 2009, which was very well received by the readers. His second book, *Blown Together: The Trials and Miracles of Katrina* was published in August of 2010. *Blown Together* also captures 25 stories from individuals (community members, civic leaders, clergy, and volunteers from across the nation), who were affected one way or the other by Hurricane Katrina. Plans are underway in writing his next book, featuring biblical characters from the New Testament.

To contact the author, e-mail him at sebymy@hotmail.com or sebymy1@gmail.com